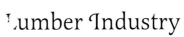
Boards, ~~~~ and Bins

S. M. Simpson and t ~~~~ Lumber Industry

Boards, Boxes, and Bins

S. M. Simpson and the Okanagan Lumber Industry

Sharron J. Simpson

Edited by Stuart Kernaghan

Manhattan Beach Publishing

Published by

Manhattan Beach Publishing,
1850 Abbott Street,
Kelowna, B.C., Canada.
V1Y 1B5.

Cover and page layout by Jack Thompson, Ehmann Printworx.

Cover photo by Joan Simpson

All photos are from the collection of Sharron Simpson, unless otherwise indicated.

Printed by Ehmann Printworx, Kelowna, B.C., Canada.

National Library of Canada Cataloguing in Publication

Simpson, Sharron J., 1938-
Boards, boxes, and bins : S. M. Simpson and the Okanagan lumber industry /
Sharron J. Simpson ; Stuart Kernaghan, editor.

Includes bibliographical references and index.
ISBN 0-9688435-1-4

1. Simpson, S. M. (Stanley Merriam) 2. Sawmills—British Columbia—Okanagan Valley—History.
3. Wooden box industry—British Columbia—Okanagan Valley—History. 4. S. M. Simpson Ltd.—History.
5. Okanagan Valley (B.C.)—History. 6. Kelowna (B.C.)—Biography. 7. Okanagan Valley (B.C.)—
Biography. 8. Businessmen—British Columbia—Kelowna—Biography. I. Kernaghan, Stuart, 1971- II.
Title.

HD9764.C33B75 2003   338.4'7674'0092   C2003-906736-X

Boards, Boxes, and Bins

S. M. Simpson and the Okanagan Lumber Industry

Contents

This book is dedicated to the employees of

S. M. Simpson Ltd.

and the other companies that grew from
its early beginnings. Their stories
and recollections have added a unique
dimension to this history.

Acknowledgments

I am indebted to many people for helping me pull together this story of Stan Simpson and S. M. Simpson Ltd. While taking a course in memoir writing a few years ago, I came to the conclusion that I didn't know much about the man who was my grandfather. He was so much a part of Kelowna's history and I didn't know much of that either, but little did I realize that researching and writing his story would take almost four years to complete. I am grateful to Dona Sturmanis for nurturing those early ideas and Rhoda Moss, Holly Yasui, and Beth Greenwood for their comments and guidance along the way. Early versions of this story were also workshopped at Oxford University Summer School in the U.K. and The Banff Centre for the Arts.

The search for information about Stan took me across the country – both physically and through the internet. I developed a new appreciation of Canada's public archives whose mandate is to preserve our individual and community heritage, and make it available to those of us searching for our stories. The archival resources that made much of this book possible include the B.C. Provincial Archives; the University of Saskatchewan Archives; the Sir Andrew Galt Museum and Archives, Lethbridge; the Penticton Museum and Archives; the Vernon Archives; the Kelowna Museum and Archives and particularly, Wayne Wilson and Donna Johnson; the Owen Sound, Ontario Archives; the Glenbow Archives, Calgary; the City of Calgary Archives, and the online resources of the National Archives of Canada. Public libraries are a vastly under-valued asset and I spent a great deal of time at the main branch of the Kelowna library and found its microfiche newspaper files particularly useful. Similar resources were also accessed at the Penticton Library, the Vancouver Public Library, and the B.C. Ministry of Forests Library in Victoria.

Much information is unique to a particular location and I appreciated both its availability and the helpfulness of the staff everywhere I went. Norm Garcia at IWA headquarters in Vancouver provided invaluable assistance searching among the union's archives for the material I was looking for and then allowing me to use their photocopier. His generosity lent credence to the notion that our collective history should be available to everyone.

Without the help of those who actually lived this story, however, the tale could not have possibly have been told. Many former S. M. Simpson Ltd. employees wanted to tell their stories – some telephoned, some wrote, others emailed. Some were happy to talk on tape but told me to turn the recorder off when they were telling a story that might have reflected badly on someone else. Sometimes, a group would gather and as they started to remember, others added their comments. The stories were sometimes hilarious, other times reflective, and occasionally selective – perhaps because the memories were too painful or they were embarrassed. I never knew. But times have changed and whatever happened, happened. I am a generation away from it all and if there were hard feelings or misgivings, they are long-past.

I am especially grateful to Arthur Marty, who wrote so many wonderful memories of his years at the mill and patiently helped me learn the machinery of the sawmill business. As well, I appreciate the many chats I had with Ray Ottenbreit, who is a great storyteller and has a remarkable memory. Ray introduced me to people he thought I should speak with, and searched out some missing IWA history for me.

I wish my father, Horace, had written down his some of his stories but he insisted no one would be interested. Even if he had committed them to paper for his children and grandchildren, we would have more vivid memories of him and a better understanding of the world he lived in. Like his father before him and most men of their generations, my dad didn't talk much about himself but he loved to tell a story and had a great repertoire of not-very-good jokes. It would certainly have made my job a lot easier if he had been more willing to share his experiences, but I hope some of them have been captured in this book.

I would also like to thank the friends who have encouraged my often-interrupted literary efforts, and my fellow writers in our *Memories into Memoirs* class, who regularly remind me how important it is to write our stories. I am also grateful to my daughter, Catherine, for her support and encouragement, and my son, Stuart, who as the book's editor has provided insight and guidance, along with liberal doses of encouragement and technical expertise as he helped to link the memories of five generations of the Simpson family together. Not only have I come to know both my grandfather and father better through writing this book, but I have also had the unique, and wonderful, opportunity to work with my son in finally getting it to press.

Because this is a Kelowna story, I felt it was important to have it printed here. I would like to acknowledge the assistance of Ehmann Printworx, and particularly Jack Thompson, for his creative input. Ehmann's is located immediately across the railway tracks from Riverside's Manhattan Beach mill operation, and it seemed fitting to print the book so close to where most of the story took place.

Sharron J. Simpson
Kelowna, B.C.

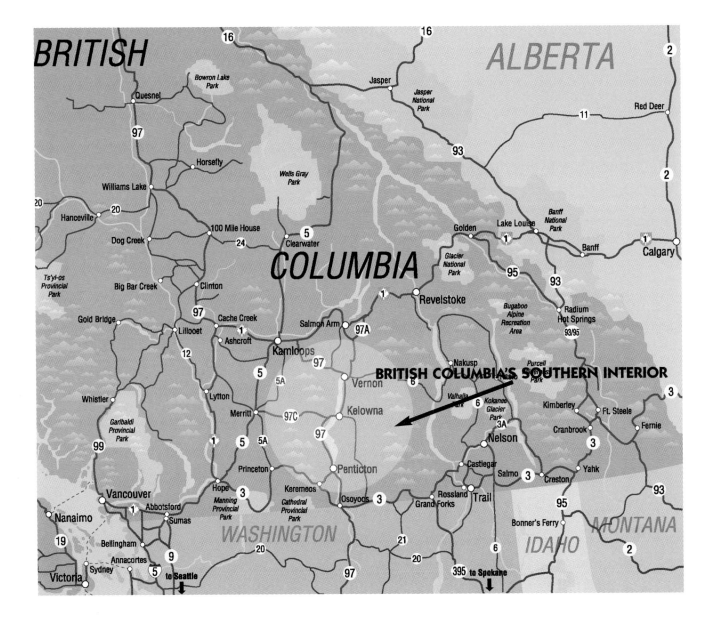

Introduction

Stanley Merriam Simpson arrived in Kelowna, British Columbia in 1913 on board the sternwheeler SS *Okanagan*. He was a modest, mild-mannered man who built screen doors that were guaranteed not to sag, repaired the town jail, opened locked safes, and sharpened dull saw blades. During his first years in the small town, he did whatever he could to earn a living. His one-man carpentry shop grew into a sawmill, box factory, veneer plant, and plywood operation that employed more than 800 men and women throughout the southern interior of British Columbia by the time the company was sold 52 years later.

In those early days, Stan's quiet demeanour masked the fierce independence of a young man who had struggled against formidable odds to make a living and support his family. He spent almost five years transforming a tree-covered quarter section of land (160 acres) on the Saskatchewan prairies into a homestead before acknowledging he wasn't cut out to be a farmer. Stan earned much-needed cash in the depths of the Prairie winters and during spring thaw working as an itinerant handyman carpenter in various parts of Saskatchewan and Alberta, but he chose not to abandon his homestead until he had fulfilled the residency requirements and became its legal owner. This early determination and persistence served Stan well throughout his life, and he never wavered from the notion that hard work and hard times created the qualities and character a person needed to cope with the challenges of everyday life.

Stan's role as provider and caretaker began when his father died suddenly, leaving a family of seven with few financial resources. He took responsibility for them throughout his life, making sure their medical needs were met in an era before health insurance. He brought his mother and younger sister west to live nearby when he decided to settle in Kelowna, and with the help of his older sister, Ruth, provided for them throughout their lives and then eventually for Ruth as well.

Stan went to work in 1901 when he completed Grade 8, shortly after his father's death, and worked seven days a week for most of his life until a stroke slowed him down at the age of 69. Even then he continued to go to the mill a few hours each day. He learned self-reliance at an early age and didn't expect, nor would he have ever accepted, a handout. This didn't stop him from giving some deserving person an occasional hand-up, however, and Stan cared about the welfare of others who were not part of his family. He would deliver a message to an employee on the nightshift whose pregnant wife was in the hospital and then drive the new father to see them. Stan gave jobs to people who needed them – even when there was no job opening – and was known to withhold part of a paycheque from an employee with a drinking problem and then deliver it to his wife and children. Stan didn't make decisions quickly. He thought, and pondered, and weighed the pros and cons before making up his mind, and expected others to do the same. Stan's objections to the union's arrival at his sawmill had more to do with its recruitment tactics than the union itself – he would have respected his employees' decision to join if he felt it had been made freely, but Stan knew many had been intimidated and were fearful of what might happen if they didn't sign up. For years, Stan defended his employees' right to choose whether they would join the union or not and frequently told them so.

He was also an opportunist and risk-taker. Stan worked at his cousins' sash and door plant after leaving school, and when he had mastered those skills he headed to Toronto where he went to night school to learn more. He tried homesteading in an attempt to find the security that came with owning land, but he had never been a farmer and soon realized that his carpentry skills could earn him a better living than his tough, inhospitable Prairie acreage. The only record of these years is a little black book in which he marked down the hours he worked, dollars he earned, and dates he was employed, and the answers to questions on his government homesteading forms. There were no words written to tell about his journey westward from Ontario and he never talked about it. As his company, S. M. Simpson Ltd., grew and prospered Stan made decisions that were questionable at the time but later proved to be wise and profitable. His sawmill pioneered new products, fought for a place among larger competitors, expanded, and explored new opportunities when many other independent sawmills were being bought out by their larger rivals.

Stan was frugal and admonished family members with the advice that "if you can't pay cash for something, then eat porridge until you can," which he had apparently done himself on several occasions. As his business grew, his employees soon learned that waste was not acceptable and he lived the adage that the debtor was a servant to the lender. There were times when he had no choice but to borrow money, but Stan always disliked being obligated to anyone. Most of what he needed to run his business was bought used. He hauled discarded equipment from as far away as Tennessee to upgrade and improve his sawmill. Hoarded bits and pieces of steel, chain, cable, and old machinery were piled in a storage shed that both he and his employees rummaged through when a yet-to-be invented piece of equipment or replacement parts were needed. Stan had an innate mechanical ability and was a hands-on problem solver, using whatever materials were available, and expecting everyone else to do the same. Bill Sinclair, the mill's first blacksmith, remained on the payroll long after the horses were replaced, to modify and extend the life of the machinery, or when nothing else was available, improvise under Stan's direction,

The men and women who worked for Stan were an important part of his life, and he cared about both them and their families. He implicitly trusted them, knew them by name, and knew if they were on the job – or not – when he expected them to be. He also knew most of their families by name. Some 50 years later, one of those employees remembered Stan's kindness when, as a youngster the boy had brought lunch to his dad, who was working as the dry kiln operator. Stan had picked up the boy as he walked home and bought him an ice cream cone along the way. During the Dirty '30s, Stan started the company tradition of delivering turkeys to employees' homes on Christmas Eve; this carried on during strikes and walkouts, as well as the good times, until the company was sold in 1965. Stan gave work to men who had very little formal training, and to women who had few employment choices. Stan, or S. M., as he was often referred to, would step in to ease a bottleneck when the heavy planks came down the green-chain[1] too fast for the men to grab. He never hesitated to pick up a shovel or the end of a load when an extra pair of hands would help, and when employees needed lumber to build their houses, they got enough to finish the job and paid for it with part of each paycheque.

Stan was quiet and reserved, and few people, including his family members, recall having conversations or being involved in any activities with him that were not related to work. He had high expectations of those around him and came across as a tough taskmaster – if you didn't know the answers to his questions, you'd better find out, and fast. He didn't tolerate any fooling around and if you were caught, he wasn't amused. Stan didn't swear and his employees knew he didn't want to hear it from them. He worked hard and expected those around him to work just as hard. He had high expectations of people and if you didn't measure up, you knew he was disappointed. He was even more intolerant of his family's shortcomings, and while he abhorred weakness, he could sometimes understand and work around it. But the closer it was to him, the less forgiving he was.

S. M. had a few personal quirks, which seemed to soften his prevailing demeanour as the hard-working, no-nonsense businessman. When he was relaxed, he had a fine sense of humour and was known to do a gentle, good-natured roast if someone in his office was getting married. He was colour-blind and when traffic lights came to Kelowna, driving became a challenge because he couldn't tell the difference between red and green. A trail of chuckles would often follow him through the mill yard as the men recognized one black shoe and then a brown one coming around a corner. Stan always wore a suit to work and usually went home with it covered in oil and grease, as he found the underside of the truck far more interesting than the topside. His wife, Blanche, removed the stains by dipping the soiled clothes into a large container of gasoline she kept in the garage just for that purpose. While Stan's usual summer Sunday best of white slacks might have deterred the more sartorially-aware from tinkering with a greasy motor, he often wore them when he dropped down to the mill for a few minutes on a Sunday afternoon. Everyone remembers that he carried a stub of a pencil in his pocket and wrote the dimensions of doors, or saw blades, or floor space in a small notebook. He wrote unidentified measurements on whatever scrap of paper happened to be available if the notebook wasn't handy.

Stan worked hard his entire life, and rarely took a holiday. He was at the mill every weekend, although in the early days he also played tennis and an occasional game of ping-pong or bridge. He was active in the community and industry organizations, and served as a school trustee in the early 1930s, as well as being a member of the Kelowna Gyro Club, a vice-president of the Canadian Manufacturers Association (CMA), and a founding member of the Interior Lumber Manufacturers Association (ILMA). S. M. also served on the Box Shook Committee of the Wartime Prices and Trade Board during World War II, which necessitated several lengthy trips across Canada.

S. M. also built a company that became the largest year-round employer in the Okanagan Valley, as well as an entrenched part of the community and a focal point for many people's lives. Generations of families worked for S. M. Simpson Ltd. as the men married the sisters of their co-workers or women working in the box factory. They had safety dinners and dances – which sometimes ended in a brawl, but were nonetheless the most anticipated social event of the year. For many the mill was more than the place they worked, it was a way of life. Stan also left a larger legacy to his adopted hometown when he sold just over 11 acres of land to the City of Kelowna for a civic centre. Today, this area is at the centre of the revitalization of Kelowna's downtown core and the newly declared Cultural Corridor. A trust fund was set up upon Stan's death to pay for improvements to Knox Mountain Park, the major geographical feature overlooking Kelowna, and that trust has just helped to finance significant improvements on the mountain.

Although it is possible to get an idea of the man by looking at what he did and how he related to others, Stan Simpson still remains an elusive character. He never talked about what he had done or why he did it, nor did he talk about the good times or bad. He came from a generation that simply didn't talk if it wasn't necessary. By looking at the business he created, his relationship with the men and women he worked with, their memories, and the legacy he left his adopted community, a picture of the man gradually comes into focus. He was a self-reliant pioneer who expected the best of those around him, and gave the best of himself. There were no airs about him and he lived a life that was true to his unassuming beginnings. Stan was humble and quiet and never liked to be publicly acknowledged or have his name in the newspaper, and he would think all this speculation and story-telling about him was unnecessary nonsense. Life was just the way it was, so get on with it.

↟ ↟ ↟

Few people today still remember Stan, and even fewer recall much about him. Those who can always tell stories of S. M. being involved in things that went on in the sawmill. I, like most of those who knew him, recollect very little about the man, even though I am his granddaughter and was in my teens when he died. Stan spent most of his time working, and while I remember him at the head of the table during the requisite Sunday lunches, I don't recall ever having a conversation with him. I also knew there were no breaks for being part of his family – he had toughed out far worse situations than we would ever have to deal with and had survived, and he expected us to do the same. Like most grandchildren, I regret not having asked him about his past but I also knew this quiet self-contained man never spoke about feelings or hardships, so perhaps he wouldn't have told me about his early days even if I had.

In writing this story of S. M. and his involvement in the early days of the lumber industry in the Okanagan, I have taken a few liberties in interpreting some of the events, made a few assumptions, and drawn some conclusions that seem appropriate under the circumstances. Though Stanley M. Simpson may have wished to leave few personal traces behind him, a picture of the man – who happens to be my grandfather – emerged as I spoke with the old-timers who remember him, read through old newspapers, and scoured the few remaining family records. I hope you enjoy his story.

Sharron J. Simpson
Kelowna, British Columbia
November 2003

Chapter 1

Ancestors and
Early Days – to 1913

At the age of 20, Stan Simpson registered his homestead in 1906 and posed for this photo before clearing got underway. The land was near Spalding, Saskatchewan – NE Quarter of Section Number 21, in Township 40, Range 17 W of 2nd Meridian.

S tan's early years likely played a significant role in forming his character and ensuring his later success, though his older sister, Ruth, dismissively noted that "the influences which led to character formation may go back to childhood and early life but if one drags in details ... it becomes verbose and irrelevant."[1] She typified the Simpson family's attitude that the past couldn't be used as an excuse for not being successful in the future. But Stan learned the important lessons of tenacity and responsibility from his pioneer ancestors and most specifically from the maternal side of his family.

S. M. could trace his roots back to the 1600s in the United States and the 1700s in Canada, when his family joined thousands of United Empire Loyalists[2] and headed north across the U.S.-Canadian border in support of the British monarchy. His mother's family, the Merriams, were a hardy, devout lot that bore large families, hacked their way out of the Ontario wilderness, and as staunch Methodists, made appropriately modest livings while achieving neither great wealth nor notable distinction. Permelia Elizabeth Merriam, Stan's mother, was one of 11 children, the sixth-born and one of two surviving daughters of Justus Johnson Merriam and Caroline Honeywell. For several years, the family had lived in the small farming village of Chatsworth, near Owen Sound, Ontario, about 185 km north of Toronto.

The paternal Simpson ancestors are more elusive, though George Simpson and Ann Thackray, Stan's grandfather and grandmother, were known to have left Yorkshire, England on separate ships in the early1800s. The adventurous Ann left home at the urging of a brother who had preceded her to the New World, which forced a smitten George to follow if he truly wanted to marry her. George booked passage on another ship soon after Ann's departure, but the three to four week trip proved hazardous as passengers risked disease and death in the cheap and squalid quarters below deck. George's ship arrived first in spite of his later departure when an outbreak of smallpox on Ann's ship caused all those on board to be quarantined for a month. They eventually found each other and married in Peterborough, Upper Canada (Ontario) in 1835. William Bramwell, Stan's father, was the fifth of 11 Simpson children, a number of whom succumbed to the family's impoverished circumstances and died in infancy. Bramwell was variously employed as a lay Methodist minister, bailiff, auctioneer, and sometimes farmer. He and Permelia were married on May 12, 1880, and had seven children. When

Bramwell died in 1896 at the age of 52, Permelia was left with four sons and three daughters ranging in age from one to 14 years, a mortgage on their home for $400, and few financial resources. S. M., Bramwell and Permelia's second son, had been born in 1886 and was ten years old at the time of his father's death.

The family's only source of income upon Bramwell's death was a $1,000 insurance policy from the local Masonic Lodge. Ruth noted some years later that "there were no local or government funds available, and if there had been, a fierce pride would have been a deterrent to their use,"[3] so the family coped as best it could. Soon Vern, the eldest at 14 years of age, went to work on a neighbouring farm; the 1901 Dominion of Canada Census noted his occupation as a domestic servant, although he likely worked as a farm hand. Ruth, the second oldest, left school and went to work as a live-in domestic helper with a nearby doctor's family. Stanley, the third eldest, was still in school in 1901 but left later that year at the age of 15 after completing Grade 8 at the local village school. Permelia continued to care and provide for the younger children at home.

Stan's parents – Permelia Elizabeth Merriam and William Bramwell Simpson on their wedding day, May 12, 1880, in Chatsworth, Grey County, Ontario.

The Simpsons' small and unassuming wood-frame home in the village of Chatsworth was within sight of the main wagon road between Toronto and the bustling Lake Huron port city of Owen Sound. In the shadow of several large elms and nestled beside the Anglican Church, the house was typical for its day. It was heated by a wood stove, had a cistern of rainwater for bathing and washing up, and a well out back for drinking water. The barn behind the house was originally used for the horse and carriage, but those soon became luxuries when the family breadwinner was no longer around; Permelia replaced them with a milk cow. A large garden enabled the family to be self-sufficient during the summers and preserve enough fruits and vegetables to see them through the long Ontario winters. Each family member contributed towards their survival: the older children went to work, while the younger ones sold produce from the garden, and several times a week took Permelia's home-baked bread to town to sell. On their way home, they would collect laundry for their mother to do during the long dark nights she was on her own. There were fewer mouths to feed with the older children living and working elsewhere, and the small amounts of money they sent home helped the other family members carry on. Little by little, enough money was saved to pay off the outstanding mortgage.

Shortly after their father's death, the three eldest Simpson children left school and went to work. This photo was taken about 1900 with their mother, Permelia. Standing on the le[ft], Nellie Ruth became a mother's helper in a nearby doctor's home. Standing center, Edwin Vernon (Vern) became a farm labourer and seated next to his mother, Stanley Merriam w[ho] upon completion of Grade 8 worked for his cousins' manufacturing and construction company.

Permelia seemed undaunted by the enormity of the task of raising and providing for seven children, and while her own family was moderately well off there is no indication they came to her assistance. Bramwell was 11 years Permelia's senior and in a group photo taken at her parents' golden wedding anniversary, he clearly stood out from the men in Permelia's family. His firmly-placed bowler hat and expansive handlebar moustache drew the eye when all the other men were hatless and sported full-bearded faces – it appeared that he did not quite comply with the family norm.

Had Permelia strayed from her parents' expectations in her choice of husband? There were persistent rumours of the rakish-looking Bramwell having a 'wee bit' of a drinking problem,[4] and Permelia's children were all known to be staunch teetotallers, so perhaps there was some truth to it. However, Bramwell was also a respected member of the community and was acknowledged as the "Esteemed Superintendent of the Chatsworth Methodist Sabbath School" on December 29, 1882, in a copy of *Gleanings from the Sacred Poets* "as a Slight Token of their Esteem for him as their Superintendent."

Four years later, Bramwell was again feted by the Sabbath School and given an upholstered armchair with an appropriately engraved plaque. If there was an alcohol problem, it was likely kept within the immediate family and Bramwell continued to serve as a valued member of his church community. Much of Permelia's strength came from her devout religious faith, and for all of her 97 years she regularly attended the Chatsworth Methodist Church and later, Kelowna's First United Church.

Although Chatsworth was a small village of a few hundred people, it was the largest in the immediate area and a gathering point for farmers, as well as a way-station for weary travellers heading north or south. The community's social and cultural life centred around the churches, and Catholic, Anglican, Presbyterian, and Methodist congregations flourished. Sunday was a strictly observed day of devotion for the Simpson family, and three times each Sunday they walked the two blocks to the Methodist Church to attend services, attired in their best outfits.

While it is unlikely Permelia had much, if any, formal education she was able to instill in her children the importance of self-sufficiency, and recognized that education was essential to getting ahead in the world. All her children attended the village school, which offered the basics of reading, writing, and arithmetic up to Grade 8. Chatsworth boasted a library of a few hundred volumes and the Simpson family made good use of this resource, as there was little money available for luxuries such as books. The children's future achievements were a testament to the value Permelia placed on education, and the considerable efforts she put into ensuring the younger ones finished high school. Vern was the first to leave school, but he could identify any quotation from the complete works of Shakespeare, as volumes of the playwright's works were his only companions during idle winter months on a Saskatchewan homestead. Ruth graduated in nursing from New York's Columbia Presbyterian Hospital in 1909, and travelled the world for many years as nurse / companion to various wealthy ladies. She spoke several languages and was enormously knowledgeable about art, world history, and politics. Anne, a younger sister, became a schoolteacher and then a nurse. George, another son, became a professor and head of the History department at the University of Saskatchewan. Stan never went beyond Grade 8 and while his spelling was always atrocious and his handwriting that of a 15-year-old, his innate mechanical ability and steely determination made up for what he lacked in book learning.

Because Bramwell had died without a will, half the property and all the mortgage was left to Permelia; the other half was registered in the names of the seven children. It took the family seven years to pay off the $400 mortgage, with each child and their mother contributing whatever they could to pay off the debt. Soon after Permelia and the children had clear title to their house, Alfred, the youngest son, completed Grade 8 at the local school and the family moved to the larger community of Owen Sound, 12 km to the north. With four children now in secondary school, Permelia sold the original Chatsworth family home and rented a small house near the children's new school. She was eventually able to purchase a larger home, which enabled her to take in 'paying guests' – the polite term for boarders – to help with expenses.

An independent young man

When Vern and Ruth left school they also left home, but Stan stayed to help his mother after completing Grade 8. It wasn't long before he went to work for his maternal cousins at Merriam Bros., Manufacturers, Builders and Contractors in Chatsworth. The brothers had a flourishing home-building business, and also manufactured screen doors and windows, step ladders, ironing tables, and clothes horses. The two years Stan spent working for his cousins enabled him to pick up the finer points of woodworking and carpentry, and while he might not have appreciated it at the time, the experience set the future course of his life. Years later when S. M. set up his first workshop in Kelowna, he supported himself by making the same screen doors, storm windows, and fruit ladders

Pages of the little black notebook where Stan tracked his expenses while in Toronto, dates he was in residence on his homestead, and dates while working away from his homestead – 1904 to 1909.

he had been taught to make many years earlier at his cousins' factory.

Stan felt he had learned all he could – or wanted to – after working in Chatsworth for a couple of years and joined the exodus of young people leaving rural Ontario to see what Toronto had to offer. Known even then as 'The Big Smoke,' Toronto typified many early industrial cities with its busy and polluted harbour, factory chimneys endlessly spewing dirty soot into the air, and railroads criss-crossing the land between the city and the lakeshore. Toronto's population was just over 210,000 when Stan arrived in early July 1904, and the city was still trying to recover from an enormous fire that had destroyed over 12 acres and 400 buildings in the downtown wholesale district just six weeks earlier.[5] Ruth had also tired of her job as a domestic helper and was already in Toronto, where she had settled into a new position as an assistant to the head matron at Toronto General Hospital. Stan was able to find a boarding house in an area that had escaped the fire, near Central Technical School, and signed up for a night wood-working course at the school shortly after making the journey south. His timing couldn't have been better. The city was in urgent need of carpenters as it began to rebuild, and it didn't take Stan long to find a job.

Living on his own for the first time, Stan knew he had to keep track of expenses and soon after his arrival in Toronto, purchased a small black notebook. This little book is the only surviving record of Stan's life between July 1904 and 1909 or perhaps 1910, as it became more difficult to decipher the information as time went on. The notebook's first entry was the cash Stan arrived in Toronto with – $28.75 – on July 2, 1904, which also happened to be the day before his 18th birthday. Stan's room at the boarding house cost him $6 a month, but his meals were extra and usually added another $14 a month to his expenses. He was earning about $16 every two weeks at this time; that figure increased to $27.50 by the time he left the city just over two years later.[6]

The little black book provides an interesting glimpse into S. M.'s everyday life, as well as his living situation. He acquired a bicycle soon after moving to Toronto so he could get to school and work, but it seemed to be in rough shape as rarely a month would go by that repairs were not recorded. It may have been just 35¢ or a dollar, or $3.25 for new tires; at one point, he resorted to bicycle cement to keep the run-down vehicle on the road. Stan began to acquire the tools of his carpentry trade – a rule, nail sets, an apron, files, and a hammer handle. A plumb bob, a bevel square, drills, and saws were also recorded in the notebook, with the prices noted beside each entry. By February 1906, Stan had acquired so many tools that he needed a tool box and built his own, spending 35¢ for the lumber and another 45¢ for a good lock.

He would send $10 home to his mother as often as he could, and regularly purchased necessities for other family members – $3.75 for knives and forks for his mother, and several times 50¢ for Ruth's laundry, 25¢ for toothpaste for Anne, a book for George, or a Christmas gift for Alf. Stan also took out a life insurance policy, payable to his mother, to ensure that the family would not suffer the same way it had when his father had died should anything happen to him. The premium on the policy cost $25.40 a year and money order receipts for this amount were attached to S. M.'s little black book, showing he had paid it from various towns as he moved westward. Though he no longer lived at home, Stan continued to be responsible for his family and would be for the rest of their lives.

S. M.'s life in the big city was probably quite typical for a young single man recently arrived from the countryside. He had a job, lived in a boarding house, went to technical school in the evenings and, following his family's church-going habit, attended services each Sunday, depositing 50¢ or a dollar in the collection plate (and recording the amount in his book). This seems substantial compared to his other expenses, but Stan likely only went to church once a day in Toronto instead of the three times each Sunday with his mother, so perhaps the amounts going into the collection plate were comparable. Stan's piety went without question, and his indulgences were few – gratifying his sweet tooth occasionally cost him 5¢ for candy, or perhaps 10¢ or 15¢ for fruit. In February of his first year in Toronto, Stan found 50¢, which was significant enough to be noted in the book. S. M. learned to watch every penny while still living at home and when he left for Toronto, he closely tracked his income and expenses; that habit would last for many years until he could hire a bookkeeper to do the job for him. His frugality became a lifelong trademark, but even at this early date, Stan was careful with his money. He purchased needles and thread to do his own mending, and spent 50¢ to replace half the sole of his shoes rather than buying new ones.

There was more to life in Toronto than just work and school, however. Stan attended the opera, a Shakespearean play, and lectures, likely at Ruth's urging. There were also hockey games, which cost him 25¢, a lacrosse stick and boot skates purchases, and he even went to a rifle range a few times. Fall visits to the Canadian National Exhibition, the country's premiere agricultural fair, were a highlight for Stan as it provided both great entertainment and an opportunity to revisit his rural roots. Living in Toronto was an adventure compared to the small community he grew up in, and both his carpentry skills and his horizons broadened substantially. Stan maintained contact with his family while in Toronto, but his visits home were infrequent and he never moved back.

Go west, young man

By 1906, two years after he had arrived in the city, Stan had decided his future lay beyond Toronto. The flood of immigrants heading west to the newly-opened Prairie provinces was already well underway. Advertising campaigns at home and overseas by the Canadian federal government and the Canadian Pacific Railway (CPR), which had been given massive land grants as compensation for the cost of building the transcontinental railway, touted the great opportunities for free – or almost free – land for homesteading, and the fortunes that could be made quickly.

CPR lands could be purchased with clear title for $5 an acre, payable over five years at six per cent interest, but many people did not have that kind of money. Quarter sections (160 acres) of federal land available for a $10 registration fee and a commitment to fulfill certain conditions became the only reasonable option for many people, including Stan and his brother, Vern. Homesteaders had to live on the land for six months and clear 10 acres each year, and plant crops or raise cattle. Once these requirements were met, the homesteader could file for title with the Local Agent for Dominion Lands in the nearest district office.[7] Homesteading was the only opportunity most people would ever have to own land, and since many came from families or even countries where they had no choice but to work for others, the autonomy and potential benefits of land ownership and self-employment became an intoxicating lure. Government advertisements seemed to omit information about long, harsh winters and the emptiness of the land, however, and many newcomers arrived with crates filled with fine china, crystal, linens, and elegant furniture only to find themselves settling into buildings cut from prairie sod. Others, like Stan and Vern, came with nothing but their willingness to work hard. They started from scratch.

The location of Prairie communities was determined by the railway's need for coal and water, and the distance a farm family could travel by wagon in a day, which meant towns were rarely more than 30 km apart. These villages took on a sameness about them, as the homesteaders' needs varied little from place to place. The general store carried most of what was required, and when there were no trees in the area a lumberyard would be located near the rail line. Where the land was covered with bush, a small sawmill, sash, door, and shingle operation would be kept busy cutting logs brought in by homesteaders as they cleared their property. Settlers would buy doors, windows, nails, and hardware, and load everything back onto their wagon and return home. Hopefully, the neighbours would have gathered for a house and barn raising. A blacksmith and harness maker was also a fixture in every village until the Eaton's mail-order catalogue came along and undercut their prices.

Vern had joined other Merriam family members and a contingent of men from the Grey County area around Chatsworth on a 1905 trip to Saskatchewan to scout homesteading opportunities. Many were encouraged by what they saw and over time, several Merriam cousins headed west, but Vern was the first and on May 31, 1906, he registered his homestead near the village of Watson in the Quill Lake area of central Saskatchewan. By that October, when S. M. arrived in the area, the 24-year-old Vern had already built and moved into a 12' x 14' log house and dug a well nearby for drinking water.[8] This area was thick with good-sized cottonwood and poplar trees, and since Vern had one of the few ox teams in the area, he frequently hired out to pull his neighbour's stumps and clear their land before he cleared his own.

Stan heads to the Prairies

The lure of free land convinced Stan to overlook the fact that he had never been a farmer, and in October 1906 he also registered his homestead. Little did the Simpson brothers know how terrible their timing was. The following two winters were so fierce that the resulting tales stand out among the annals of horrendous Saskatchewan winters. The blizzards came early, and blew night and day for weeks. Snow was still on the ground in May and the Chinook winds, which usually provided some relief from the relentless cold, never came. Cattle froze where they stood and when spring finally arrived, over 40,000 carcasses were found stacked in the gullies and ravines where the animals had sought refuge. Even the combs and feet of chickens in the barns froze, and the only option for some farmers was to stop passing trains and beg for coal to save their families from freezing to death.[9] There is no record of how Stan and Vern survived their first Prairie winters, and they never talked about it, but there is little doubt it was an extremely difficult experience for them.

Stan stayed on his homestead from October 6 until Christmas of that year before leaving to find work

Stan's homestead house which, with its doors and multiple windows was considerably more substantial than many in the area. When Stan decided his future was not in farming, his brother Vern, combined his acreage with Stan's and moved into the original farmhouse where this photo was taken.

elsewhere. He was away for a good part of 1907, and carefully recorded the important dates on the homestead in his little black account book so he could prove he had fulfilled his residency requirements. When the crippling winter conditions returned in 1907, Stan reluctantly realized the futility of trying to make a go of it entirely on his own and chose to abandon his first homestead and re-file for another closer to Vern. He registered the second on October 20, 1908. With the curious checkerboard pattern of federal land sections alternating with CPR sections, the corners of Stan and Vern's sections were now touching and the new arrangement allowed for easier access from one property to the other. The document Stan filled out to register for this second property asked, "When absent from your homestead, where have you resided and what has been your occupation?" Stan's answer was, "working as a carpenter in Prince Albert." Realizing that he had his carpentry skills to fall back on, Stan was willing to try homesteading again – he liked the opportunity it offered for him to become a self-sufficient land owner, but he also knew he had an alternative if need be.

Stan's new land was covered with poplars and cottonwoods, sometimes more than a foot in diameter, that had to be cleared before any planting could begin. The trees provided both firewood and building materials, but they also delayed any grain planting. Many new farmers resorted to planting potatoes around the tree stumps as food for their families, as well as an interim cash crop. Fields could finally be seeded with cash crops like wheat, oats, rye, or flax once the stumps were cleared.

Within two months of filing for his second homestead, S. M. had built a 14' x 18' log house valued at $320, along with a stable worth $300, a 12' x 12' frame granary worth $60, a well that cost him $80, and enclosed 70 acres with wire fence valued at $80.[10] Hard work had never deterred Stan, but this was quite an accomplishment in such a short time and with their properties relatively close, Vern and perhaps some of his other neighbours helped Stan get set up before another winter descended on the area. Stan was able to put his carpentry skills to good use and his little house had both windows and a board roof, which was considerably more substantial than the windowless shacks with sod roofs that dotted the Prairie landscape. Stan's house had required three wagonloads of lumber, which meant three trips into town to have the logs cut and three trips back with the finished lumber. The inevitable chinks between uneven boards were filled with mud and moss, and then covered with layers of newspapers or pages from catalogues to stop the winter gales from howling through. Furnishings would have been minimal, with the brothers likely building their own or simply improvising with the boxes their food had been shipped in. Since they relied on the wood stove for both cooking and heating, an abundance of handy firewood was a bonus.

S. M. and Vern's homestead years were dreary and isolated, but the brothers were hardy and determined, and their lives were not out of the ordinary for the single young men who came to settle the Prairies. Without the help of a wife and companionship of a family, many of these bachelors were without any domestic skills and didn't know what food to buy, how to cook it, or what they should be eating. They survived on jam, graham crackers, and tea for the first while, with porridge and potatoes becoming their staples. For breakfast they would add a few dried blueberries or Saskatoon berries and a piece of salt pork. Lunch would consist of tea and salt pork, and potatoes might be thrown in for supper. If they were lucky enough to have a neighbour lady who baked bread, they could indulge themselves until they had devoured the treat and were again left to their own devices.[11]

Although he was mindful of meeting the residency requirement on his homestead, Stan, like many others, had to earn some cash and frequently left the farm to find work elsewhere. His black account book recorded $86.80 for work done in June and early July of 1909 in the nearby community of Aberdeen, Saskatchewan. When that job finished, he caught the transcontinental CPR to Lethbridge, Alberta, where he worked as a carpenter for several months. Another trip took him to Medicine Hat, where he mailed his annual insurance premium back to Toronto. Stan travelled to wherever he could find work and didn't leave much of a record of when or where he went other than in the random figures and occasional names in his account book.

Stan arrived back at his homestead on April 7, 1910, and this time stayed for a full year. By now, a full 33 acres had been planted and he had lived on the land for the required six months of each of the preceding three years, which meant he could now apply for title to his property. Stan filed the papers to become the registered owner of his 160 acres before he left his homestead that April, with two of his neighbours attesting to the truth of his claim that he had fulfilled all the necessary requirements. He never returned to the land, but documents show that he officially became the owner, in absentia, of 160 acres of Saskatchewan prairie on August 9, 1912.

Stan didn't hold onto the homestead, and an early 1920s map of the Simpson homesteads show V. Simpson as the owner of his original section as well as the section previously registered to S. Simpson. Vern had likely worked his own section as well as his brother's while S. M. was off earning the cash that would sustain the farm until their crops could be sold, and by the time Stan left his homestead for good in 1911, he knew he could make a better living as a carpenter than as a farmer. Once the land was in his name, Stan transferred it to Vern, who had chosen to stay on. Vern wouldn't have paid Stan much, if anything, for the additional homestead and he soon moved into S. M.'s larger and more substantial house. Stan did not return to the property for another 40 years and then only to collect his older brother and drive him back to Kelowna, where Vern lived with his mother and sister, and worked at Stan's mill for a number of years.

No further west

After leaving the farm, Stan spent several months working as a carpenter in the bustling coal mining towns of Alberta, but he was itinerant and never stopped long enough to settle down. Just as winter was returning to the Prairies, Stan decided he had had enough and departed for the Okanagan Valley on the CPR. The rail journey from Lethbridge took him to Sicamous, British Columbia, where he transferred with the other passengers and boxes of freight to the Okanagan Shuswap Railway for the

82km trip to Okanagan Landing, at the north end of Okanagan Lake. There, everything was again transferred onto one of the sternwheelers that travelled up and down the lake, stopping at the many small communities nestled along the shoreline. Stan probably disembarked during the boat's scheduled stopover in Kelowna, but his destination was Penticton at the south end of the lake, and he got back on board and continued to the final stop. The trip from Prairie winter to benign Okanagan autumn took Stan two days to complete.

The first record of S. M.'s presence in Penticton came in the form of a mention in *The Penticton Herald* on December 11, 1911, as the newly appointed Second Vice President of the Literary Committee of the Union Sunday School Society. This may seem like quite an achievement for a man with a Grade 8 education, but since Penticton was the frontier, the Committee took whoever was available and Stan had walked through its door at an opportune time.

No one knows why Stan chose Penticton as the final destination on his journey westward. Perhaps he visited one of the Okanagan fruit exhibitions in Lethbridge and was attracted by what he saw. Maybe he struck up a friendship with someone heading west to participate in the mining boom underway in Hedley, which used Penticton as its bustling supply base. Perhaps Stan was looking for an alternative to the harsh Prairie winters and since he now knew he could use his woodworking skills to make a living, he might as well find a more pleasant climate to do so. Whatever the reason, Stan liked what he saw in the Okanagan and stayed in Penticton for the next year-and-a-half – the longest he had spent anywhere since leaving Toronto.

Stan never travelled without his tool box and soon after his arrival, he met Oswell C. Etter, a building contractor who had recently emigrated from Nova Scotia, and his wife, Flora Anna, a leading figure in the local Methodist Church. Stan's church roots drew him towards the Union Sunday School Society where the small Presbyterian, Baptist, and Methodist congregations joined together for social and educational activities. Penticton was in the midst of a construction boom and Etter had set up his own business to take advantage of the opportunities, and Flora Anna, as president of the Society, became the link between Stan's church activities and her husband's construction business. A friendship developed between the two men and S. M. was hired on by Etter. He and Oswell had worked together for over a year when they heard of a carpentry business that was for sale in Kelowna and on July 17, 1913, they joined the annual Union Sunday School excursion to Kelowna. Their intention was to check out the carpentry shop to see if it would be a good opportunity for them to form a partnership and go into business together.

This trip took place nine years to the month after Stan had left his family in Chatsworth. He had ridden his bicycle around the busy streets of Toronto, homesteaded in some of the wildest weather and toughest conditions ever experienced in Saskatchewan, and led a journeyman's life throughout the western Prairies. Stan had just celebrated his 27th birthday and whether he knew it at the time or not, his wanderings had finally come to an end.

Chapter 2

"Don't Simply Exist – Come to the Okanagan and L-I-V-E"[1] – 1913 to 1920

When Stan decided to go to Kelowna that sunny day in July, he must have wondered if this would just be another in a succession of jobs that had already taken him across much of the country. He had managed to pick up work wherever he went, but the jobs had only lasted for a few days or at most, a couple of weeks. Apart from homesteading Stan had always worked for someone else, but that was about to change.

A better opportunity

The picnickers turned as they walked down the gangplank of the SS *Okanagan* at the CPR wharf in downtown Kelowna, and continued along the lakeshore towards City Park. The small town was busy and festive as members of the Kelowna Union Sunday School group joined their visitors in City Park. According to *The Penticton Herald*, "everyone from the child of four up to the old grandmothers and grandads [*sic*] … forgot their worries as the park was the scene of mirth and enjoyment … and their hearts were lightened by the fun and floric [*sic*] of the kids."[2]

Stan and Oswell disembarked from the ferry along with the other passengers, but instead of joining in the festivities right away, walked east on Bernard Avenue, the town's main street. A block later, they turned right onto Water Street and walked to a short lane just beyond the wooden fire hall, where they found George Ritchie's carpentry shop, a 40' by 50' building that still had the appearances of the blacksmith's shop it had once been. Stan continued to be mindful of his spending, and a chance to combine business with pleasure had considerable appeal: the day had been declared a civic holiday in Penticton, so he didn't have to miss a day's work and the reduced excursion fares offered to the picnickers meant it didn't cost him much to check out the new business opportunity.

The SS Okanagan *docked at the end of Bernard Avenue as local citizens enjoy a day at City Park beach. Knox Mountain in the background. (Kelowna Museum photo)*

As the men looked around the dark workshop, they discussed the equipment that was there and what more they would need, considered the possibilities, and quickly decided to purchase the business. They had come prepared and immediately put $25 down and provided a note for the remaining $300. Etter was an experienced business man, 23 years older than Stan, and had been involved in a number of partnerships. Stan, on the other hand, had never run his own business but what he lacked in experience in that area, he made up for with his wood-working skills, energy, and determination. It was a promising combination as Oswell became something of a mentor to Stan and perhaps even a father-figure, sharing his business experience and offering guidance and friendship. Stan brought his youth and practical skills to the table, and over time was able to gain confidence and learn the business skills he didn't have before. It is unlikely either man appreciated the significance of the day's events in setting the stage for future developments, and both were probably just hopeful their new partnership, the new business, and their move to another town would be successful. It had been a busy, eventful day but the partners still managed to find time to participate in some of the picnic festivities before boarding the sternwheeler later that afternoon for the return trip to Penticton.

A new business

It didn't take Stan and Oswell long to relocate from Penticton to Kelowna and establish the Kelowna Manufacturing Company. The Okanagan Telephone Directory listed the O. C. Etter residence phone, and the company's longer title, Etter and Simpson, Cabinet Makers and Sash and Door Factory, in the December 1913 issue. Their business telephone number – 312 – stayed with Stan for many years, through many moves. S. M.'s tastes were simple and since he was still on his own, a room in one of the town's many boarding houses was fine. The partners had been a little hasty in choosing their company name, however, and soon discovered there was another Kelowna Manufacturing Company in town and reverted to Etter and Simpson to match their telephone listing. Stan and Oswell added some much-needed machinery to the few pieces they had purchased with the shop to provide

The Kelowna Courier & Okanagan Orchardist, *September 11, 1913.*

the kind of service they had in mind. A plant ledger, compiled some years later, noted a September 1913 purchase of a five-horsepower motor (with a note in Stan's handwriting, "our first motor purchased"), a buzz planer, and band saw, as well as mortise-and-tenon machines for screen doors, and lathes, sanders, and saws to make the office fittings and cabinets they advertised; the cost for the additional equipment was over $2,000. Stan must have been very confident in his new venture as this was a huge financial commitment even if it was shared between the two men.

The years leading up to 1913 held the promise of good times for Kelowna. The city's population had grown to about 1,800 people, and a mini-building boom had been underway for a few years. A sense of permanence and optimism prevailed as new brick buildings along Bernard Avenue were beginning to replace the earlier false-fronted wooden structures. The partners couldn't help but be encouraged, and had few reservations about buying the business or spending substantial amounts of money to equip it. Although there were other sash and door and carpentry businesses in town, there seemed to be more than enough work to go around. It wasn't long before Etter and Simpson were busy and with Oswell's congenial wife, Flora Anna, making sure the men were involved in both the church and community, the demand for their services grew quickly. As 1913 gave way to 1914, however, life in Kelowna began to change as the threat of a world war became reality.

Lost opportunities

Business activity in the area slowed substantially as the overseas money that had developed Okanagan Valley orchards soon vanished, along with many of the British settlers who now patriotically departed to fight for their homeland; over a thousand men left the Okanagan in 1914 to join the battle. The flow of new settlers into the area also slowed to a trickle and those who stayed spent as little money as possible. Etter and Simpson gave "Prompt attention … to all jobbing" as the two-man company did whatever would provide them some income. City Council accounts show the partners being paid $8.55 for repairs to the jail, $2 for sewerage supplies, and $3.30 for hospital repairs, none of which required either their carpentry or cabinet-making skills. As the war dragged on and the city stopped collecting taxes on the homes of fighting men, there was little money to make repairs or improvements to municipal facilities. Businesses closed their doors, and more people lost their jobs. Government-sponsored make-work projects were introduced to help the unemployed, resulting in fewer and fewer opportunities for the partners to find work, and they struggled to earn enough money to support the two of them.

The partners' financial situation worsened over the next several months, and they soon realized their future wasn't as nearly as promising as it had been at the outset of the venture. After much deliberation, S. M. and Oswell concluded there was only enough business to support one of them, and when they couldn't decide who should stay and who should leave, they agreed to make the difficult decision by tossing a coin – heads, the company was yours and tails, you moved on. Stan called tails and lost, but Oswell changed his mind and decided he wasn't prepared to risk his future, especially since he had the added responsibility of a wife and two young sons to support. Etter and his family would return to Penticton.

The sole proprietor

S. M. Simpson Sash and Door on Water Street[3] was in business by the early part of 1916, and while O. C. Etter still had a residential telephone listing in Kelowna, the Etters had re-established themselves in Penticton by the following September. Subsequent telephone directories noted Etter and Pearson – Sash and Door & General Contractor, and Etter and Killick – General Contractor in Penticton, with Oswell always being the first partner, and he continued to work in the construction business until his death in 1937 at the age of 74. His obituary recalled: "A pioneer builder, Mr. Etter's mark on the structural developments of this community during his residence and building career were well-known … his Christian principles and beliefs always made him an outstanding member and supporter of the Church."[4]

The Etter and Simpson partnership only survived in Kelowna for two years, but during that time the men had become involved in the church and business life of the community. When Stan took over, he enjoyed a good reputation for quality work at fair prices and had a substantial clientele among the town's business community. Oswell had left Stan with a solid company and taught him enough about operating a business that Stan could continue – as long as he could find customers. S. M. was confident enough now to run the business, he liked being his own boss in spite of the inherent risks, and most importantly felt settled enough in Kelowna that he didn't see any reason to pack up, move on, and work for someone else again. It was a big step for the 31-year-old, but the decision to stay seemed to be the best option available to him at the time. Though their friendship probably continued, no one remembers Stan ever talking about his mentor and first business partner, and like many other parts of his life, that information simply died with him.

Early Kelowna

When Stan arrived in Kelowna in 1913, the small town's dusty main street, wooden sidewalks, hitching posts, and false-fronted buildings belied the changes already taking place in the community. While many frontier towns were ungoverned and grew haphazardly, a small group of early residents had much higher aspirations for this new town and spearheaded its incorporation in May 1905. The first city council had enacted bylaws to ensure that public health, street construction, and fire protection made Kelowna attractive and safe for the growing number of settlers that were arriving each year from overseas and the east. The swaying lantern of the horse-drawn 'honey' wagon could be fol-

Kelowna's main street, 1911.

lowed through the town's meandering back lanes in the early morning gloom, as the wagon driver, known locally as the scavenger, took care of the town's sanitation needs by regularly emptying residents' galvanized backyard privy buckets.

Law and order were essential in turn-of-the-century Kelowna, and ordinances were enacted to deal with cases of "furious riding by thoughtless bronco-busters who gave exhibitions of their prowess on the public streets or those who did not hesitate to fire off their fire arms and sorely try the patience of the city authorities."[5] Later, when automobiles became a daily reality on the dusty streets, "those driving in excess of the 10 mph speed limit and given to indiscriminate parking or driving on the wrong side of the road"[6] were also prosecuted.

Bernard Avenue was a vibrant main street for Kelowna's residents in 1913. Efforts were made to keep the summer's road dust to a minimum, but mud from infrequent rains and occasional flooding created horrendous problems for those trying to get around town. William Haug & Co. laid a cement sidewalk along part of the south side of Bernard Avenue, which was a great benefit for the ladies in their fashionably long skirts, though in other parts of town they had to manoeuvre on varying widths of unsteady wooden planks or on the dirt roadway itself.

The Okanagan Valley's transportation system had also evolved in the years since the CPR had finally driven its last spike in 1885. Transcontinental train passengers could disembark from the main line at Sicamous and catch a stagecoach to Okanagan Landing until 1892, when the Shuswap and Okanagan Railway line was completed. This was also the year the sternwheeler SS *Aberdeen* was launched to carry passengers and freight down Okanagan Lake. With ever-increasing volumes of both passenger and freight traffic, the *Aberdeen* was retired from regular passenger service in 1907 and replaced by the larger, more luxurious SS *Okanagan*. It was possible to drive down the west side of Okanagan Lake by the time Stan arrived in Kelowna, but the dirt track was perilous and narrow. Kelowna, along with the rest of the country, was mesmerized by the new automobile and racy motor bikes even though the area had few roads and even fewer places to drive to. The Okanagan's love / hate relationship with the motor car and the challenges of crossing Okanagan Lake at Kelowna had its origins just after the turn of the last century. S. M. would have to contend with that very issue as his business grew and expanded.

The valleys of B.C.'s Southern Interior originally supported large cattle ranches, but as the gold rush brought more people to the area, the need for food and supplies provided an impetus to begin using the land for other agricultural purposes. Settlers initially planted small orchards for their own use, but as the trees flourished, so did their interest in expanding production, and by 1901 apples and other fruits, vegetables, tobacco, and cigars were being exported out of the Okanagan. Much was destined for the mining camps of the Kootenays, but produce was also shipped to the Prairies and overseas.

During a time when boom towns came and went with amazing speed, Kelowna planned from the outset to become permanent and prosperous. The Bank of Montreal, the Royal Bank, and the Canadian Bank of Commerce all had branches on Bernard Avenue by 1913. The post office was established in 1893, and the early *Kelowna Clarion* newspaper became *The Kelowna Courier and Okanagan Orchardist* in 1905. George Rose was its editor for the next 33 years and what was once a small four-page weekly newspaper advertising local businesses[7] and reporting on the small town's activities, eventually evolved into a multi-sectioned daily with worldwide coverage.[8]

Services had to be provided for the new arrivals in this frontier community and by

While the sternwheelers carried passengers and freight north and south along Okanagan Lake, Captain Len Hayman operated three scows plus the MV Klatawa *(on the left) and the MV* Aricia *(on the right, between the barges) to carry passengers and livestock between Kelowna and the west side of Okanagan Lake. Stan later bought the* Klatawa *and used it for many years to haul log booms around the lake.*

1892, Kelowna's first school was organized on the second floor of Lequime's general store. Growth was so rapid that by October of the following year, another school was built and by 1913, the tender was let for the large brick Central School, which is still in use today. In 1908, the city raised $10,000 to construct the first Kelowna General Hospital on land that is still occupied by today's much-expanded facility. The Oblate Missionaries settled in the Okanagan Mission in the mid-1800s and seemed to set a tone of relative sobriety and earnestness for the community. They were followed by several other denominations, with the Benvoulin Presbyterian Church founded in 1892 and the cornerstone laid for St. Michael's and All Angels Anglican Church in 1911. In 1925, the separate congregations of the Methodists, Presbyterians, and Congregationalists merged and moved downtown to the Presbyterian church, which then became the First United.

Kelowna was not without its diversions. The Lakeview Hotel and the Palace Hotel had lively bars and round-the-clock poker and Blackjack games for those who were looking for a little more excitement. Both hotels provided lodging for single men, but numerous boarding houses around town also offered room and board for 'respectable gentlemen' as a less expensive and quieter alternative. Kelowna's early sporting life also flourished, and the Kelowna Regatta and Water Carnival began in 1905. When City Park was purchased in 1908, a permanent grandstand and clubhouse soon followed.

Stan would have been able to sample all sorts of cultural events upon his arrival in Kelowna. A two-day fall fair at the Exhibition Grounds in the city's north end, with its famous suicide race down Knox Mountain, drew spectators and participants from all over the Valley. Gilbert and Sullivan were great favourites and talented residents were known to stage a very credible *Mikado*. The opera house seated 600 and was the scene of a curious array of events, including wrestling. Frontier culture was provided by those who ventured off to the colonies[9] and pianoforte, violin, and elocution lessons were offered by 'Professors of Music' who were also "at liberty for concerts, songs, recitations, and monologues."[10] Travelling shows offered alternatives to the local productions with moving pictures or plays like *Charley's Aunt*, *Birth of a Nation*, or *Uncle Tom's Cabin*.

Community activities filled the void in the lives of many people whose families lived elsewhere, but it was up to the churches to protect the moral fibre of their flocks. Socials, teas, and dinners, as well as public lectures on "How to meet the evils of the white slave trade," or "Be it resolved that novel reading is not beneficial," or "Defeat through Drunkenness" were regularly presented in small Valley towns. Given Stan's religious upbringing, he would likely have been more inclined to frequent these events than some of the other 'less appropriate' activities that were available.

Before equipment was developed to stack piles of lumber left to air-dry in mill yards, agile Chinese men carried the heavy green boards up the sides of the tall lumber piles on protruding narrow boards that served as a precarious ladder.

Kelowna, like many other small towns across the province, had a flourishing Chinatown. Known as "celestials" because of their perceived ties to the mystical universe, the predominantly single male Chinese population came to work on the railroads. When that construction was finished, they stayed on and often ended up doing the menial jobs no one else would take. Most never made it back to China and efforts to bring their families to this country failed when a succession of federal Exclusion Acts and costly head taxes effectively eliminated immigration, and the men were left to establish their own communities. Dr. Sun Yat Sen, the first nationalist president of China, visited Kelowna in 1911 and it was not long after that about 500 Chinese (about 10 per cent of Kelowna's population at the time) developed a vibrant neighbourhood of rooming houses, shops, restaurants, laundries, and a Masonic Hall (which doubled as a hospital) in a small three-block area. The Chinese often worked at area sawmills, clambering up the sides of the lumber piles, stacking the heavy green boards higher and higher.

The early fruit industry

Small orchards had been thriving in the Okanagan for about 40 years before Lord and Lady Aberdeen planted their 480-acre Guisachan Ranch near Kelowna and 1,300 acres in Coldstream, near Vernon, at the turn of the 20th century. Their holdings became the first commercially viable orchards in the Valley and laid the foundation for what has become the area's most defining characteristic – its orchards and vineyards. Lord Aberdeen became Governor General of Canada in 1893 and left the Valley for the nation's capital, but during his time in the Okanagan, Aberdeen's high profile and contacts in Britain drew considerable attention to both the area and its fruit growing potential. By 1915, orchards were already surrounding the Kelowna town site and the commercial potential of the burgeoning industry was just beginning to be realized. Several development companies bought thousands of acres of grazing lands and turned them into orchards: the Kelowna Land and Orchard Company (KLO) irrigated and subdivided land near Mission Creek and gave the town property for its new hospital; the Belgo Canadian Fruit Lands Co. Ltd., using capital from Belgium, developed land in the Black Mountain area; and the Central Okanagan Land and Orchard Co. subdivided much of what is now Rutland, east of Kelowna's downtown core. Once the large cattle ranches had been subdivided into smaller, more marketable acreages, the need for irrigation soon became apparent. Creeks were dammed, and flumes and channels were built to bring water from the surrounding hills to the newly-cultivated orchards. Development companies ran aggressive marketing campaigns that lured settlers from other parts of Canada, Britain, and Europe to the Okanagan in the early part of

Trees in the Valley's early orchards were widely-spaced with irrigation ditches running between the rows. Today's high-density, sprinkler-irrigated compact orchards are dramatic alternative to orchard techniques in vogue at the turn of the last century.

the last century. They made enthusiastic claims that fortunes would be made quickly, that owning an orchard held little financial risk, and that the undertaking required only a minimum amount of work. Many of the people who responded had no idea how to operate a farm or an orchard, or even survive without servants, but in these early days they saw life in the colony as an adventure and rarely seemed deterred by the possibility of hardship.

The Kelowna Board of Trade was established in 1906 to promote the Okanagan and invite people to the Valley to set up their businesses. Advertisements ran in the *Winnipeg Free Press* and elaborate displays of the Valley's apple crops began to appear in Toronto, London, and Spokane. As Britain was the preferred source for new immigrants, advertisements were placed in *The London Times* and a thousand brochures were sent to the B.C. Agent General in London in an effort to lure people to the area. The rapid pace of orchard development in the first decade of the new century was fortunate, as the early plantings and irrigation works, often paid for with foreign capital, created the base for the fruit industry's future growth and expansion. The flow of money dried up with the outbreak of World War I and the orchard community had to rely on its own resourcefulness to survive.[11] Once it was established, however, that same fruit industry grew over the next century and continues to flourish in the Okanagan today, although many of the trees have been replaced and crops have often changed to meet the demands of a different marketplace.

Tobacco production was thriving in the Okanagan as early as 1894, and Kelowna's British and North American Tobacco Company produced 800,000 cigars annually. By the first decade of the new century, trade shows in London were praising the Valley-grown product, but a large part of the area's tobacco and cigar market came from the gold miners who passed through the Okanagan and nearby Kootenays on their way north. When they moved on, much of the demand for Okanagan tobacco left with them. The loss of this market, along with significant financial mismanagement, drove the British and North American Tobacco into bankruptcy and the area's tobacco industry soon disappeared.

Kelowna's first permanent sawmill

Around 1891, Bernard Lequime, a pioneer entrepreneur, decided to move his small sawmill from Okanagan Mission, south of present-day Kelowna, to a flat area 10 km to the north, beside Okanagan Lake. It was a curious decision at the time, as most sawmills were portable and frequently dismantled so they could be moved closer to the trees being cut, but Lequime saw the benefits of reversing the practice. Okanagan Lake had been the Valley's main transportation route for a number of years and he figured it would be easier to float logs to the mill instead of having to move his equipment every year or so to stay in business. Shortly after the mill was set up, a new town site – which would soon become Kelowna – was laid out around it, and the wharf Lequime built for his log-hauling boat was taken over by the CPR, which needed a wharf for the sternwheeler SS *Aberdeen*. With the increasing passenger and freight traffic on Okanagan Lake, the railway company saw an opportunity and the *Aberdeen* became the first of three sternwheelers it would have on this lake.[12] Lequime built another wharf and stacked his lumber over the still-unoccupied town site, but it is highly unlikely he would have realized his sawmill would remain at the same location for more than half a century while Kelowna's downtown business district grew and eventually surrounded his original mill site.

Lequime also ran a general store across the dusty main street from his sawmill[13] where a young man named David Lloyd-Jones worked for him. Lloyd-Jones was a carpenter who left his Ontario home in 1893 and headed for B.C.'s Interior via San Francisco, Esquimalt (on Vancouver Island), and New Westminster, where he caught a steamer down the Fraser River to Hope before finally horse-packing over the Hope-Princeton trail to Okanagan Mission. Lloyd-Jones met up with his brother, William, who was already in the area. The two men pre-empted land in Summerland before William departed for points unknown, and David worked as a carpenter before joining Lequime in his store. It didn't take long for the restless Lloyd-Jones to also begin working at Lequime's mill, and within a few months he had become the manager. The small business was turning out 28,000 board feet of lumber a day at the time, mainly for the new homes and businesses being built in Kelowna, although some lumber was also delivered to small communities springing up along the lakeshore. After a decade in business, Lequime decided it was time to sell his Kelowna sawmill and move to the Kootenays to open another mill.

The lumber and dock in the foreground are part of David Lloyd-Jones' Kelowna Saw Mill at the foot of Bernard Avenue in the early 1900s. Bernard Lequime, the first owner of the mill, also ran the general store across the street. (Kelowna Museum photo)

He had a ready buyer in David Lloyd-Jones, and the mill manager bought out Lequime in 1901. Disaster struck almost immediately, however, when Lloyd-Jones' Kelowna Saw Mill burned to the ground before the new owner had a chance to insure it. While he was staring at the smoking ruins, three local business men, F. A. Taylor, T. W. Stirling, and Arthur Day, offered Lloyd-Jones the money necessary to rebuild. Lloyd-Jones offered to pay off his debt when the mill began making money, but the men chose to become shareholders in his company and remained partners until the business was sold in 1944.[14]

There were benefits to having a permanent sawmill close to a growing community, but there were also some drawbacks. Logs were often cut high up the Valley's hillsides, and since there were few roads, horse teams had to haul the logs as close to the lakeshore as possible. That often left them perched at the top of a rocky bank and it took some ingenuity to build chutes[15] to get the logs down the steep hillsides into Okanagan Lake, where they would be collected from various sites and hauled back to the mill by tug. The mill was destroyed by fire again in 1906, and Lloyd-Jones moved the buildings a little further north so he could sell the increasingly-valuable property fronting onto Bernard Avenue. As the business grew, and the unsightly sawmill, planning mill, and lumber piles took over the lakeshore adjacent to Kelowna's City Park and a large portion of the growing downtown business district, the mayor of the day attempted to convince Lloyd-Jones to move his sawmill even further north, away from the town centre. The mill owner was reluctant, however, and said he would only consider it if the city gave him a ten-year reprieve on property taxes. The city fathers declined and the mill remained in its original location until it was finally destroyed by fire four decades later.

From despair to optimism

Now that Stan was running the carpentry shop he and Oswell had bought in 1913, he decided to use his own name for the new company. But he still had to buy out his old partner before he could do that. The two men had been regular customers of the Royal Bank, and Stan naturally applied there for the $350 loan he needed. To his astonishment, he was turned down. For a man who had tracked every nickel spent since he was a teen, it was a grievous insult. When it happened with no explanation, it was even worse. Stan learned many years later that the influential Lloyd-Jones had sug-

Kelowna Saw Mill – this photo may have been taken about 1920, but very few changes were made to the buildings between 1910 and 1944.

Kelowna Saw Mill – the white horse in the foreground is standing where the front entrance of today's City Hall is located.

gested to the bank manager that S. M.'s struggling business was probably a poor credit risk. Lloyd-Jones' assessment may have appeared right at first glance, but neither he nor the bank manager had factored Stan's determination into the equation. The real motivation behind Lloyd-Jones' actions have been lost to time, although the the animosity would resurface in the future. This was not an auspicious beginning for Stan's solo business venture but fortunately Kelowna had more than one bank, and he was able to walk across the street to the Bank of Montreal and get the loan he needed. As Stan's company grew and eventually became the town's largest employer, the relationship with his new bank continued to their mutual benefit for many years.

On with business

Securing a loan was just one of the hurdles Stan had to overcome when he ventured out on his own. Times were tough everywhere during the early part of WWI, and it was difficult to find enough work to keep his small shop running. Everyone became miserly with their limited incomes as the war continued, including the town council that had been one of his regular customers. To make matters worse, Stan had no money for advertising and had to rely on repeat business to survive. Now that he was once again in charge of his finances, Stan started to keep track of his business transactions in two red 3" x 5" notebooks. Each expenditure and sale was meticulously itemized, including bad debts, goods on sale, his customers by name, and the amounts they owed. Stan extended credit when his customers couldn't pay cash and noted their debt, the interest charged, and repayment dates. He had his own system of record keeping as "Xs", penciled-out amounts, "OKs," "interest,"

and "contra" were scattered through the pages. The list of ledger entries doesn't mention the kind of work Stan was doing, but it does show how little money he was making on each job. Thriving was out of the question, but Stan was managing to survive.

The names found in the small notebooks are a who's who of the town's early businesses and as Stan was becoming better known, many of his customers were among Kelowna's recognizable pioneers, including: the Hewetson & Mantle insurance company; Fumerton's Department Store; Mr. Dumoulin, the manager of the Bank of Montreal who had enough faith in Stan to extend him the loan; the Kelowna Club, a gentleman's club founded in 1904; and the Methodist Sunday School, whose debt was always crossed out. The Kelowna Garage, which sold the new-fangled Ford Touring car, was also on Stan's list of accounts, as was

Stan kept his accounts for 1914, 1915, and 1916 in two small red notebooks, itemizing amounts owing and crossing them off as they were paid or cancelled. The names include the town's pioneers and early companies.

Rowcliffe's cannery and packinghouse; Leckie's Hardware;[16] Leathley, the publisher of *The Kelowna Record*; the Casorso Brothers, and Pridham, who became well-known orchardists. Stan's small business had a cash flow for February 1915 of $336.81 for 41 transactions, plus credit notes for a further $225.10 – Stan wasn't the only one finding it tough going, and when his customers couldn't pay, he extended their credit. But many other businesses in the area were not so lucky and had little choice but to close their doors.

Stan always forgave an oddly recurring and unexplained monthly $2.55 debt of the Epworth League, a Methodist youth organization, but nonetheless recorded it as one of his regular accounts. Life in the small community did carry on during the war, and there were still accounts for the Philharmonic Society, the Mason-Riche Piano Company, the Kelowna Land and Orchard Company, and Lloyd-Jones' Kelowna Saw Mill. The provincial government, the town's fire hall next door to his shop, the jail, and Aquatic Club would also show up in the little red book, and there was even a listing for Stan's old partner, Oswell Etter, whom he charged $12.40 in May before Oswell left town. At the same time, the Kelowna Furniture Company was selling some of the furniture Stan had been making as part of his cabinetry business, and his account book noted the store had two small tables, a chair, and a small billiard table of his. The billiard table keeps reappearing in the account books, but whether it is the same table having difficulty finding a buyer or whether Stan was doing a modest business in billiard tables is unknown.

S. M.'s unmistakable handwriting filled most of the books' pages but on occasion, he hired a book-keeper and the odd page in a much more elegant and flamboyant script would appear. Two pocket-sized Bank of Montreal account books also remain, with the hand-written entries first checked off with a red pencil and then again by the vigilant Stan, who double-checked each item with an "X." He also had a habit of writing dimensions of some unknown door or window on whatever was handy, and the back pages of one of the bank books has penciled specifications of some now forgotten project.

The number of Stan's clients grew over time, but the value of each transaction was usually small and charges in the amount of 35¢, 50¢, and 75¢ were not uncommon; the largest single amount on a page of 22 entries might be $10. Stan's was definitely a volume business, but gradually the value of each transaction grew, and as the turmoil of the early years of the war subsided, the local economy became less fragile and fewer credit notes were listed. By June 1, 1916, Stan's books showed an opening balance of $117.98, which dropped to $2.12 two months later, but the following months showed gradual improvements as the 35¢ and 50¢ amounts were replaced by more substantial figures.

The business grows

Stan began getting orders for the custom-made cabinets and furniture he had been making before the war as the town's economy picked up, in addition to the small jobs that had sustained him over the previous few years. It wasn't long before the original carpentry shop became too small and overcrowded. Stan was looking around for larger premises when he noticed a small headline in *The Kelowna Courier and Okanagan Orchardist* on December 27, 1917, reporting: "Cannery Narrowly Escapes Destruction." The newspaper went on to explain that a recently installed chimney in George and Frank Fraser's Abbott Street cannery[17] proved faulty and the resulting fire had carried the blaze up to the building's second floor. Damage had been confined to the centre of the premises, and when Stan checked the building, he found the outside walls and most of the floor area still intact and felt he could easily repair the rest. The timing was opportune as the brothers also had a cannery in the north end of town and decided to consolidate their two operations, which left the Abbott Street building vacant at the same time Stan was looking for larger premises. He bought the building, gathered up the tools of his trade, and moved around the corner to the other end of the block from his original shop.

Since the cannery was so close to Stan's first workshop, he was able to repair the building while carrying on his day-to-day business and move equipment to his new premises on evenings and weekends. Stan was still operating a one-man shop at this time but with the larger site, he could now do the custom work he was getting orders for as well as hire help to provide odd-job services to his many customers. With a building four or five times larger than his first shop, Stan began to expand his production to include orchard ladders, as well as store and office fittings. He was already making custom windows, so it was a logical expansion to do glass replacements and it wasn't long before the company became one of the largest glass installers and auto glass replacement operations in the Valley.[18]

Stan took some time to settle into his new building and ponder the direction he wanted his business to take. He had been making orchard ladders for some time now and was becoming more familiar with the Valley's fruit industry, and realized the maturing apple trees – the largest crop in the Kelowna area at the time – would be producing more and more fruit in the coming years. Fruit growers and packinghouses would need more boxes for picking the crop and exporting apples out of the Valley, and while S. M. was cautious about expanding too quickly, he was both optimistic and ambitious, and looking for a new venture. Several sawmills around the area were already making fruit boxes, but Stan speculated that the steadily increasing harvests would create a demand for boxes well beyond their capacity. Stan had other things going on in his life at this time, however, and while he knew there was an opportunity for him in the fruit industry, he needed to think about it, gather more information, be comfortable with a decision to expand again so soon after buying the cannery, and make sure his finances were in place to support such a move. Whether he recognized that a decision to get into the fruit box business would be the first step in establishing the major thrust of his business over the next 30 years is unknown. Regardless, it would be another few years before he would commit to making boxes.

On a more personal note

Stan was primarily focussed on his business during the years following his arrival from Penticton, but he did take a little time to become involved in his new community. Shortly after landing in Kelowna, Stan began attending the Methodist Church and probably took advantage of the offering of the Methodist Ladies' Aid who:

> served a most excellent chicken supper in Raymer's Hall ... where the liberal attendance must have been gratifying to the energetic ladies in charge of the function. The meal was dainty enough to make a bachelor commit matrimony, for the roast chicken, home-made bread, cakes, pies, salads and other good things were certainly the real old-fashioned article. Every table in the hall was well filled, and the onslaught on the fowl continued from 6 o'clock to after eight.[19]

It was during this period in his life that Stan met Thomas Birch and his three daughters, Eva, Laura, and Bertha. The Birch family had arrived in Kelowna from England in 1911 following Tom's younger brother, John, who brought his family to the area a few years earlier and had taken up farming in Benvoulin, on the outskirts of Kelowna.[20] Thomas' wife, Jane Mary Gibbons, had succumbed to consumption (tuberculosis) and died in 1905, 26 years after they married, leaving Tom to care for 23-year-old Eva, 22-year-old Laura, and 20-year-old Bertha. With the three daughters still unmarried six years later, Thomas thought the prospects of finding them husbands would likely be better in the New World and the family of four immigrated to Canada to join his brother in Kelowna.

Thomas and his daughters each found work to help support the family on their arrival in the Okanagan. Eva and Laura worked as domestics, and Bertha, the most independent of the sisters, set herself up as a dressmaker and continued the trade she had learned in England.[21] Thomas was variously employed as a stableman for Dr. Knox, the town's first physician, and as a butcher, though one presumes not at the same time. Subsequent newspaper accounts told of the family's involvement in the social and musical activities of the small town's only Methodist Church. Stan would have undoubtedly met the Birches in church, where he had become an active member of the congregation; S. M. was even asked to propose toast at the fifth annual Methodist Missionary Banquet to "Canada's Unparalleled Opportunity at Home and Abroad." While referring to the role of church missionaries in "laying the foundation for the social, moral, and spiritual life of new immigrants in the new country of Canada,"[22] Stan was likely thinking that Kelowna held some of those same opportunities for him as well.

Now that he was settled in the community and running his own business, Stan decided to bring his mother and sister, Norma, from Owen Sound, Ontario, to Kelowna. With financial help from Ruth, who was living in New York City at the time, he bought a small home on Sutherland Avenue and moved out of his rooming house to join his family. The friendship between Stan and the Birch family that had begun at church grew to include his mother and sister, and it took on an added level of seriousness.

Bertha disappeared from the family's history upon her death. This unidentified lady is presumed to be Bertha.

The relationship between Stan and Bertha flourished, and after a respectable Methodist courtship, the two were married on May 11, 1916, at the home of the bride's sister and brother-in-law, Mr. and Mrs. W. J. Clement. Stan was 30 years old at the time and Bertha was 31, and according to the newspaper:

> only the immediate relatives and most intimate friends of the happy pair were present for the ceremony ... After receiving the congratulations and well-wishes of the assembled friends, and after partaking of refreshments, Mr. and Mrs. S. M. Simpson motored to Vernon, where they took the train for the Coast ... among the most popular young people of the community, a large number of friends have united in wishing them every

happiness. Upon their return, the young couple held an Open House at their Sutherland Ave home, on June 1.[23]

The first year of Stan and Bertha's marriage was busy, with Stan moving his business to larger premises and the birth of their son, Horace Birch, on March 17, 1917. A small announcement was sent out by Stan telling of the arrival of "Baby Simpson (boy)," and mentioning that "Bertha had a rather hard time but both her and baby are doing nicely now." This was the first hint of problems. Bertha fought a virulent infection for several days and when nothing seemed to help, medicine was ordered from Vancouver. It was delivered via the Kettle Valley Railway to Penticton, where a friend collected the medicine from the train station and drove along the treacherous road to the west side of Okanagan Lake opposite Kelowna. Stan and his friend, David Leckie, were waiting on the beach for the package to arrive and rowed back across the lake through the blackness of night, but by the time they arrived at the hospital it was too late. Bertha had died shortly before their return. A small headline in *The Kelowna Record* told of:

> Mrs. S. M. Simpson Passing Away … from complications arising out of confinement … The deceased was very well known in the city, and the sad event has awakened much sympathy for the bereaved husband … Service will be held in Knox Church, April 5, 1917.[24]

Permelia and Norma took care of three-week-old Horace, and Bertha quickly disappeared from their lives. While no one recalls any mention of Bertha ever being made after her death, there are two unidentified photos of a slight, dark, attractive young lady who might have been her. One was taken in Dover, England, where the Birch family lived before coming to Canada, and the other was taken in Kelowna. A headstone in the old part of the Kelowna Cemetery is the sole reminder that Bertha Elizabeth Simpson, née Birch, once lived in the town.

Signs that Stan's world had changed came from small clues in his everyday life – his account books are the only hint that his world seemed to stop during March and April of 1917. There were few billings for those two months: the Bank of Montreal deposit book had six entries for March and two for April. In March of that year, the telephone directory also noted that Stan had installed a telephone in his Sutherland Avenue home, likely in anticipation of the baby's arrival. Stan undoubtedly mourned Bertha's death but with a new son, his mother, and sister relying on him, he couldn't afford to be incapacitated for long. He picked up and returned to work, and with an advertisement in *The Kelowna Courier and Okanagan Orchardist*, reminded the community he was still in business.

Bertha's death wasn't the only tragedy that struck the Simpson family in 1917. Stan's youngest brother, Sergeant Alfred Simpson of the Canadian Expeditionary Force, was "Killed in Action" on the Belgian front on June 28, 1917. Alfred, 22 years of age at the time, was the baby of the family and looked far too young to even leave home. He had stayed in Owen Sound when his mother and sister came west to live with Stan and had enlisted in Grey County, Ontario, as one of many Canadians to serve in the "war to end all wars."

SCREEN DOORS
AND WINDOWS

(if they fit) protect your health by keeping out the (typhoid) fly.

——Mine are——

Made to Remain True, Made to Last, and Made in Kelowna.

Fruit Ladders, Windows and Repairs

S.M. Simpson
Next Door to Fire Hall.

The Kelowna Courier & Okanagan Orchardist, *April 26, 1917.*

Kelowna after the war

Canada's population was beginning to shift from its early 20th century rural base to urban centres in the immediate post-war years as many people who had settled the vast open spaces of the Prairies left in search of a better life. Families with few resources flooded into cities ill-prepared to deal with them. Housing was inadequate and few social services were available to look after those without jobs, which were particularly difficult to come by. As the foreign war was ending, social and labour unrest became a daily reality in many cities and with a still-sluggish economy, veterans who thought they were returning to a better world found little to be optimistic about. The country's collective frustration and discontent culminated in the Winnipeg General Strike in the summer of 1919, a strike that was brought about in part by a lack of effort from mainstream political parties to deal with the underlying causes of discontent. It wasn't long before both the Communist Party and the newly created Co-operative Commonwealth Federation (CCF) – the precursor to today's New Democratic Party (NDP) – stepped into the leadership vacuum. While no one realized it at the time, the activities of these parties during the years following the war and into the early 1920s set the stage for the strife and protest that would become commonplace during the Great Depression and the trade union activities of the '40s. Most of this discontent and labour unrest passed by Kelowna – the city was remote and mostly rural, and neither the news of the day nor the people involved had much direct impact on the area. The pressures of great social change that followed these events would eventually be felt, not only in Kelowna but also in Stan's sawmill.

The Kelowna Courier & Okanagan Orchardist, *September 25, 1919.*

The 1919 edition of Wrigley's *Provincial Directory* noted that the population of Kelowna and district was now about 5,000 people, with a substantial number of residents employed in fruit and vegetable growing, packing, and shipping, as well as dairy farming. When it came to opportunities in the area, Wrigley's noted that because of the "recent abnormal conditions" [i.e. World War I] it was impractical to provide details for investment or employment opportunities. Nonetheless, the directory did give "Reasons why Kelowna is a Desirable Place to Live":

> Spring opens as early as March and good weather lasts until October. Winters for the most part are clear and bright and not severe. The climate is healthy and long dry summers, short bracing winters, good motor roads, attractive scenery, splendid bathing, good hunting and fishing, excellent schools, reasonable rents, and a good class of people.[25]

As the second decade of the new century came to a close, Kelowna was still dependent on sternwheelers to carry people and produce to trains at either end of lake. It wasn't isolated enough, however, to be protected from the ravages of the 1918 Spanish influenza pandemic, which killed over 40 million people worldwide. Many Valley families lost sons and daughters, and sometimes parents, to the terrible disease. The aftermath of the flu, coupled with social unrest and wartime losses, seemed to cast a pall over the entire country. In an attempt to bolster morale, His Royal Highness The Prince of Wales visited Canada – and Kelowna – the following year as local soldiers guarded the streets and formed an impressive military welcome; even the most "stolid socialists were seen to effuse over his affable comradeship."[26]

Land speculation has always been an integral part of Okanagan Valley development and early promoters aggressively marketed land that was often unsuitable for fruit growing. Gradually, unproductive areas were abandoned, and as trees began to mature and produce good crops, the orchard industry became more firmly established as the area's major economic activity. Kelowna had the largest fruit acreage of all Valley communities, with almost 5,000 acres under cultivation, consisting of 28 varieties of apples, seven varieties each of pears, plums, and prunes, and six varieties of cherries, while the soft fruits – peaches and apricots – were more often found in the south end of the Valley. Each area had its own packinghouses and canneries, and as the provincial government began to provide loans to build the necessary irrigation work to sustain them, the fruit industry's future looked promising. Markets for Okanagan produce had moved beyond the mining and gold camps in the Kootenays to the Prairies, and through the port of Vancouver to Australia and New Zealand. After the Panama Canal opened in 1914, shipping to Britain also became a great deal easier, and with fast freight boats rushing the more perishable crops from Kelowna south to Penticton or north to Okanagan Landing, the Valley could now access markets almost anywhere in the world.

By the time Stan arrived in Kelowna in 1913, the town had grown beyond its early pioneer days and had a sense of permanence about it. The fruit industry, though still in its infancy, was being recognized across the country and overseas for its potential, and newcomers to the Valley – Stan included – were pleased with the opportunities they found to build a better life. He likely saw himself as a carpenter and although he would eventually have greater aspirations, S. M. continued to struggle to make ends meet and run his own business. The Kelowna Saw Mill would have been the source for wood he needed for his carpentry business, but Lloyd-Jones ran a pretty basic operation and Stan was often forced to go further abroad if he had special orders to fill. That meant having lumber sent to him from Brookes McKenzie, a supplier in Penticton, and while it was a short-term solution it was one that Stan's expanding business would outgrow before long.

S. M. seemed to have found a congenial place to live and had been able to establish and then expand a business with prospects for long-term growth. He had suffered personal tragedy with the loss of his wife, but his young son was well and with the arrival of his mother and sister, he now had the most important members of his family with him. Stan was cautiously optimistic about his business: he had a home, family, and friends around him, and he was becoming an integral part of the town's growing business and social community. S. M.'s life had been transformed from its early itinerant homesteading years to one of stability and his own business. Much had transpired in the relatively few years Stan had been in Kelowna, but it is unlikely he had any idea of the changes that would occur in the coming decade. He would have had even less of an idea that his ingenuity, perseverance, and determination would be tested in ways that he could never have anticipated.

New Directions – the 1920s

S tan had an uncanny knack for being in the right place at the wrong time. His arrival in Saskatchewan coincided with the first snowflakes that marked the onset of the two worst winters in recorded history. A few years later, he started a new business in Kelowna just before World War I broke out; the resulting economic slowdown left him with so little income that he barely survived. S. M. persisted through the uncertainty and gradually his company began to thrive. But was this to become a pattern?

New opportunities

British Columbia's economy had more or less recovered from WWI by the early 1920s and the Okanagan Valley's maturing apple orchards were producing one bumper harvest after another.[1] As the decade wore on, however, apple markets became saturated. Prices dropped, and growers began receiving bills for packing and shipping instead of income from the sale of their crops. For a few years, orchardists faced tough times and while Stan was certainly aware of this – the local newspapers were full of stories of the growers' dilemma – he must have thought the over-supply problems were temporary. Increasing orchard productivity would eventually mean that more boxes were needed, and while there were already a number of box makers in the Valley, S. M. felt there was still room for one more.

A multi-functional Day-Elder truck. Circa 1925.

Stan took time to consolidate his operation and build up some cash reserves after moving to the new premises, so it wasn't until 1923 that he began buying the equipment necessary to get started in the box-making business. He also took awhile to learn the ropes, and there were a few missteps along the way: part way into his first season, he realized the single-colour printer bought to stamp the packinghouse name on box-ends was inadequate, and traded it in for a two-colour machine. Stan decided it was better to take the $299 loss on the original printer and move on rather than make do with inadequate equipment. In spite of this small setback, the new box making venture was so successful that most of the machinery had been paid for by the end of that year.

It didn't take Stan long to see that his expanding business needed even more space, and he purchased an empty lot to the north and added a single-storey extension onto the existing two-storey cannery building. Sheets of corrugated iron were delivered for the walls and roof, and electricity was brought to the site before the more equipment began arriving in January 1924. Once the decision was made to expand, there was little delay in getting the new production line up and running for that year's box-making season. Along with the business' constant growth came the need for a better method of record keeping than S. M.'s red account books could provide. He also needed an infusion of cash to pay for new equipment and in January 1924, S. M. Simpson Ltd. was incorporated, with Royal Stanley Moe as authorized agent, bookkeeper, and Stan's business partner. Sandy Camozzi, the sash and door foreman, became another shareholder, as did Stan's sister, Ruth. The shares of Simpson's, as locals called the company, didn't cost his partners much at the time, but they did provide Stan with some cash and he was confident they would be worth much more, eventually.

Earliest photo of S. M. Simpson Ltd. sash and door building on Abbott Street. The person in the foreground is thought to be Jim Davies, who worked as a finishing carpenter for many years. The second storey portion of the building was originally a cannery.

The evolution of box industry

Western Canadian growers had decided that the American 40 lb. – or bushel – box was more convenient than the barrels that had previously been used for packing apples by the time Stan began making boxes in 1923. The barrels, used in many apple-producing areas, weighed about 150 lbs., contained just over three boxes of apples, and were heavy and awkward to handle, whereas the bushel boxes could be easily lifted to pour apples onto packing tables, and they were light enough that "even a woman" could do the lifting. A 1909 British publication identified the standard that the industry continued to follow:

> All apples in British Columbia, irrespectively of the variety and irrespectively of the size, are packed into a box of uniform dimensions and on one end of each box the law imperatively demands that the grower or packer place his name and postal address, the name of the variety, the grade, and the number of tiers of apples, counting from the bottom upwards. A box of these dimensions, no matter how large or how small the apples packed into it will almost invariably weigh 40 lbs.[2]

The abundance of large-diameter pine trees in the Okanagan Valley enabled local box makers to cut boards to the right size and set a 'no-knot' standard (knots rubbed against the fruit and caused bruising) for the 1" x 11¼" box ends. The waste caused by this no-knot standard was enormous, but the hill-

Logs from the area were huge, but most ended up as fruit boxes.
(Peter Simpson photo)

sides were covered in pine forests that had never been cut; everyone thought they were inexhaustible and there was very little concern about waste. A decade-and-a-half later, however, yellow pine stocks had been greatly reduced by the growing box industry and standards changed to allow for a knot as large as man's thumbnail in box ends. As the years passed and pine stocks diminished even further, box ends would have to be pieced together with squiggle nails to achieve the same 11¼" size. Today, surviving wooden apple boxes can be dated by their construction – single or pieced-together ends, single board tops, bottoms and sides, or two - or three-pieced veneer tops and bottoms, with single components indicating older boxes. Paper labels, many of which have become collector's items, were introduced about this time and glued to boxes by the packinghouses or shippers.

When Stan started in the box business, he purchased lumber from a variety of sources and sometimes had to go as far away as Penticton to find enough. Boards would be cut and shipped by sternwheeler or freight barge from the south end of the lake, but he also bought locally from the Kelowna Saw Mill and Crawford's mill in Okanagan Mission; both mills also made their own boxes. At times, Stan purchased the needed boards from Jenkins Cartage, "Kelowna's Leading Livery Stable," which advertised "Birch, Pine and Fir Wood For Sale."[3] Jenkins' horses hauled rough lumber into town from the portable mills scattered throughout the surrounding hills and took back some of the wood as payment; a number of independent loggers also supplied S. M.'s new box factory with lumber from their bush mills.

Stan bought his first sawmill in 1925 when he became a partner in Fred Munson's Ellison mill.

A pattern begins

Stan quickly realized he needed to have a guaranteed lumber supply to sustain his expanding business. The network of suppliers was fine when the operation was small, but as it grew Stan also became their competitor and the survival of his box business would be in jeopardy if he had to rely on them for basic supplies. That realization pushed Stan towards further independence and a new business venture that would guarantee his supply of raw lumber. This need for ever-increasing amounts of timber became a recurring theme in S. M. Simpson Ltd.'s history, and Stan's first steps to rectify the problem also set the tone for how the company would deal with the issue in the future.

In 1925, Stan went into partnership with Fred Munson, who owned a sawmill in Ellison, about 20 km north-east of Kelowna. Fred had worked with his father, Robert, for years in a succession of bush mills and had the practical experience running a sawmill that Stan lacked. Munson's small mill was little more than a makeshift shed covering a steam-powered saw that used waste slabs and sawdust to feed its boiler. The 6' to 7' diameter pine trees that surrounded the mill were rough cut into boards of the approximate sizes Stan needed and delivered to the Abbott Street factory, where they were planed and finished to the required 1" x 11¼" box-end widths. The factory also cut box sides, tops, and bottoms – the unassembled component parts of a box – that were collectively known as box shook. The term 'shook' likely transferred to box manufacturing from the barrel-making business, where it referred to the set of staves and headings for a cask before they were assembled.

The box factory was located at the edge of Kelowna's expanding business district, with City Park at its front door and a well-established Chinatown immediately to the south, so there was little manoeuvring room to handle the large boards arriving from the bush mill. Stan became creative with the limited space available, and when the rough lumber was delivered, it was unloaded, passed into the building through the window overlooking Abbott Street, re-sawn or planed, and then sent to the box-making area. Stan also used some of the lumber for his ongoing sash and door operation, but supplies were limited and no dimension lumber was being sold at the time. Space was so tight that lumber-handlers had to compete with mounds of slabs, shavings, and sawdust that accumulated in the lane behind the factory.

Box making started in March each year so a good supply would be on hand for the orchardists when harvesting began in June. As production continued, stacks of shook were stored in every available space until the ice melted in the curling rink behind the box factory, and the building was rented as storage space for $10 a month.[4] The timing was perfect for Stan and he filled the building to the rafters with box shook awaiting delivery. Hauling shook bundles from the box factory to the curling rink, stacking them, and then after a few weeks reloading them onto wagons for delivery to the packinghouses and orchards was hard, back-breaking work, and those involved were glad they only had to carry the bundles across the lane.

Another business venture

The growing piles of sawdust and shavings produced by the box factory were also creating space problems for Stan, until he realized the solution was close at hand. Just south of the Abbott Street location, the town's engineer had been trying to re-route the meandering Mill Creek and reclaim some waterlogged, but potentially usable, land. Simpson's bought the land – it was swampy and not worth much at the time – filled up horse-drawn carts, and dumped load after load of sawdust into the bog. Gradually, the sawdust soaked up the water and when it was later covered with gravel, the land became the foundation for today's Abbott Street heritage conservation area.[5]

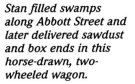

Stan filled swamps along Abbott Street and later delivered sawdust and box ends in this horse-drawn, two-wheeled wagon.

During the 1930s and into the '40s, the land further south of the original fill area was so wet it was possible to paddle a canoe up to Kelowna General Hospital – two blocks in from the lakeshore – but it too was filled with slabs and shavings from Simpson's and built upon. Much of Kelowna's prime lakeshore was also regularly inundated during spring floods, as were parts of City Park, the area north of the downtown core around the new Grand Hotel, and the neighbouring railway lands; each area was gradually filled with mill waste. The company also provided other businesses in town with sawdust and shavings for boiler fuel, while house builders used sawdust for insulation. Many homes constructed during this era still have the original sawdust insulation in their walls; and while it has settled, the sawdust is usually left if the homes are renovated.

Turmoil in everyone's ranks

Things seemed to be going well for the Valley's fruit industry in the mid-1920s. It had survived the heady exhilaration of early land speculation, as well as the demise of several well-marketed orchards that should never have been planted. Orchardists outlasted inadequate irrigation projects and marketing organizations that promoted co-operative schemes with guaranteed returns on investment. Attempts to keep independent-minded growers within the confines of those schemes[6] failed when large apple crops in Washington and the Maritimes threatened the Okanagan's traditional Prairie markets, or perceived biases in the co-op's leadership resulted in discontented growers abandoning the organization and going their own way.[7]

Things may have been unsettled for growers in the mid-'20s, but they were worse for Interior box makers. On May 13, 1926, a meeting took place between Okanagan fruit shippers and the area's box shook makers in an effort to reach an agreement on that year's shook prices.[8] Two local box makers had broken away from the now-defunct B.C. Box Makers Association, which set industry-wide shook prices, and were offering shippers lower prices than other box makers. At the same time, the organization said its members could not operate unless they were guaranteed a certain – and higher – price for their shook. Since the survival of the Valley's emerging box industry was at stake, the shippers and the box association felt they should try to reach an agreement on that season's pricing.

It had already been established that Interior box makers could not provide pine shook (the preferred species) at the same price Coast suppliers could supply hemlock shook, so the real purpose of the meeting was to decide how much of a premium shippers were prepared to pay to sustain Valley box factories. Shook makers presented their arguments: the premium was worth paying for pine shook; Washington apple growers had already established a precedent by paying a 1¢-per-box premium for pine boxes; Interior box makers could supply the Valley's fruit industry except in unusually heavy crop years; and if the premium was not paid, Okanagan box factories would be forced out of the box business and would restrict themselves entirely to the lumber industry.

Stan's second sawmill in Winfield was substantially larger than his first. Rough cut lumber was loaded onto carts at the mill and sent by elevated track out to a field for stacking. It would then be brought into the Abbott Street factory to be planed and cut into the necessary sizes for making boxes.
(Kelowna Museum photo)

By the end of the meeting, the shippers agreed to pay a ½¢-per-box premium for Interior-manufactured pine shook. The threat of the two break-away companies meeting Coastal prices gave Interior box makers little choice but to accept the reduced premium. The following year, however, fruit growers received a better price for their fruit and box makers raised their price by 1¢ per box. But when another ½¢ increase was proposed in 1928, shippers were outraged and suggested that if B.C. mills were not more reasonable in their pricing, they would be compelled to buy shook from the U.S. as the shippers didn't feel they should have to pay such inflated prices for their patriotism.[9] The shippers' outrage was somewhat self-serving as they charged growers for packing and shipping, and the box makers' price increases impacted the amount the shippers could charge, so they were in fact protecting their own profit margins.

S. M. had only been making boxes for a few years by the late '20s and his factory was still small, but the outcome of the talks was important to his future plans and he would have been keenly interested in the negotiations between the shippers and the box makers' association. Stan would have ample opportunity over the next few years to reflect back on these discussions when he challenged the Coast berry-crate makers and Ontario grape-basket manufacturers for their share of the Valley's box market.

More sawmills

Most of the best trees within a 5 km radius of Stan's first mill in Ellison had been cut by 1927, and the saws were packed up and moved a further 8 km north up the road towards Winfield, where a larger, more substantial mill was set up. Logs would be brought down Beaver Lake Road with a crawler tractor and a track-type trailer called an Anthey wagon. The tractor and a crew of two or three men headed up the road in the morning, felled and bucked enough timber to make one load, and returned to the mill later the same day.[10]

Logs were brought down Beaver Lake Road in Winfield by Anthey wagon – a trailer with both wheels and tracks. It was slow going, but an effective way to deal with the mud and debris of the roads and cutting areas.

With a secure source of lumber, Stan began to expand the type and variety of containers being made at his box factory. The selection of wire-wrapped bundles delivered to the Fintry Ranch on the west side of Okanagan Lake was typical of the kind of orders he was filling at the time. An invoice dated 1928 showed that Stan was supplying the Ranch with apple boxes for 16½¢ each, 3¼" prune boxes for 9¼¢; plum crates for 10¾¢; and tintop veneer baskets for soft fruit and tomatoes for 14½¢. A further invoice included cabbage crates at 35¢ each, pear boxes for 15¢ each, and cherry lugs for 13¼¢.

Another timber shortage was looming by 1929, however, and Stan again needed to find more trees. He packed up his mill, loaded the boiler onto a trailer behind a team of eight horses, and headed west on what is now Highway 97 towards Kelowna, up Benvoulin Road to KLO Road,[11] across Mission Creek, and up through East Kelowna to Hydraulic Creek. He set up shop there, and as was typical of many early portable mills, dealt with the waste – the slabs, edgings, and sawdust – by send-

All the large trees surrounding Stan's Winfield sawmill had been cut by 1929. The mill was dismantled, the boiler was loaded onto a trailer, and hauled to Hydraulic Creek in south-east Kelowna.

It wasn't long before a frame was devised to lift the logs onto the back of a truck. Cecil Metcalf, pictured here, was a contractor/hauler who owned a Dodge Brothers truck, the farrier and cross-haul horse team in the photo were still an integral part of the operation in 1929.

Logging went on during the winter, when sleighs were used to haul substantial loads of logs out of the bush. (Kelowna Museum photo)

Pete and Elmer Luttens at Canyon Creek, 1924. Logs would be pulled up the makeshift ramp by a team of horses and loaded onto the truck.

ing it into the bush. 5' to 6' trees were cut with wide-blade circular saws that reduced one out of every four boards to sawdust; that sawdust was carried away by a specially built flume that ran underneath the saw. Traces of this waste can be found scattered around Valley hillsides to this day. The Hydraulic Creek mill lasted for about two years, but by the end of the '20s Stan's business was thriving and he needed to move beyond a portable mill and establish a more permanent location that could meet all his needs. It was time for Simpson's to build its own mill in Kelowna.

In the space of six years, Stan's box business had become the company's main focus. The box factory and the original sash and door plant covered every square foot of space in the Abbott Street building, and even beyond into the adjoining lanes; there was no room to expand. S. M. knew there was a market for more boxes but he also knew there was an opportunity to make tintops, (veneer fruit containers with a strip of tin around the top) and grape baskets on site instead of importing and reselling them as he had been doing for the past few years. To expand into this market, he needed a steady supply of veneer. With planning now underway for a new sawmill and larger box factory, Stan knew a veneer plant could be integrated into the layout and allow Simpson's to make these containers itself.

Portable mills had provided Stan with some much-needed experience, but they were limited in what they could produce and with their distance from his main centre of operation, transportation and manpower were becoming a problem. With the nearby example of Lloyd-Jones' Kelowna Saw Mill, Stan had a good working model of how a permanent sawmill could use Okanagan Lake to haul and store logs, as well as for delivering finished products up and down the Valley. It was time once again for Stan's business to grow, and this expansion would be much bigger than anything he had attempted before.

A choice location

Prior to World War I, plans were in place to construct a cannery on a large parcel of land approximately 1 km north of Kelowna's downtown. A wharf had been built in anticipation of sternwheelers delivering fruit and vegetables to the site, and then picking up the finished products for export out of the Valley. Uncertainty following the war resulted in the project being abandoned, and the land sat empty until Stan decided it was the best location available for the new sawmill he wanted to build. While there was more space there than he needed, S. M. bought what was available with the thought that it could accommodate any future expansion. Even the water-logged land wasn't a deterrent – Stan had dealt with the same conditions before. This new site soon became known as the S. M. Simpson Ltd. Manhattan Beach operation, and Stan had a telephone hooked up to a pole in the yard before construction on the buildings was even underway.[12]

Life changes at home

Things also started looking brighter for Stan on a personal level when he met Blanche Mowat shortly after her arrival in Kelowna in 1919. Blanche was an independent, entrepreneurial woman in an era before such behaviour was appropriate; she studied dietetics in Wisconsin, sold encyclopaedias to support herself, and then returned to New Westminster to teach Domestic Science. When a similar position became available in Kelowna, Blanche moved again and taught at the town's original high school. Stan and Blanche married two years after they met, and moved into a home Stan built on the lakeshore, just six blocks south of his sash and door plant. Horace, Stan's son who had been cared for by Permelia for the five years following Bertha's death, came to live with the newly married couple; the following year another son, Bob (Robert Mowat), was born. Stan's habit of working long hours didn't change after he mar-

Stan, Blanche (Mowat), and Stan's son, Horace, shortly after the couple was married.

REMARKS.

I did not keep a set of books that would enable me to answer all the questions but if there is any thing else I can let you know I shall be pleased to do so

S.M.Simpson

Stan's skills were mechanical and not in record-keeping, so when he had to file his 1923 tax return he felt compelled to add this comment.

ried Blanche, and she created a life for herself as a dedicated volunteer, teaching dietetics at the Kelowna General Hospital School of Nursing and judging cooking competitions at local fall fairs. She was also a long-time supporter and judge at Valley music festivals, as well as being a stalwart member of Shakespeare Kelowna and the First United Church, and was instrumental in founding St. Paul's United Church. The '20s were a happy time for Stan, with his business growing, and his personal life more settled than ever before. With the arrival of his daughter, Rhoda Blanche (R. B.) in 1929, his young family was complete.

The ultimate betrayal

While renovating the Abbott Street building in 1927, Stan fell through an open stairway and ended up with a severe concussion. He was unconscious and away from work for several weeks, and when he finally returned he was confronted with an unexpected crisis. Moe, the company's secretary-treasurer, shareholder, and his friend had, as was noted in subsequent correspondence from the investigating auditors, "manipulated the records at various times." The auditors continued, noting, "Owing to the fact that there is evidence that the irregularities have existed for several years," they were of the opinion that "the amount of your loss in this connection would be far in excess of the amount shown above" – $7,602.47.[13] Stan had asked that the auditors only prove $5,000 was missing and not to track down anything further – perhaps because that amount would establish intent in Stan's mind and there was little to be gained by spending more time or money to identify additional losses.

The investigation was done quietly, with much of the work carried out by Vancouver lawyers and accountants, but the embezzlement must have been difficult for Stan. The Moe and Simpson families had been good friends for some time, and S. M. had loaned Moe money to buy shares in his company. Moe eventually made partial restitution by returning the shares, as well as a Studebaker car valued at $1,250 and a small interest he held in an estate. Stan never pressed criminal charges, although the theft was considerably larger than the amount Moe paid back. Stan always believed people were honest and trustworthy, and unfortunately this was one of the few times he was proven wrong. The motivation behind the embezzlement remains unknown, but the resulting loss of a trusted friend and business partner likely weighed more heavily on Stan than the considerable financial loss.

39

Still more boxes

Kelowna had become the agricultural centre for the Okanagan Valley by the end of the 1920s, and orchards that had been planted earlier in the decade were producing the greatest array of fruits and vegetables the area has ever seen: there were 274,000 apple trees of 54 different varieties, 17,000 pear trees of six different varieties, as well as six kinds of cherries and peaches, three varieties of apricots, and two of crab apples. Thousands of wooden crates of tomatoes were picked and hand-wrapped, as well as thousands of crates of cucumbers, peppers, celery, cabbage, vegetable marrow, pumpkins, and cantaloupes. The box industry was also booming and becoming more and more innovative as different sizes and shapes of wooden boxes were needed to pack and ship the increasing array of produce. Briefcase-sized containers were made for the large crop of Italian plums; open-style crates were made to stand celery stalks on end, as well as 'coffin' crates that enclosed the stalks; wooden-slatted crates were made for marrow, squash, and pumpkins, while asparagus crates had tapered ends and layers of wet moss spread between the stalks to keep them fresh; octagonal crates bound with wire to allow air flow were made for exporting onions, and junior-sized apple boxes were more consumer-friendly and at half the size of a regular apple box, were easier to handle. With the huge volumes and variety of produce leaving the Valley, there is little wonder Stan saw opportunity in the box-making business.

Kelowna was the last of the Okanagan communities to receive direct rail service to the Coast and eastern Canada and the much-heralded extension of the Canadian National Railway in 1925 enabled packinghouses to load fresh fruits and vegetables directly into rail cars that were then attached to transcontinental trains, without first having to be loaded onto barges and sent to either end of Okanagan Lake. It looked like there was nowhere to go but up for the Valley's growers, and along with them, box makers like S. M.

Stan had come a long way during the '20s. He had expanded from a small sash and door operation and portable mill to a major box manufacturing plant. He also understood the box business itself better and as he assessed its opportunities, knew he needed a more integrated operation to achieve his goals. S. M. likely pondered and scratched out on a piece of paper where logs could be delivered and stored, how a sawmill would be laid out, and where a veneer plant would fit into the overall plan. With the additional space, Stan would figure out how to design a bigger box factory and where the railway tracks should be to pick up shook for delivery beyond the local market. What he was planning was a far cry from his bush mills and the earlier in-through-the-window, out-through-the-back door operation he started with. Plans for the new Manhattan Beach plant were well underway before the decade ended, and Stan was full of optimism for his growing business. What S. M. didn't know was that he, along with the rest of the Valley, he would soon be dealing with astoundingly difficult times.

Storm clouds on the horizon

Life at the end of the decade was good for most people in Western Canada. Grain production was at record levels, and B.C.'s mining, forestry, and fishing industries were providing high-paying jobs to an expanding work force. Local fruit and vegetable industries were thriving, and Stan was developing his business plans around their continuing growth. But elsewhere things weren't quite as rosy.

Europe was still struggling to recover from the devastation of the first world war, and the booming U.S. economy, which had been absorbing about 40 per cent of Canada's exports, began to collapse in 1929 along with the American stock market. The onset of a devastating drought on the Prairies seemed to catch everyone by surprise. Canadian factory production slowed and then ceased altogether, unemployment grew, banks began to call in loans, and the bumper wheat crop of 1928 remained unsold as the huge 1929 crop ripened. The chaos of the '30s, later known as the Great

Depression, was about to descend on the country. Kelowna was still relatively isolated, and it took a little longer for the economic downturn of the Prairies and central Canada to be felt in the Valley. Stan didn't seem to be aware of the impending disaster and with the Valley's orchardists and vegetable growers continuing to harvest bumper crops, he carried on with plans to make more boxes: construction of a new sawmill, veneer plant, and box factory was well underway at the Manhattan Beach location by March 1930.

The Day-Elder truck - again

Chapter 4

No One Could Have Known
– the 1930s

No one knew the Great Depression was coming, including Stan, and he carried on with plans to build a new sawmill and box factory. What was initially thought to be a temporary slump in the economy evolved into a recession, but it was business as usual for Stan in the first years of the 1930s.

Carrying on

Rhoda Simpson christening the tug MV Manhattan in 1939. Art Jones, the local builder, is on the far right beside Jack Riley, tug captain. On the left is Jack Coops and long-time boom man, (Klondike) Mike Paly. The tug on the right is the MV Klatawa, purchased by S. M. from Captain Len Hayman, about 1930.

Window frames, doors, and fruit boxes were still being made at the Abbott Street factory as plans were finalized for the Manhattan Beach expansion. The box factory continued to operate out of the original building while a sawmill and then a veneer plant were being built, and it wasn't until three years later that it became an integral part of the new site. Although a small mill office was set up at Manhattan Beach, the company's main office remained on Abbott Street along with the sash and door operation until 1948.

Stan must have either set aside some extra working capital or had a very good relationship with his bank in the early '30s in order to proceed with construction. Even in the early years of the Depression, thousands of companies and individuals were defaulting on their loans and it was almost impossible to get new financing from any source. No company records remain from this time, but upheaval in fruit industry during the years the mill was being built must have left Stan wondering if there would be enough demand for his boxes to stay in business.

Nation-wide chaos

Depression spread across the country, and there seemed to be no political will or national strategy to deal with Canada's growing unemployment crisis. Calvinist principles more suited to another time and place continued to prevail, as politicians rationalized that "any healthy man could always find a job … and if he was idle, it was deliberate."[1] Financial assistance was seen as shameful, though many depended upon the meagre dole for their very survival. 20,000 jobless people had congregated in Vancouver by the summer of 1931, and soup kitchens were set up to feed thousands of women, children, and unemployed men. Canada had become a nation of hobos as thousands of young men rode

the rails, travelling back and forth across the country hoping that some rumour of a job might be true. Times were tough everywhere and even Kelowna had its own hobo jungle, euphemistically called 'Honolulu'; whether this was because it was as close as these men were going to get to Hawaii or because it was a nice place to be isn't clear.[2] Transients knew it was best to arrive in the Okanagan during the spring and summer when fruit and vegetables were plentiful; they wouldn't starve to death – at least not during those months.

The Canadian government grew alarmed with so many unemployed young men across the country agitating for change, fearing they might be recruited by various radical groups such as the Communists or the newly organized Co-operative Commonwealth Federation (CCF). As thousands of them congregated in cities, the men became an increasing menace and grave threat to the strongly held Canadian values of peace, order, and good government, and it wasn't long before the RCMP and federal government decided these undisciplined transients should be removed from the cities. By 1932, rural relief camps had been set up for nearly 19,000 young men,[3] and with 27 camps in B.C. it was inevitable that some would be in the Interior.

One was at Wilson's Landing, across Okanagan Lake from Kelowna, another at Oyama, and a third in Vernon. Most B.C. relief camp workers did road construction, and those in the Valley were provided with shovels and wheelbarrows to tackle the rocky stretch of highway between Oyama and Winfield, to the north of Kelowna. While the camps were 'voluntary', they were run with military discipline: the men were issued army surplus clothing; the food allowance was meagre and inadequate for young men doing hard physical labour; there was little recreation, few opportunities to find other jobs, and no chance to speak freely, protest, or vote. The men were known as the Royal Twenty Centers – the amount they were paid each day – and to make matters worse, they were so segregated there were never any young ladies in sight. If a man left a camp for whatever reason, he was blacklisted and could not return or collect the dole elsewhere.

The isolation and sense of hopelessness overwhelmed many, but others chose to fight and protest against the government's questionable social experiment. Within two years, relief camps across the country – referred to by many as slave labour camps – became breeding grounds for high profile and often violent anti-government protests. As Stan would later discover, the social unrest of the Depression laid the foundation for a militant, combative Canadian labour movement that would exert its influence on Interior sawmills.

Turmoil at home

The fruit industry, which by the '30s had become the core of Kelowna's identity, lurched from one marketing and distribution crisis to another and usually took the community along for the ride. Several attempts were made to implement co-operative marketing schemes to better organize the sale of the Valley's fruit, but dissidents always surfaced and every effort failed. Federal and provincial politicians were preoccupied with trying to keep their jobs in the midst of the worsening Depression, so local voices demanding a legislated solution to the Okanagan's marketing problems were lost in the chaos. Traditional Prairie fruit markets were struggling with their own crises, and there was little money available to buy Valley apples. Shippers tried to find ways to make their fruit more affordable; part of the 1931 apple crop was shipped in sacks to eliminate the cost and weight of the traditional wooden boxes. Another year, even the sacks were eliminated and:

> straw was scattered on the floor of the boxcar to a depth of about six inches. Paper was spread over this and up the walls. Lumber walls or bulkheads were built down the lengths of the car about every ten feet. Orchard-run loose apples were then poured into these bin sections to a designated height, which was dictated by the weight of the cargo.[4]

While the fruit industry was adjusting to shrinking markets, Stan continued to build his new box factory. At one point, however, he changed his assembly line and switched from the standard-sized box that held 40 lbs. of apples and built a simpler, less expensive, lighter, topless crate that held 50 lbs. of apples. An elaborate production line was set up at the Manhattan Beach box factory, where automatic nailing and stitching machines operated 24 hours a day. A truck-load of boxes was produced in about four hours, and vehicles arrived day and night to carry them back to the packinghouses.[5]

Orchards were still producing abundant apple crops when the usually strong Lower Mainland and Prairie markets began to disappear, and the average price for a 40 lb. box of apples fell to 85¢ – 25¢ lower than the year before – and then continued to drop further; it wasn't long before a box of Okanagan apples could be bought on the streets of Vancouver for 25¢. Even more troubling was the fact that it cost shippers 50¢ a box to sort and pack the apples, and between 33¢ and 70¢ a box to grow them, so orchardists were getting bills from shippers and receiving no money for the year's work.[6] And frequently, there was no money to buy the wooden boxes that had become the foundation of Simpson's business.

Stan wasn't the only one distressed by disappearing fruit markets. By 1933, the Okanagan's apple growers were so angry about falling prices they took matters into their own hands and rallied around the slogan "A Cent a Pound or on the Ground!" They refused to deliver apples to the packinghouses unless they would receive a guaranteed minimum of 1¢ a pound. Pickets were set up in desperation at each of the three bridges coming into Kelowna from the fruit growing areas, and all trucks carrying fruit were challenged until a written price guarantee was produced; if no guarantee was forthcoming, the loaded truck was turned back. Most shippers agreed to the growers' demands, but Joe Casorso and the Rowcliffe brothers remained independent and defiant, and proceeded to fill two (and eventually seven) rail cars with loose Macintosh apples.[7]

The leader of the "Cent a Pound" campaign called a mass rally, and evoking the passive resistance of Mahatma Gandhi as a model, called for a non-violent response to the independents. Other growers became so angry they forgot about Gandhi and threw stones and cut off power to the packinghouse in attempt to halt the loading. They weren't successful, and locomotives headed down the track to pick up the loaded cars but they were met by a wave of growers' wives and children surging over the tracks shouting, "Only over our dead and mutilated bodies will those cars ever move out on the tracks!"[8] Huge bonfires lit the night sky as the engines retreated, and the victorious protesters could be heard singing well into the early morning hours.

It was all about boxes

Between 500 to 600 million wooden boxes were made in the Valley during the 30 peak years of their use – and Stan made the majority of those. When S. M. built his Manhattan Beach sawmill, veneer plant, and box factory he planned to have the most efficient production line for making the boxes that had become the focal point of his expanding business. Stan had the innate mechanical ability and ingenuity to shape the layout and design for the new operation, as well as the determination to see it through. There is no record of any long-term overall plan, but S. M. was building what would become the largest integrated sawmill and box factory operation in the Valley. He was also becoming the Okanagan's largest supplier of orchard products and was moving beyond traditional wooden boxes to also make veneer fruit containers and ladders, as well as providing flume lumber. Stan's soft-spoken presence masked a shrewd business sense and steely determination, and while he took business risks others might not have been comfortable with, they were well-calculated and he seemed to know where to draw the line. Sometimes he got into price wars with Vancouver suppliers but he was more determined to service the local market than Coastal companies and he held out as long as was necessary to gain that control in the Okanagan.

Stan was able to produce a wide range of products with the new operation. Lumber was now cut on site, and even though most was still sent on to the box factory, there was enough being produced that some could now be sold to the local construction trade as dimension lumber. Select logs also were sorted and sent to the veneer plant, and with veneer now being readily available, Stan began replacing solid box tops and bottoms with the lighter, more flexible veneer. Box parts – 25 plain ends, 25 printed ends, 50 sides, 50 tops and bottoms, and 250 cleats, which together provided enough material for 25 finished boxes – were bundled and wrapped with wire ready to be shipped out. The top and bottom pieces were attached to the box ends with cleats – four per box – with extras included in case they split, and it wasn't long before S. M. built up a considerable business selling tops and bottoms to other box makers who didn't have their own veneer plants.

Simpson's was a driving force in the box-making business, but continued to let others assemble the boxes. Early box makers were a unique lot, and each demanded a certain organization of their work area out in the orchards or in the packinghouse. With a small hatchet as their only equipment, each box maker would shave and whittle the hatchet handle to get the balance and fit he needed. Once the men got into a rhythm, they could produce an extraordinary number of boxes each day. This was hard, skilled piecework but with an early start most of the boxes needed for a day could be produced before the summer heat became unbearable. A good box maker could assemble about 1,000 boxes a day and with the going rate of 1¢ a box, the $10 he made was double the wage of the average labourer. Automation gradually took over but itinerant box makers travelled up and down the Valley well into the '50s,[9] and they remained closely tied to the box production that went on at Simpson's.

Stan had been buying veneer fruit containers and grape baskets from Coast and Ontario manufacturers for a few years and reselling them to area growers, but with his own veneer plant he no longer needed to be the middleman. The expansion into veneer was only the start for Simpson's, with tintops, the small containers used for soft fruits such as apricots and peaches, being the next item in S. M.'s ever-growing business, and by 1935 the annual production of tintops was between 1,250,000 and 1,500,000 units. Tin arrived from England in 6" x 16" x 20" sheets that covered the floor of a rail car in a single layer. The tin was cut into strips so the machine operators – usually women[10] – could form the strips into a "V," which would be wrapped around the top of two folded pieces of veneer. With a leg-operated lever, tin strips were crimped around the top of the basket to hold the veneer pieces in place; an experienced operator could make about 2,000 tintops in an eight-hour shift. Although these light veneer boxes looked fragile,

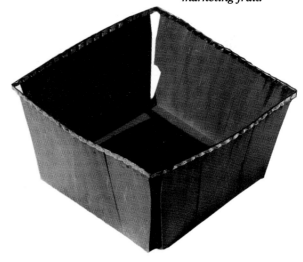

A veneer basket referred to as a tintop because of the strip of tin around the top that held it together. They were used for marketing fruit.

Berry crates were taken to the fields where small individual veneer cups were removed, filled with strawberries or raspberries, and returned to the crate in a double layer. Each crate held 24 cups.

they were remarkably sturdy.

Tintops were used much as Styrofoam or pressed cardboard containers are today, and were either thrown out or used for other purposes at the end of each season. In addition to the tintops, Simpson's also made about 35,000 shallow wooden-slatted berry crates annually, which in turn held 24 hallocks – a small stapled-together veneer cup. The box factory produced 840,000 veneer cups each season for the huge strawberry and raspberry crops grown in the north Okanagan and Kootenays. Concord table grapes were also becoming a popular addition to the fresh fruit market at the time and were packed in six-quart baskets with vented lids. Stan decided he could also produce these baskets locally instead of importing them, and began turning out about a 1,000 grape baskets a day, or 75,000 during the season.[11]

Okanagan orchards kept producing bumper crops as the Depression continued in other parts of the country, and in spite of the instability at the beginning of the decade, Stan's box factory expanded in the mid-'30s. An endless stream of trucks would arrive at the factory at the height of the summer fruit season to pick up load after load of box parts and deliver them to packinghouses or orchards for assembly. Stan somehow continued to purchase new machinery and automate his production line during these years, and by running a double shift during the summer, made about 120,000 units a day, or over 10 million box tops and bottoms each season.[12] Millions of new boxes were needed annually as it was standard industry practice to sell Interior fruit in clean, new boxes each year; old boxes were used in the orchards during picking season and repaired each winter but they were never used to ship fruit out of the Valley. The new 50 lb. box standard was maintained during most of the '30s with only a few exceptions, and Stan's box factory established itself as the Valley's main supplier of wooden fruit containers.

Shook being stacked for drying in the mill yard.

Grape baskets with vented lids were filled by pickers in the vineyards. (Kelowna Museum photo)

Logs to the mill

Changes were also taking place in the forest industry during the mid-'30s. Better roads provided greater access to more remote areas, but they were often so rough and treacherous that winches had to be used to get trucks up steep grades, and drivers would have to make several attempts to manoeuvre their single-axle trucks around a tight hairpin turn. They were also not sure the brakes would hold and sometimes truckers would drag a huge log attached to the rear axle on the down-hill run as an extra bit of insurance. Even that wasn't enough in some cases: the old Bear Creek Road on the west side of Okanagan Lake was too steep to drive a loaded truck all the way down to the lake, so a log chute was built. The chute was slathered with bear grease and logs would shoot across Westside Road at a tremendous clip down to the shore below. Although many trucks used during the '30s were ingenious adaptations of early Republics and Day Elders, they were barely a step above the horse-drawn wagons when compared to today's high-tech logging machines.

Horse logging and portable mills continued to operate throughout the Interior for many years, and networks of overgrown logging trails, mostly two wagon-wheel or sleigh-ruts wide, criss-cross Valley hillsides today. The derelict remains of portable mills or logging camps, the stable, or cookhouse, and sometimes a tell-tale cache of rusty cans, pieces of chain, or an old saw blade are the only remnants of years of logging and life in the camps.

Logging trucks delivered their loads to the beach by transferring them to log chutes or by dumping them over the bank. When enough logs had been accumulated near the lakeshore, horse teams would sort them before the logs were rafted into booms and hauled to the mill.

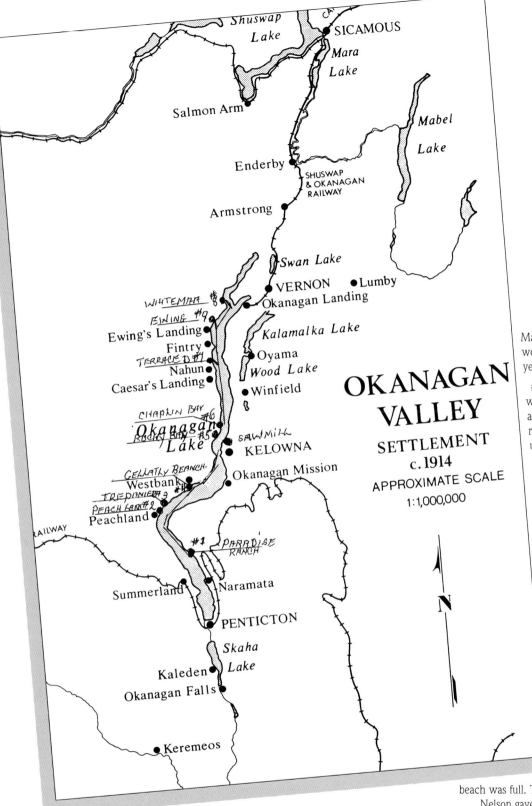

OKANAGAN VALLEY SETTLEMENT c.1914 APPROXIMATE SCALE 1:1,000,000

Map courtesy of Arthur Marty, who worked on Simpson's tugs for many years. Art's key to his map:

#1 – The Paradise Ranch, where logs were dumped in the water. Fred Kitsch and (Klondike) Mike Paly would round them up for rafting and towing until about 1940-45.

#2 – Logs were dumped on the beach near Trepanier Creek, which faced south. When the beach was full, we rolled the logs into the water, and rafted them up as soon as possible and got away from the beach before the south wind would blow in.

#3 – The Trepanier Creek log dump. When the beach was full, we rolled logs into the water, rafted them, and usually towed them at night.

#4 – Gellatly Beach, where the logs were initially dumped on the beach; boom sticks were later anchored out in the lake.

#5 – Rocky Bay, where logs were hauled down from Bald Range, dumped on the beach, and rolled into the lake when the beach was full. This is where Otto Sandberg and Eric Nelson gave a small rattlesnake a taste of hooch.

#6 – Chaplin Bay, where the log booms were stored.

#7 – Terrace Mountain log dump. Cecil Philpot hauled logs here and often lost his cable wrapper in the deep water.

#8 – Whiteman's Creek log dump and wharf. The logs were scaled on the trucks and then the trucks drove onto the wharf. A 4' x 12' x 20' - long wedge on one side of the wharf tilted the trucks and when the chains around the logs were released, most logs would roll off the truck into the lake.

#9 – Sometimes logs were dumped on this beach, and had to be rolled into the water for rafting. Once or twice we would tie up on shore for the night, and when we woke up in the morning we'd have to try and figure out where on earth we were – across from Whiteman's Creek or over by Otter Bay.

Stan's record of his dealings with logging contractors was kept in a coverless notebook.

Logger Abe Thompson's 1934 invoice.

When Stan expanded his operation to Manhattan Beach, he needed to be sure he had an adequate timber supply. That ultimately meant getting into the logging business. S. M. hired the crews and bought three, three-ton Chevy logging trucks, but soon realized he didn't have any experience and decided independent loggers could do a better job; several contractors were already supplying the mill with pine, spruce, fir, and smaller amounts of poplar and cottonwood from locations around the Valley by 1933. Most delivered their loads to log dumps around the lake, where they were boomed up and hauled by the company's tugs to the Manhattan Beach operation as needed. Stan kept track of the logging contractors and what they supplied in a coverless school notebook that also recorded the log marks unique to each area being cut, the dates, types of timber supplied, location, royalties, and stumpage paid. The book remains intact, though a child's coloured scribbles fill its unused pages.

In order to get the logs to Manhattan Beach from the booming grounds around Okanagan Lake, Stan bought the tug *Klatawa* from Len Hayman in 1932. The small boat had ferried passengers and cattle between Kelowna and the west side of the lake twenty years earlier, and Len had been its legendary,

The Stanley M. *hauling logs from Bear Creek.*

colourful captain.[13] The *Klatawa* stayed in service until 1939, when it was replaced by the more substantial *Manhattan*, built by local boat builder Art Jones. The men who worked on the tugs formed a unique group, and often transferred from tug to tug as the sturdy boats worked through their useful lives.[14] The *Manhattan* was hauled to Mabel Lake in 1962 and replaced by the *Stanley M.*, which is still in service today. Getting logs to the mill wasn't S. M.'s biggest concern during the '30s, however.

Out of money

Stan was fortunate for a long time, but he didn't escape the ravages of the Depression entirely. As the decade wore on and many of his customers couldn't pay their bills, he found himself without money to pay his employees and would occasionally have to shut the mill down for a few weeks. That didn't stop some employees from showing up, loading the trucks, and delivering fuel to houses in town that had no other source of heat – and not expect to be paid. On other occasions, small groups of men could be seen waiting around the office hoping to get a few hours work, which reminded those who had jobs that didn't pay well or only paid sporadically that they were still better off than those who never got paid at all.[15] New equipment was out of the question by this time and blacksmith Bill Sinclair or Dan Hill, with his innate mechanical ability, would rebuild, adapt, or repair whatever was on hand. During these lean years, everyone knew there was little choice but to make do with what was on hand.

Tough as times were, a strong bond of loyalty developed between Stan and his employees. They knew he was doing what he could to provide them with jobs and when that wasn't possible, they understood and stepped in to help out where they could. The mutual respect developed during these years was deep and it lasted for a long time, but when the labour wars of the '40s broke out, the bond between S. M. and the men at the mill would be tested. There was more than just an emotional bond at the mill, however. As the Depression deepened and cash became even more scarce, Stan told employees to go to Capozzi's grocery store and get what they needed. 'Cap' had agreed to extend credit until the men were paid, although Stan had said he would make up any loss; it is unlikely he ever had to. It would have been wiser for Stan to shut down his mill as many other owners were doing, but he rarely took such a drastic step.

The fire in 1937 destroyed the machine shop, garage, and storage sheds. The rail line looks unused, although stacks of shook are still drying on the right.

Apples kept growing and the public kept buying despite the Depression, though often at reduced prices and in reduced amounts. Stan somehow remained optimistic and seemed to think better times were just around the corner and even went so far as to start distributing Johns-Manville roofing products and building supplies[16] in 1937, as an added convenience for people thinking of buying lumber for the homes they hoped to build some time in the future.

A glimmer of hope

There was a glimmer of hope for a short time near the end of 1936 and into 1937 that the much longed-for economic recovery might have started. That optimism was short-lived, and the nation soon plunged back into despair as destitute and ragged young men continued to gather on street corners. These were uneasy times for the Canadian establishment, particularly when loosely-structured Communist organizations tried to fill the political vacuum by rallying the homeless and occupying the main Vancouver post office, the Hotel Georgia, and the Vancouver Art Gallery in May 1938. The protestors soon abandoned the hotel and art gallery, but remained at the post office for several weeks until the police got tired of waiting, for the men to leave their posts and attacked. The resulting newspaper photos of 'Bloody Sunday', with clouds of tear gas and police wielding lengths of lead pipe against the cowering protestors, shocked the nation: the graphic violence that characterized the 1919 Winnipeg strike and the 1935 Regina Riot had arrived in Vancouver. Even as the despair and desperation of the Depression continued to spread across the country, politicians and business leaders insisted that "the worst was over" and "Canada has survived the crisis."[17] What they didn't see at the time was that the Depression had become the birth place of an impending struggle that would involve many of these same disenfranchised young men.

The 1939 fire destroyed the sawmill and veneer plant. The box factory, which survived, is in the background.

The band resaw survived, but everything around it was destroyed. The saw was later sold to Gorman Brothers sawmill and used for many more years.

This truck had been loaded with shook the day before the fire and only charred remains were left the following day. The truck was subsequently restored.

The boiler for the portable sawmill that had been set up in the yard to begin cutting lumber as soon as possible. (L. Bouvette photo)

Fire – and more

Stan was somehow managing to stay in business in the midst of the ongoing national crisis when the first of two major fires nearly wiped him out. The first destroyed buildings along the west side of the Manhattan property – the office, blacksmith and machine shops, and the long sheds used for storing retail building supplies. The blaze was spotted at noon on July 23, 1937, and it wasn't long before strong winds spread the flames along the row of buildings. It took firemen over two hours to contain the fire, although most of their efforts went toward preventing the flames from jumping the narrow road separating the shops from the sawmill and box factory. The cause of the fire was never discovered and crews soon set to work replacing the destroyed buildings.

The second fire, two years later in April 1939, was at the time the most spectacular in Kelowna's history. The night watchman turned in the alarm at 1:30 a.m. on April 13, but by then flames were already raging through the sawmill and tinder-dry stacks of veneer. The fire was out of control when the fire brigade arrived, and they quickly made a decision to try to save the box factory and nearby stacks of lumber. According to the *Courier:*

> It was only through heroic work that the rest of the big plant was saved. First task confronting the firemen was to carry out the planer from the burning building. This they managed to do, with the flames licking not a dozen feet away. Then efforts were made to save the building but the blaze had too great a start and the firemen had to be content with protecting the neighbouring property. The large sawdust pile directly east of the building had caught on fire when the fire brigade arrived, but it was dampened down and the fire kept from spreading in that direction.[18]

Fortunately for the rest of the plant and the entire Manhattan area, high winds that had been blowing through the Valley for several days had died down just hours before the fire began. Flames filled the night sky, and the threat of the fire spreading into the neighbouring houses was very real despite the recently installed fire hydrants; even with the upgraded system, water pressure was barely adequate to contain the blaze.[19] By morning, all that was left of the sawmill and veneer plant was a heap of twisted, charred equipment.

The box factory escaped destruction and as soon as it was safe to walk through the debris, cleanup began. Stan quickly put the near-calamity behind him and set about planning a new sawmill and veneer plant. Business had been slow for months so there was plenty of lumber and materials on hand to get on with rebuilding, and the box factory started up as soon as lumber was available.

53

The lathe was put in place in the new veneer plant when it was still under construction. (L. Bouvette photo)

Although fewer boxes were needed than earlier in the decade, S. M. did not want to risk losing his customers and set up an extra planer beside the box factory to continue making boxes. He needed to get some money flowing back into the company but also felt an obligation to Simpson's customers and didn't want them to have shortfalls because of his fire. Then, a startling revelation:

Suspicion of Incendiarism in Simpson Fire Aroused by Finding of Bottle of Kerosene and Oiled Rags
(The Kelowna Courier, April 20, 1939)

Spencer Howie, a Canadian National employee, discovered the kerosene and rags on Saturday afternoon and reported his discovery to Mr. Simpson, who immediately notified the provincial police. A search of the district began immediately in an attempt to ascertain any possible grounds for such an outrage. Why should any person, unless he had evil intent, place such inflammable material in the third row [of stacked lumber] from the end of the line? If a man was intent upon such a form of sabotage, would he take two bottles of kerosene with him or was the second bottle intended for a second conflagration, which was foiled by lack of time or some interruption? The police would value any advice as to recent purchases of kerosene by any suspicious persons in this district as the task of locating such a marauder is a difficult one.[20]

Piles were driven into the water-logged ground to provide a solid footing for the new sawmill floor. The sheds in the background were used for storing retail lumber supplies and were untouched in the 1939 fire

Stan was at a loss why anyone would set fire to his mill: he knew of no one who wanted to destroy his business or even a disgruntled employee who might have sought revenge. But the timing was curious. Simpson's was one of the largest box makers in the Valley – was someone trying to eliminate their competition? No suspect was ever arrested and the origins of the fire were left to speculation.

Few Kelowna residents can remember this fire, and fewer still can recall Stan's response to the potential demise of his struggling business. Fire was a fact of life in the sawmill business – as David Lloyd-Jones knew all too well – and many operations ceased to exist when a fire of this magnitude struck. But Stan's cautious nature had served him well: he had paid his insurance premiums throughout the Depression, even when the company's cash flow had been almost non-existant. In response to a query from the newspaper, Stan said, "The loss was as adequately covered with insurance as possible."[21] Not completely covered, but adequately enough that he now had cash to replace the destroyed equipment and buildings, and get his business up and running again.

Getting back to business

Stan used the fire to reorganize his operation, and in addition to the extra planer beside the box factory, a portable sawmill, began supplying the box factory with lumber and the heavy timbers and joists needed for the new sawmill and veneer buildings. This temporary production line gave Stan enough time to redesign the mill and search out the latest equipment. According to his son Horace "The only good thing about the destruction of the plant by fire was that it provided an opportunity to replace the original equipment with more up-to-date, efficient machinery."[22]

The veneer plant was up and running in early July 1939, even before the roof was on, and the new sawmill cut its first piece of lumber on September 5 – less than five months after the original building was destroyed. This time, Stan installed a sprinkler system throughout the reconstructed buildings as well as in the old box factory – he wanted all the protection he could get against the same thing happening again. The suspected "incendiarist" had failed to eliminate the competition – if that was in fact the motive – and S. M. Simpson Ltd. was only shut down for a few days. In the end, the 1939 box season was pretty much business as usual, even though much of the work was done in the open yard.

Survival against the odds

S. M.'s decision to expand during the early days of the Depression was either courageous or naïve, as the economy in the rest of the county had already started to collapse by the time construction on the Manhattan plant got underway. Stan must have wondered if he had any future in the box business when the fruit industry tried to eliminate the cost and weight of boxes by shipping apples in sacks and loose in rail cars, but he adapted and changed his production lines, and did whatever he could to help the fruit industry – anything that would keep his factory operating.

Perhaps he was also blessed with the eternal optimism of the politicians who kept saying the worst was over. S. M. must have seen opportunity where others did not, and felt the risk was one he could live with. He would have been called foolhardy and blind in the face of such obvious risks if the company had not survived, and as the Depression deepened and times became even tougher, Stan must have wondered about the wisdom of his decisions. By the end of the decade, however, even he recognized that a combination of good luck and dogged persistence had enabled him to survive. The burned-out sawmill had been replaced with the latest, most up-to-date equipment, and Stan was uniquely prepared to take advantage of huge demands that would present themselves within a matter of months.

Finally ... some relief!

The country was exhausted by the strife and desperation of the '30s. Jobs were still almost impossible to find, as the decade drew to a close, and over a million people remained on the dole. Rumours of impending war in Europe were everywhere, as well. One of the few bright spots during this otherwise dark period was George VI and Queen Elizabeth's visit to Canada in May 1939. The royals' train trip created an aura of enthusiasm that seemed to re-energize the whole country. The outpouring of joy and adoration likely surprised even Their Majesties, as the reality of the pervasive despair that had gripped Canada was likely never conveyed to them. Hundreds of people from Kelowna headed to Revelstoke – the closest scheduled stop on their cross-country journey – to greet the couple. Even the relentless rain that fell all day failed to dampen the celebration and the visit turned out to be one of the few high points in a decade of despair.

By September 3, 1939, however, the nation's mood had become much more sombre once again. Newspaper accounts told of the increasing unrest in Europe, which ultimately came to a head when Britain and France declared war on Germany. Canada joined the Allied ranks five days later and began to mobilize for war. The Great Depression was finally over.

Chapter 5

War On Two Fronts – the 1940s

After surviving two fires, the stress associated with building a new sawmill, and the uncertainty of the Great Depression, Stan looked like he might finally be in the right place – at the right time. Only a small portion of the 4½ million feet of lumber stockpiled in the yard had been used to rebuild the sawmill and veneer plant after the fire in the spring of 1939, and since there had been little demand for building materials during the Depression, lumber inventories were unusually high when Canada declared war in September 1939. Mills that had managed to stay open during the Depression – including S. M. Simpson Ltd. – quickly cleared out their lumber inventories and what would have been a burdensome over-supply suddenly turned into a windfall.

Mobilizing for war

H. R. MacMillan, B.C.'s first Chief Forester[1] and later head of the province's signature lumber company, MacMillan Bloedel, was named national Timber Comptroller soon after war was declared, and given the task of organizing the country's forest industry. Prior to this time, Britain had purchased most of its wood products from the Scandinavian countries but when German U-boats made shipping on the North Sea too hazardous, Canada became its most readily available source for all things made of wood. The tentacles of MacMillan's organization reached into every corner of the province, searching for more and more material, and Interior sawmills and box makers soon found most of their production diverted to the war effort at home and overseas.

Kelowna's industrial area in 1948. The Memorial Arena is in the foreground with the KSM building, warehouses, and yard to the north. Several packinghouses and rail yards are between the KSM and Stan's Manhattan Beach sawmill on the lakeshore. Newly-built wartime housing is at the foot of Knox Mountain.

Increased demands on Interior sawmills significantly changed the way they did business. Lumber and shook had largely gone to local markets in the years before World War II and because time wasn't of the essence, the practice of air-drying green lumber had served the industry well; there wasn't much need for kiln-dried lumber. With the massive mobilization, however, the huge inventories of dry lumber that had accumulated in mill yards during the Depression were quickly shipped out and the only option left was to ship green, undried boards. So much lumber was required for ships, hangars, barracks, docks, and munitions factories that sometimes the order simply read, "send everything you've got,"[2] and it wasn't long before green lumber was all that was available. This undried lumber became part of every hastily-constructed structure across the country and the resultant gaps, twists, and warps were incorporated into whatever was being built.

With the high wartime priority rating given to the Interior's lumber and box production by the federal government and the low rating given to the fruit industry, the resulting shortages of boxes soon became a crisis for the Valley's fruit and vegetable growers. Rutland Sawmills was created early in the war as a public co-op in an attempt to deal with the problems and ensure farmers along the benchlands northeast of Kelowna had adequate lumber for flumes and boxes. Five Okanagan co-op packinghouses also bought the Norris Lumber & Box Factory (later known as Boundary Sawmills) to maintain a supply of boxes, but as the war progressed many packinghouses were reluctant to risk purchasing their own box factories only to find their inventories commandeered by the government.

Local demands

As Canada mobilized for war, the federal government provided start-up funding for many B.C. sawmills that had closed during the Depression and then guaranteed owners a market for their lumber. Mills that didn't reopen became a source of much-needed equipment for those that needed to retool for the war effort, and while Stan replaced some of the machinery damaged by the fire with new equipment, it was against his frugal nature to spend money when abandoned mill sites and mining operations left derelict equipment lying around. Stan was able to refit parts of the sawmill and veneer plant with equipment that worked well for many years for little more than the cost of hauling used machinery back to Kelowna and re-conditioning it.[3] The insurance settlement from the fire also provided cash to buy the newest, most up-to-date equipment during the five-and-a-half months between the blaze and the outbreak of World War II. Once the war got underway, new mill equipment became impossible to purchase as wartime supplies and munitions took priority on assembly lines.

When Canada declared war on September 10, 1939, hastily organized efforts to send troops to Britain and the European front soon brought an end to the political problems caused by the unemployed, homeless, and underfed. Public funds were made available to re-start factories and armed forces recruitment depots were overwhelmed by the same young men who had earlier filled relief camps and ridden the rails. Suddenly, there were more jobs than there were people to fill them and the same women who lost their jobs to unemployed men during the Depression were now in great demand. By 1942, lumber and logging were declared essential services[4] in B.C. and given high wartime priority ratings. In spite of efforts by mill owners, however, neither their employees nor the loggers who were a key part of the mill's supply line were classified as essential personnel and the shortage of workers in both mills and the woods reached crisis proportions as more men were sent off to war. Women and the Japanese men who had been interned at camps throughout the Southern Interior and Kootenays when war broke out kept many sawmills operating, but the Japanese were declared a security risk and banned from going into the woods; loggers remained in short supply throughout the war. Getting the logs that were available to the mills was also difficult during the war years with gasoline and tires being rationed; horses were used for loading and hauling, and loggers had to make do with axes and crosscut saws.

S. M. Simpson Ltd. was one of the Interior's largest wood product suppliers for the war effort, and the Manhattan Beach plant worked at maximum capacity as Stan continued to turn out fruit and vegetable boxes for local customers in addition to dimension lumber, different-sized boxes for the British Boxboard Agency, and dynamite boxes for the Canadian Industries Ltd. (CIL) plant on Vancouver Island. Boxes made for the export market were locally referred to as butter boxes, but as was the case with much wartime production, their destination and actual usage were classified. Once cut and bundled, box shook was loaded into a never-ending line of rail cars that were shunted onto the track beside the box factory, and then sent to Vancouver where the shook was transferred to ships heading for Britain via the Panama Canal.[5] Not all the shook produced at the Simpson mill made it

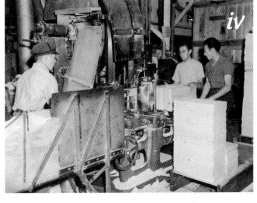

The Box Factory

i   *Blythen unitizer for stapling box tops and bottoms together*
ii   *Making cleats for use on box tops and bottoms*
iii *Planer*
iv *Bundling shook*
v   *Veneer sorting table*

to Europe, however. Some years after the war, Bill Greenwood was sorting through old company files and found a memo saying one of the ships carrying Simpson's boxes had been torpedoed in the mid-Atlantic and the company was asked to quickly replace the lost order. Horace, Stan's son, gave an account of what was happening at the plant in the early part of the war:

> Things are keeping pretty busy at the mill. No apple boxes moving now but lots of apple tops. We're not shipping any carloads of lumber now but very busy making export shook and that is a headache in itself. We were loading a car on Friday and Saturday containing 26 different sizes of shook and nearly 5,000 bundles. We only worked until about 10:00 that night, which wasn't too bad compared to some other nights.[6]

Lumber shortages had reached crisis levels in the Valley by September 1942 but that didn't stop Terry Greenwood, on behalf of S. M. Simpson Ltd., from declaring that "as far as lumber is concerned, it is war purposes first, last, and at all times. If there should be any left over, it may be released for domestic consumption."[7] That sentiment didn't do much for local fruit growers desperate for boxes, and the B.C. Fruit Growers' Association (BCFGA) and the Fruit Shippers' Association sent a delegation to Ottawa to plead for an increase in their priority rating. Their concerns fell on deaf ears, and the availability of boxes for Okanagan growers remained an ongoing problem.

This situation was made even more complicated by a dilemma faced every year by the Valley's box makers. Growers would estimate the size of their crops when the blossoms set and order boxes accordingly; and box makers would base their production plans and schedules on these estimates. Then, depending upon rain, hail, sunshine, insects, and a few other factors, they would find themselves either scrambling to fill orders for more boxes or with extra stock on hand if the crop was less than anticipated. Box factories would make and stockpile shook during March, April, and May, and then ship it out to the packinghouses as crops were picked and packed. Production continued if more boxes were needed. If not, employees were either laid off or put to work elsewhere in the plant.[8] It was almost impossible to predict what was going to happen, however:

> Wynndel Box and Lumber near Creston, in the Kootenays, had pretty well slowed down during the Depression. When the phone call came telling them to gear back up because their boxes were needed for the war effort, Monrad Wigen responded, "If you want our boxes, I need money!" He was told to go to the local bank. "Already done that – no luck." He was told to try again. This time, MacMillan got there before him and soon the retooled Wynndel plant was adding its production to the area's wartime quota.[9]

Taking out the competition

As the war continued and the demand for lumber and boxes increased, Stan realized he needed more timber if he was to be able to keep up. He decided his best option was to purchase an existing mill and the timber supply that went along with it, and the best prospect was the Kelowna Saw Mill (KSM):[10]

So much lumber was needed for the war effort that sales to civilians were restricted and S. M. Simpson Ltd. explained its problem in the newspaper. (The Kelowna Courier, May 13 and 14, 1943.)

Stan Simpson, 'Uncle Willie' Lloyd-Jones, and Terry Greenwood in 1949, when they were collectively managing S. M. Simpson Ltd.

Saw Mill Control is Changed: S. M. Simpson Ltd. Purchases Control of Kelowna Saw Mill Co. Ltd.

(The Kelowna Courier, December 10, 1942)

David Lloyd-Jones[11] had owned the downtown Kelowna Saw Mill since the turn of the 20th century, and had supplied both Kelowna and its neighbouring communities with dimension lumber and boxes for 40 years; he and Stan had been competitors for about 20 years of those years. Lloyd-Jones was even tighter with his money than S. M., and as a result the old KSM buildings had remained relatively unchanged during that time. The plant and equipment hadn't seen many upgrades, either. The Kelowna Saw Mill, like all early mills, had had its share of fires and each time some part of his mill was destroyed, Lloyd-Jones rebuilt a little further north along the lakeshore from his original Bernard Avenue location. Eventually, the dilapidated mill filled an area of the city's downtown now occupied by the Kelowna City Hall, Memorial Arena, Centennial Museum, and the Kelowna Yacht Club. Access to a sizeable portion of the lakeshore adjacent to City Park was cut off by several acres of the mill's wharves, equipment, and hundreds of piles of air-drying lumber.

Stan wasn't interested in the obsolete equipment or buildings but he knew the Kelowna Saw Mill's timber supply would help him keep up with the ever-increasing demands for lumber and boxes, as well as enable his company to expand in the future. Negotiations for the sale began some time in 1941, despite recollections from company old-timers that "there was no way in hell David Lloyd-Jones would ever sell his mill to Stan Simpson." S. M. had few enemies, but the rift between the two men that dated back to 1915 when Lloyd-Jones apparently prevented Stan from getting a bank loan had never healed. Stan was likely aware that Lloyd-Jones's ongoing animosity would be an obstacle to his purchasing the mill and engaged a Vancouver agent to act on his behalf. When the offer came from the Coast, Lloyd-Jones assumed it was from either the Koerners or Bentleys, both relative newcomers to the province's lumber industry, and sold his company.

The *Courier* revealed the identity of the buyer shortly after the sale closed, noting that "contrary to reports that have been current on the street, no Vancouver company is interested in purchasing the old mill."[12] Lloyd-Jones was an old man by the time the papers were signed in 1942 and wanted out of the business that had consumed most of his life, but he must have been furious that his archrival had out-manoeuvred him on their final deal and died shortly after. Business at the newly-acquired mill carried on as usual with Terry Greenwood, who had arrived a few years earlier from Saskatchewan with log-buying and lumber-industry experience, becoming the general manager while William (Uncle Willie) Lloyd-Jones, David's cousin, stayed on as secretary-treasurer.

Back to the war

The federal government moved quickly in the early days of World War II to establish the Wartime Prices and Trade Board (WPTB) to minimize the profiteering, hoarding, and inflation that had plagued Canada during the previous war. The Board set maximum prices and allowable price increases for all products – including lumber and box shook – and services deemed to be of national importance during the war and post-war period. Stan was appointed to the Board's Box Shook Committee in 1943 as a representative of the country's box makers, with the job of assisting the government in ensuring enough boxes were available for the country's war effort and dealing with potential shortfalls. The Committee's meetings required Stan to travel to Ottawa several times a year, and as he became more familiar with the workings of the federal government and its wartime demands, the Valley's box manufacturers and fruit shippers asked him to represent their interests in the nation's capital as well. When tight price controls prevented box makers from recovering their production costs and boxes continued to be diverted to the war effort, Stan went back to Ottawa to plead for relief on behalf of the fruit industry.[13] S. M. saw his involvement with the national committee and his efforts on behalf of his Valley colleagues as part of his patriotic duty, and if there was a personal cost for his involvement, he never mentioned it.

The box industry faced a series of ongoing crises during the war but none were severe enough to halt the flow of apples. Bombing raids on transatlantic convoys stopped apple shipments to the United Kingdom by 1941, but they resumed in January 1943 and the number of carloads of apples leaving the Valley soon reached a five-year high. Loaded rail cars also headed to Texas, Florida, Nebraska, and to the Maritimes, and on April 15, 1943, B.C. Tree Fruits shipped a record 10,000th carload of fruit out of the Okanagan. The event was such a milestone that the CNR and CPR flipped a coin to see who would have the honour of hauling the car. MacDonald's Consolidated, a big grocery wholesaler based in Regina, also conducted a raffle to see which of its many retailers would win the right to sell the high-profile shipment. As important as boxes were for the war effort, Okanagan orchards were producing larger crops year after year and Stan had to factor their growing needs into his operational plans.

 S. M. took his first-hand knowledge of the box allocation and shortage issues to a meeting of the government's Box Shook Committee when it met with other box makers and fruit industry representatives in Kelowna in March 1945, where he gave concrete examples of the challenges the Valley box industry was having to deal with. Box makers calculated they would need 54 million board feet of lumber to make all the required fruit, vegetable, and berry containers after growers provided crop estimates for the coming year. About 40 million feet of that could be obtained locally, but box factories needed federal assistance to make up the difference and the government's guarantee that there would be a supply of lumber from elsewhere in the province. In order to do this, packinghouses would have to place firm orders immediately and accept whatever shook was delivered, regardless of what their final needs would be. Growers, realizing they might have to buy more boxes than they actually needed, were not willing to take the risk, and box makers felt they would be in a similar predicament if labour shortages prevented them from delivering all the boxes that had been ordered. If this were to happen, the box makers wouldn't qualify for the subsidy that had enabled then to purchase the lumber in the first place, and they would have to pay full price for it without being able to pass these costs on to the packinghouses. Labour shortages were such a problem toward the end of the war that growers asked the National Selective Service if prisoners of war could be made available in the Central and South Okanagan to work in the orchards, packinghouses, or box plants, but nothing came of the initiative when no one would take responsibility for housing the prisoners, and orchardists were left to manage with whatever boxes could be supplied to them from the lumber box makers had on hand.[14]

The Interior's box manufacturers were working at full capacity in the spring of 1945 and still unable to keep up with the demand. Eventually, special permission was given to the Alaska Pine and Universal Box plant in Vancouver to ship 10 railcar loads of box sides and tops to Kelowna, on the condition that S. M. Simpson Ltd. supplied the bottoms.[15] Even that did not solve the problem as Simpson's was working flat out to build its own boxes and had little capacity to supply parts to other manufacturers. The annual supply crisis seemed unsolvable and growers began to look for alternatives to the traditional wooden box. Paper bags were their first choice but apples were easily bruised during shipment, and the bags received a mixed reception. Their second choice was corrugated fibreboard and wooden boxes, which began to appear in Okanagan packinghouses in the mid-'40s and provided some much needed relief to the ongoing box shortage. Both options were seen as temporary solutions to the problems created by the war; most people expected the problem to disappear once the war was over. It's unlikely anyone, especially S. M., could have foreseen the profound impact these new containers would soon have on the Valley's wooden box makers.

The cardboard alternative
Box Shook Situation Brighter – Corrugated Fibreboard Box Has Made Place for Itself in Fruit Industry
(The Kelowna Courier, January 28, 1943)

Foreshadowing what was to come, the fruit industry ordered 900,000 of the new hybrid wood-and-cardboard boxes for the 1943 growing season. Because measurements for the new boxes were the same as the standard wooden box, S. M.'s mill provided the national paper companies making the cardboard boxes with wooden box ends to fold the top, bottom, and sides around. All-cardboard boxes were introduced a few years later but were still not strong enough to withstand the pressure of stacking, so Stan made small triangular wooden pieces that were fitted into each of the four corners of a box, giving it the needed additional strength. The fruit industry increasingly began using this type of box as an alternative to all-wooden boxes, and with a cost of about 7¢ per cardboard box versus more than 20¢ for a wooden one, it wasn't hard to see why growers were receptive to the change. Stan was likely so busy running his company that he didn't see the cardboard box as any kind of a threat to his business – it was wartime and accommodations had to be made. In the meantime, the new containers provided Simpson's and other box makers with a temporary reprieve from the fruit industry's continual demands, and it would be a few years before Stan would have to deal with the real impact of the cardboard revolution.

Slabwood Shortage
—

Owing to inadequate stocks to meet the general demand and to protect those not having supply on hand, we will only supply to those in urgent need and in limited quantities, effective immediately.

Deliveries will be restricted to our own equipment and within restricted areas.

We would kindly ask those having a supply on hand not to request further deliveries. Their co-operation in this connection will greatly assist us to fairly distribute available stocks.

■

S. M. Simpson Limited
AND
Kelowna Saw Mill Co., Ltd.

From The Kelowna Courier, *December 10, 1942.*

Not everyone liked the change from wood to cardboard. In Vancouver and Victoria's more humid climates, suppliers would only take cardboard cartons when wooden boxes weren't available. On the other hand, wholesalers in Saskatchewan and Alberta thought it was their patriotic duty to go along with changes that made more wood available for the war effort. Winnipeg, at the hub of the Prairie market, demanded the original wooden boxes even though cardboard substitute was seen as a good alternative for soft fruits. The general consensus among suppliers was that everyone had a responsibility to adapt to the demands of war, so cardboard boxes were accepted as a short-term alternative during these extraordinary times. But everyone, including S. M., expected that the familiar wooden boxes would return once the war was over. Everyone, that is, except the paper box manufacturers who, by 1945, were aggressively going after this new market; at that year's annual BCFGA convention, a full range of paper and cardboard products were on display.

Freezing temperatures

Stan dealt with the continual shortage of boxes throughout the war, but in 1943 he was faced another shortfall when Kelowna experienced its coldest winter in years. Most of the town's residents relied on waste from the sawmill for their cooking and heating fuel, but with its usual winter slowdown, Simpson's wasn't generating enough sawdust or slab wood to fill the demand. Stan met with Mayor G. A. McKay and put a large ad in the *Courier* to let his customers know what was happening; Stan

63

thought it was both unfair and unacceptable that local farmers had been stockpiling enough sawdust to last them a couple of years and decided an ad was the best way to rectify the situation. Fiercely cold winters also compounded the wartime supply problem when log booms froze into one solid mass and the mill's corrugated iron building were too cold to work in. Many mills closed because of cold weather and log shortages, but other risks to their survival were never far away.

The spectacular fire that destroyed the Kelowna Saw Mill, October 1944. (Bud Shelley photo)

Yet another fire
Spectacular Evening Fire Destroys Kelowna Saw Mill … The City Landmark [was] Built About 50 Years Ago

(The Kelowna Courier, October 19, 1944)

While Stan was busy negotiating labour agreements and starting to get his two sawmills working together, another disaster struck. A blaze started in the KSM boiler room at 7:30 on a Friday night in October 1944. The night watchman sounded the alarm, and the Water Street fire hall was only a couple of blocks away, but volunteer firemen had to come from all over town – many on their bicycles. The old buildings were tinder dry and with oil and gas storage on site, the fire was quickly out of control. Furious winds that had been whipping through the Valley earlier in the week had fortunately died down few hours earlier, and firemen were able to contain the blaze before it spread to the nearby downtown business district. Corrugated iron roofs on the burning building also kept most of the sparks from flying around the site and engulfing the nearby sawdust piles and stacks of lumber.

Stan had considerable first-hand experience with sawmill fires by this point, and had the foresight to purchase insurance for the aged mill when he bought it. Another owner might not have thought the run-down operation was worth insuring, but Stan knew how essential it was to have a ready source of cash available to rebuild if necessary, and the $30,000 loss was mostly covered. Rather than rebuild the obsolete mill, however, he transferred the KSM employees who chose not to retire to his Manhattan Beach plant, where extra shifts absorbed the production quotas from the burned-out operation. S. M. already had bigger plans underway for his company in the early '40s, and the fire proved to be more of an opportunity than a setback.

S. M. Simpson Ltd.'s Manhattan Beach office at the foot of Guy Street. (Kelowna Museum photo)

S. M. Simpson Ltd. was operating out of three different locations near Kelowna's downtown business district in the middle of the decade. The original sash and door plant on Abbott Street was still producing custom store fittings, windows, and doors, and had become the town's major supplier of glass and car window replacements; it also housed the main Simpson mill office. The Kelowna Saw Mill, just two blocks away, produced dimension lumber, sawdust, firewood, and boxes. The Manhattan Beach operation, another seven or so blocks to the north, produced most of the company's boxes, lumber, sawdust, and firewood, as well as housing a small retail building supply outlet. Stan had been thinking about consolidating his Abbott Street operation to the more central KSM location for a while and the fire firmed up his decision to do so. But with the war and the uncertainty it brought, Stan decided to wait before making any major changes to his company.

Labour organizes

Organized labour arrived in the Valley while Stan was busy juggling wartime quotas, integrating his two sawmills, and travelling back and forth to Ottawa pleading for help for the struggling fruit industry. In the fall of 1943 the *Courier* announced:

Sawmills' Employees Return to Work After Voluntary "Holiday"

(The Kelowna Courier, September 23, 1943*)*

As the article continued, the most telling comment about the emergency labour dispute was that "tearing away the fog and touching the essentials [of the issue], insofar as possible," was difficult. There are many versions of the company's history during these years, but few who were involved in the early days of the unions in the Okanagan are still alive. Of those who are, even fewer are willing to talk about it – perhaps their actions don't seem as justifiable in hindsight as they did in the heat of battle.

Although the International Woodworkers of America (IWA) didn't arrive in the Valley for another few years, the Canadian Congress of Labour (CCL), had begun meeting in 1943 to organize the area's unskilled workforce, including packinghouse workers, though it was unsuccessful doing so at this time. Kelowna City staff were more favourably inclined, as were the employees of the Kelowna Saw Mill and S. M. Simpson Ltd., and the issue that had sparked the mill employees' 'holiday' that September had been Stan's refusal to recognize the CCL Woodworkers Local Number 4 as the official bargaining agency for his employees.

The Simpson Employees' Association, which was unaffiliated with any labour organization and made up primarily of employees who had worked with Stan for many years and not gone off to war, had been taking the employees' concerns to management in the years prior to the CCL's arrival. The arrangement had worked well and most older employees were comfortable with the organization, but younger employees at both the Manhattan plant and the KSM were agitating for change, and had already signed up with the CCL. Stan took his employees' desire to unionize very personally: he felt they had struggled through the Depression together and now that times were better, agitators from outside the Valley were intimidating his employees and turning them against him.

The Employees' Association was certified as the mill's official bargaining agent by the Provincial Department of Labour and Stan had no problem negotiating with the Association, but younger and more vocal employees felt CCL Local No. 4 could get them a better deal. It turned out, however, that they had not been members of the new organization for the provincially-required three-month period and as a result, the CCL had no legal standing and Stan refused to negotiate with the union. The CCL certification would have been automatic if employees had waited another few weeks, but the union organizers didn't want to lose their momentum and insisted on being at the negotiating table immediately. When Stan refused that as well, the employees walked out – the voluntary 'holiday' of the headlines. During the walkout, the Employees' Association kept the sawmill operating and sent excess sawdust and slabwood to local canneries, which were at the peak of their tomato-canning season and needed all the fuel they could get. S. M.'s attempts to deal with the situation expeditiously weren't very successful:

> As mill employees gathered around an empty railway flat car beside the box factory, Stan climbed up to speak to them. Just as he began to speak, one of the union reps shoved Stan off the platform and tried to take his place. Though momentarily

The greenchain at Simpson's Manhattan Beach operation, early '40s.

caught off guard, Stan clambered back up and insisted on his right to speak to his employees. Calls of "shame, shame" came from some of the old-timers and while he appreciated their support, Stan knew he could not change the minds of the majority.[16]

Because this was wartime and strikes were both unpatriotic and unlawful, the walk-out was referred to as a "stoppage of work," although, as the *Courier* commented, "Just what the difference is, is difficult for the layman to understand but apparently a strike is illegal while there is nothing illegal about a large number of workers simultaneously taking a holiday and shutting down a high-priority plant."[17] As a result of a flurry of telegrams between the company, CCL reps, and the Department of Labour, employees were told that negotiations would only get underway once they returned to work. The sawmills were back in operation a few days later and the 'holiday' was officially over. Once that happened, negotiations got underway very quickly.

Logs are sorted out of the boom, sent up the jack ladder, and sprayed to remove any grit or stones before heading into the mill for sawing.
(Bill Greenwood photo)

The Simpson Employees' Association Bargaining Committee[18] negotiated a new agreement and the old-timers found themselves swept along by the demands of the more outspoken younger group; some became reluctant union members but others refused to join the CCL and stayed on the outside until a few years later when the IWA arrived in the Interior; most eventually succumbed to the pressure to join the IWA when it arrived, but a few remained on the sidelines and chose not to get involved in its activities. Stan and

his son, Horace, signed an agreement with the bargaining representatives of the Employees' Association[19] on December 14, 1943, and then signed an identical agreement with Kelowna Saw Mill employees.

The timing of the union's nation-wide campaign to organize unskilled labour couldn't have been better, as most of Canada was distracted by the war and wasn't paying much attention to efforts to organize small groups of unskilled workers. But even then, the unions didn't have a tremendous impact on working conditions. During the war, wages, overtime pay, and vacations were all set by the War Labour Board, and hours were set by the Provincial Department of Labour, so in reality, there was little to negotiate.

That didn't mean conditions were the same for everyone:

> Special provisions were made for women employed at the mill during the war: female workers on any job formerly done by male workers were paid at the same rate as male workers, provided the female worker did the same amount of work on all jobs as efficiently and without assistance. Female workers could also have a ten-minute rest period midway during the first half and second half of regular days work.[22]

Wooden flume
(Kelowna Museum photo)

The contract Stan and Horace signed was in effect until December 1, 1944, and thereafter from year to year unless either party gave notice of termination.[20] The Canadian Brotherhood of Railway Employees and other Transport Workers, Division 217 Kelowna, signed an agreement on November 30, 1944, as bargaining agent[21] for the company's truck drivers, although the terms were the same as the contract negotiated by the Employees' Bargaining Committee. The second union's involvement was likely territorial and it was soon absorbed by the IWA contract.

With the push to organize unskilled workers, there was little Stan or other Interior owners could have done to stop the CCL from unionizing their sawmills. The owners were a self-sufficient group of hard working, risk-taking entrepreneurs who saw themselves – for the most part – as benevolent capitalists who had used their own money to set up these sawmills and they felt they had a right to control their own destiny. In the owners' view, unions threatened all this and forced fundamental changes to the way they did business.

Stan was not a demonstrative man, so the anger and betrayal he must have felt when many of his employees choose to support the union would never have been apparent. His relationship with the union and the confrontations that would become frequent in the years that followed were never easy for him to deal with, but little changed in the way S. M. related to his employees. He still knew them all by name and what was happening with their families. He helped his employees when they were in trouble and had nowhere else to turn,[23] and continued the company's tradition of delivering turkeys on Christmas Eve. But in the words of Sadie Gregory, wife of Vic Gregory who joined the mill staff in 1943, the sense of family had been shattered:

> When Vic started working at the mill, there was no union but it wasn't long before rumours were heard of union shops etc. and shortly after, a meeting was called. I remember Vic coming home and describing the scene to me. S. M. gave a talk and Vic was very impressed by it, but as other speakers voiced their concerns and desires, it became apparent that it was definitely a *fait accompli*. So,

a lot of bargaining and meetings began and these became the norm for all mills before long. After that it seemed as if there was a different work ethic in the mill, what with grievance committees, union shops, and so on and it was no longer a family operation.[24]

The IWA arrives in the Interior

Labour was organizing across the continent and by 1944, over 38,000 new union members had been signed up in B.C. alone. With wartime demands, sawmills were working flat out and while growth in productivity provided some increase in profits for mill owners, both box prices and increases were strictly controlled by the Wartime Prices and Trade Board; this same group also controlled wages and working conditions. Little had changed in either area since the Depression and many sawmill employees were dissatisfied with their jobs, and it was relatively easy for union organizers to stir up dissent.[25]

The IWA had organized most Coastal loggers and mill workers by May 1945, and was able to free-up organizers to send to the Interior. An invitation from Marion R. Holtom, secretary of the B.C. Woodworkers Union CCL Local No. 4 Kelowna, was all that was needed to facilitate the IWA's entry into S. M. Simpson Ltd. and two months later, the CCL local became IWA-CIO Local 1-423. A slate of officers for the new local was elected on July 24,[26] and within the first week they made presentations

S. M. Simpson Ltd. saw itself as a full-service provider to the orchard industry and offered both picking ladders and flume lumber in addition to boxes.

to the Board of Industrial Relations in Vernon arguing for an eight-hour-day, overtime pay, and wage parity with the Coastal lumber industry. Until this time, most Interior box factories had been working nine to 13-hour days during the busy box-making season. Operators were adamant that their circumstances were unusual and there was no justification for the union's demands for a shorter work week. The box makers also tried to use the call of patriotism to sway the union and noted that any increased costs they incurred would have to be passed on to the consumer, which they didn't think was appropriate during wartime. The union prevailed on the length of the work week in the end but not on overtime pay and parity with the Coast; this issue would continue to resurface for many years to come.

25 – 40 Union Security or Strike [27]

The IWA was already well-established in the Interior sawmills a year later when the strike of '46 – a strike that would establish a pattern of acrimony, confrontation, and turmoil that continued to plague the Interior lumber industry for many years – began. But not everyone supported the union. Several mill employees had just returned from the war as the IWA was making its presence known and felt they had little to complain about. They were grateful to have a job and their wages, without having to go on strike, were significantly higher than the 20¢ a day they had been paid to fight. Older employees were comfortable with the way things were and felt threatened by more radical employees who were prepared to fight and if necessary strike for the changes they felt entitled to. The situation was highly contentious and there was virtually no hope of a simple resolution.

William Langmead, one of the IWA's international organizers, became a frequent visitor to Kelowna in the mid-'40s. Following the IWA's 1946 Vancouver convention, Langmead met with the Kelowna local to brief it on province-wide terms that the union's members had been agreed to – a 25¢-an-hour increase, a 40-hour work week, and union security (a union shop but with voluntary dues check off, meaning employers could automatically deduct union dues from paycheques if the employee agreed). It didn't take long for Simpson's employees to respond, as the *Courier* noted:

Picket Lines Surround Mill – Province-wide Woodworkers' Strike Starts Fruit Industry in Valley Will Be Crippled Due to Lack of Boxes

(The Kelowna Courier, May 16, 1946)

At the union's 11:00 a.m. province-wide deadline on May 16, 1946, more than 37,000 IWA members left their jobs. About a dozen Simpson employees, some of whom were young girls working in the box factory, ignored the deadline and crossed the picket line amidst cat-calls from those on the sidelines, as police officers watched on. Langmead promised no violence but warned that names of those who returned to work would be recorded and they would be blacklisted by all unions in the future. Stan met with his employees in the lumberyard in a last-minute effort to avert the strike, telling them that

> it has been a long time since I have had an opportunity to speak to the staff as a whole, but things make it rather necessary at last that I should have a talk with you. I have been told by your union officers that it is the intention to go on strike at 11:00 but thought it better to call you together before 11:00 to explain our position to you.

Stan said the issues of pay increases, a 40-hour week, and union security were minor and that for him, the greater issue was that a minority group in the sawmill should not be able to compel and force the majority of employees to go out on strike. He explained his position, noting:

> To me that is the main issue on which the last war was fought. The death of millions of people, millions of dollars lost, and millions of people under starvation and misery.

69

To me this is an important factor when you limit individual security. It is not a matter of union security, but a matter of individual security. As you are aware, there has been several threats of intimidation and threats of physical violence ... Under present conditions our law will be enforced and we believe our police are strong enough to give security and protection to every individual who desires to carry on his work ... I am going to give my reaction to this strike – if it was simply a matter of business, I would prefer to turn the key in the lock and take a year's holiday. Some of these employees have been loyal to me for 20 years, and I intend to be loyal to them, and I also have certain obligations to packinghouses and I intend to fulfill my contracts ... If people wish to work, I am going to suggest they go to work if they wish to cross the picket lines. If they do not wish to work, I will not request it as I believe every person is entitled to their own right of liberty.[28]

S. M. also believed that the strike and walkout were illegal, as the original contract he had signed with the Simpson Employees' Association didn't expire until December 1946 – seven months down the road – when the IWA was scheduled to take over as the recognized bargaining agent for mill employees. Rumours abounded and Stan felt he needed to counter some of them. He told his employees he would not be intimidated by nor would he agree to the union's demands that certain employees be discharged and others hired in their place.

On behalf of the IWA, Langmead responded:

Brother union members and sisters: it is now past 11:00, the deadline set by the union and the strike is now in progress. Now, to establish picket lines and inform citizens of this community to respect these picket lines. The only danger for any worker to cross the picket line is a moral one. Any person crossing the picket line will be advertised in every labour paper in Canada and North America and every union will be informed of that person's name. That is our only weapon and it is a strong one ... If you do not support this strike, don't talk about it, go home and stay home.[29]

Stan thought most employees would return to work and shortly before 1:00 Horace, as general manager, took the names of those intending to return to their jobs: "silence prevailed as the men marched through the picket lines."[30] The mothers of the girls working in the box factory refused to allow their daughters to return to work even though several were prepared to do so. Union officials and their supporters stated that 90 per cent of the employees were union members; the few non-union employees who dared to speak out accused the union of gross misrepresentation. A dozen employees crossed the picket line the afternoon the strike began and Stan expected many more to return the next morning, but was stunned when even fewer showed up. By the end of the week, only four or five men were willing to cross the picket lines and by Saturday (a regular workday), so few employees showed up that Stan had little alternative but to shut down the boilers and his sawmill, veneer plant, and box factory along with them.

Contract expiry dates were always an issue with S. M. His original contract ran out each year in December when the box factory was closed and mill production was reduced. But this contract was being negotiated in May when the box factory was working flat-out, fruit crops were ripening, and any work stoppage would seriously jeopardize box production. It was great timing for the union because it would pressure box makers to settle and get on with making boxes but not for the box makers, who wanted to negotiate during their slow season. A strike in the spring would also cause other problems as supplies of dimension lumber were already low and more was needed to finish the wartime houses for veterans who were having to make-do in less-than-satisfactory quarters. Restaurants also had to curtail their hours of operation because they were running out of the sawdust and slabwood that fuelled their stoves, and things got so bad that the Kelowna Steam Laundry had to revert to coal to generate steam, but even that wasn't much of an alternative with wartime restrictions still in place. Fruit growers around the Okanagan were insistent that if the strike lasted more than three days, the consequences would be disastrous. In the end, it lasted 36 days.

Stan was adamant the strike was illegal because the previous contract had not expired. He insisted again that a small number of union members were intimidating the majority of his employees, who really wanted to return to work. The union denied it. Stan said they were coerced. The union denied that, too. L. R. Stephens, a Kelowna resident and frequent spokesman for the Okanagan fruit industry, waded into the dispute saying the IWA was pressuring Stan's employees to strike. The union ignored him. Stan said he would not be bound by contract terms that had been agreed upon at an IWA convention when his employees were not IWA members.

While all this was going on, growers were becoming increasingly agitated. The longer the strike lasted, the greater the shortfall in the number of boxes that could eventually be produced. They professed neutrality but nonetheless wanted the box plants back in operation. Rumours spread – either the growers or the army would be brought in to run the box factories – but both Stan and the union denied it. At one point, the BCFGA offered to pay the difference between the wage settlement that had been reached in Vancouver and the wages Interior employees were being paid at the onset of the strike, but only if the strikers returned to work. Simpson's employees would only accept if union security was guaranteed; Stan refused both options.

Railcars loaded with undried lumber began arriving from Williams Lake to make up for the shortfall in locally-available yellow pine, but strikers wouldn't allow the cars to be unloaded and demurrage[31] of $120 a day was passed on to the BCFGA, adding to its cost for shook. Stan knew he would still have to pay for the lumber even it became mouldy and unusable in the sealed rail cars. The growers were frantic and sent telegrams to the provincial and federal ministers of labour pleading with them to intervene. Not waiting for a reply, Stan and Stephens flew back to Ottawa to personally urge the government save the Okanagan fruit industry. The men were apparently very persuasive as shortly after their return, the federal government took control of Interior box factories and ordered the strikers back to work. Twenty-four hours later – after being on strike for more than a month – the IWA agreed to a settlement on June 20.

Kelowna Mill Employees Return to Work at 1 p.m. Thursday Union Leader Declares IWA Forced to Play Last Card to Save Crop

(The Kelowna Courier, June 20, 1946)

Langmead admitted the decision to settle the strike was "forced upon them by the serious box shook situation"[32] and the IWA's offer to go back to work contained conditions that neither he or any other union man would have agreed to if it were not for the desperate need for one of the parties to take action and break the stalemate. The union accused box factory operators, and S. M. Simpson Ltd. in particular as the largest operation in area, of stubbornness, lack of cooperation, and starving the striking workers into submission. The chief IWA spokesman, Verne Carlyle, blamed the "whole mess ... on the bosses and mostly upon the eight or 10 who are running the lumberman's association by their weight and high productivity. We have done all we can." Carlyle went on, noting that "today we went so far as to make an offer which I despise myself for having to agree to ... We have sacrificed nearly all our pride in the organization with this one."[33] He accused the lumber companies of refusing to sell to veterans, turning instead to the black market where they could make more money and further, that he was putting the industry on notice that the union's demand for a 40-hour work week was just the initial step towards the ultimate goal of a 30-hour week.

When Carlyle was asked by the *Courier* if there were enough workers to man additional shifts at the factory to make up for the shortfall in boxes, he claimed that 400 expert box makers from Vancouver could be put to work here, but this would only happen if working conditions and pay scales were the same as what would be paid by their Vancouver employer. These included "a cafeteria, well furnished lounge rooms, health benefit schemes, nurses in attendance, and sports clubs, all financed by the operators."[34] In spite of the threat, Coastal box makers never materialized.

Three weeks after the strikers were ordered to return to work, contract terms for the Southern Interior were agreed upon – a wage increase of 10¢ an hour, retroactive to the date work resumed, a basic 44-hour work week with time-and-a-half for overtime (with certain exceptions), and the insertion of the Coastal check-off clause for union dues (voluntary and revocable). Stan had little choice but to negotiate with the IWA and agree to a new contract expiry date. The union had made its point and was now the recognized bargaining agent for Southern Interior sawmills. It had also won a wage increase for both its members and the employees who had refused to join the IWA ranks, but the other issues that weren't resolved would reappear.

The IWA's handling of the 1946 Southern Interior strike set the stage for future negotiations. The union's provincial organization spoke for the local workers, with the provincial convention setting contract terms based on the needs of the majority, who were from the Coast, and Interior woodworkers went along. IWA leaders from Vancouver called the shots on the picket line and the strikers either went along with it or went home – until the pressure became too great and they joined the union, whether they agreed with it or not. It took many years before the voice of Interior locals was heard around the provincial negotiating table, although by then the IWA had firmly established a climate of combative and aggressive negotiations.

Hard times for everyone

While most Coastal loggers were IWA members, those in the Interior remained independent and continued to deliver logs to area sawmills during the strike. Midway through the 1946 shutdown, logging contractor Leo Doucet was stopped at the barricades set up across the mill entrance, pulled from his cab, and "cuffed around by the strikers." Further trouble was anticipated that same afternoon when:

> about 20 loggers visited the area, headed by Justin McCarthy, a local logging operator. A few pickets were on hand, including the IWA's Bill Langmead, when Mr. McCarthy issued a "hands off" warning to the strikers, and added that any more interference on the part of the strikers would lead to a feud between the mill employees and the loggers. Staff-Sgt. Thomson was on hand, and after the men "talked it over," he suggested they move on.[35]

Arguments became so heated during the strike that one of the loggers 'just happened' to have a ball peen hammer on the truck seat beside him as he crossed the picket line. The picketers who grabbed at him through the open window were unfortunately laid low for the next several days after an unexpected encounter with the hammer.

The aftermath

Strikes took a terrible toll on everyone in the Valley. Families of the pickets had to deal with threats and confrontations as well as survive on significantly less income. Employees had to show up for picket duty to receive $12.50 a week in strike pay and since most families had only one source of income, the men did picket duty whether they agreed with the strike or not. Some employees found other jobs to add to their meagre strike pay and although it was expected, they refused to give that extra income back to the union. Brothers disagreed with brothers, sons disagreed with fathers, and wives and children had to do without. Sometimes the hard feelings and disagreements were never resolved, and the fear and suspicion never truly disappeared.

Over the years, the upheaval of the '46 strike resurfaced as unresolved issues and turf disputes returned and set the stage for later strikes. But the labour disputes had other, more far-reaching effects. Stan and his supervisory staff worked long days and often throughout the night to keep the mill secure and avoid long-term damage to the plant. The town's merchants found their earnings greatly reduced and, through no fault of their own, many risked losing their businesses. Strikes also put the Interior's vital box supply in jeopardy and added yet another risk to the orchardists' already precarious existence. For the time being, everyone went back to work when the '46 strike ended. Some employees were furious and some just mad. Others were fearful and guarded, while most were just relieved to get a regular paycheque again. The strike had been a bitter experience for many Simpson's employees, and although Stan had stood his ground and stuck to his principles, he was above all a realist and knew some of the things he felt strongly about were beyond his control. His sawmill, veneer plant, and box factory started up again and everyone returned to work, but the strike of 1946 changed S. M. Simpson Ltd. forever and established an acrimonious relationship with organized labour that would endure.

Okanagan Lake had risen more than two feet during the strike and in spite of pressure from packinghouses to start producing boxes, the flooded powerhouse needed to be dried out before the boilers could be fired up again. Vernon packinghouses had about 50 per cent of the boxes they needed on-hand before the strike began, but both Kelowna and Penticton had only stockpiled 30 per cent. The number of boxes required by the growers and packinghouses varied each year, but a bumper crop was anticipated this year, and when coupled with the strike and the recently-negotiated shorter work day, box makers were scrambling to even attempt to meet the enormous demand.

There were more problems for box makers, however, who had to buy the lumber they needed on a very competitive open market. With tight wartime pricing restrictions, there was no way they could pass along their increased costs to the packinghouses. When box factories in Kamloops and Oliver threatened to close down because they were losing so much money, Stan and Stephens headed back to Ottawa in the summer of '46 to argue for the removal of the price controls that were strangling box makers. The two men had become familiar figures in the nation's capital and were able to persuade the federal government to require all logs and lumber be directed to the manufacture of fruit containers and further, that box makers would have priority when purchasing in the open market. To underscore the urgency of the situation, a federal inspector was appointed and given the power to take over any box factory that didn't comply with the government's order to operate at maximum capacity.

By mid-September, the Wartime Prices and Trade Board approved a 16.6 per cent increase the price of box shook – an apple box now cost 27½¢ – and made it retroactive to July 1 so box makers could recoup some of their losses. The already-difficult year was made worse when the nails and wire needed to assemble boxes was in short supply because strikers had shut down eastern Canadian suppliers and closed most eastern U.S. seaports, which prevented fruit orders from leaving the country. Box production never did catch up with demand and much of the Okanagan's 1946 bumper apple crop was never picked. One Kelowna grower was reported to have left 12,000 to 14,000 boxes of Macintosh apples on his trees, and others found themselves in similar circumstances. It had been a tumultuous year for everyone – for the growers and shippers, for box makers and their employees, and the communities so dependent on all of them. Everyone hoped they wouldn't see another year like 1946.

1948 – A pivotal year for the IWA
The history of the International Woodworkers of America in B.C. reads like a good suspense novel. There were allegations and counter-allegations, cross-border intrigue, secret bank accounts, docu-

ments disappearing under the cover of darkness, threats and counter-threats. The details of each story varies depending on who is telling it, but there is little dispassionate reporting among the volumes written about union activities during these turbulent times.

A large number of the IWA's leaders were active in the Canadian Communist Party, and while people today are often inclined to dismiss Communism as an archaic and inconsequential part of Canadian history, its mandate for the workers of the world to unite and challenge the domination of their sometimes-repressive employers spoke to disenfranchised workers, especially during the desperation of the 1930s and the later struggles to establish unions across the country. The Communist Party filled a political vacuum that was created when the unemployed gathered on street corners and in relief camps during the Depression and were ignored by successive Liberal and Conservative governments. Through some of the most violent protests in Canadian history, Communists leaders became the voice for thousands of downtrodden and unskilled workers, and it wasn't a big step for those same people to become active in the union movement as they found work in the mines, docks, and forests across the country. When young soldiers returned from World War II and remembered who had championed their causes during the Depression, many readily accepted the new union leaders and didn't question their Communist affiliations.

Between the 1930s and the '50s, several skirmishes took place over control of the IWA. Those challenges finally exploded in 1948 when the union split into the 'red bloc' (the Communists), who subsequently formed the Woodworker's Industrial Union of Canada (WIUC), and the 'white bloc' (the anti-Communists), who were a group of IWA locals supported by the Canadian Council of Labour (CCL) and the U.S.-based Congress of Industrial Organizations (CIO). These were confusing times for everyone as union organizers from both the white bloc and the red bloc travelled throughout the province trying to convince union locals to join their side of the battle. A history of the union suggests that

> the real issue, as internal conflict grew in the Union, was the self-government of
> the IWA by the membership. Rumblings of rebellion were heard during WWII when
> the policy of the Union shifted with the changing policy of the Soviet Union Foreign
> Office. This rebellious mood became more pronounced when, in the years follow-
> ing WWII, the Communists [i.e. the IWA executive] insisted upon adherence to the
> Communist 'line' to the point where open cleavage with the trade union movement
> at large was evident.[36]

During the fall of 1948, the two sides fought to out-manoeuvre each other, but in the end one union local after another rallied to the flag of the IWA and ousted officers still affiliated with the dissident WIUC. Various court actions recovered most of the union assets that had been siphoned off by WIUC supporters, but the fight between the red and white blocs carried on within the ranks of provincial and federal governments, the CCL, the CIO, and union locals across Canada.[37] It took a few years, but eventually the WUIC and its Communist leaders dwindled into obscurity and members, with the exception of some locals in the East Kootenays, returned to the IWA fold.[38] By the following year, the Communists had been identified, branded as traitors, and barred from membership in the IWA. The rift was so deep, in fact, that it wasn't until the IWA Canada convention in September 1998 that delegates unanimously endorsed a resolution that abolished the IWA's 'errant members' list – those who had been banned from the union after the 1948 split because of their Communist affiliations. It took 50 years to get such a resolution passed because earlier attempts to do so resulted in bitter memories being dredged up and irresolvable fights on the convention floor.[39]

Lumber and orchards as the decade ends

In retrospect, it is curious how few people in either the fruit or lumber industries thought there could be any alternative to traditional wooden fruit boxes. The Southern Interior's yellow pine had been the best, most readily available species to make the containers, but most of it had been cut down and used by the mid-'40s. Early in the decade, Okanagan box makers made up for local yellow pine shortfalls by purchasing supplies from the Williams Lake area; when that wasn't enough, hemlock from the Coast was imported, although it was a poor alternative to the pine. Wood shortages became more apparent in the Southern Interior when the less-than-perfect boards that had earlier been sold for fuel were now needed: the parts containing knots were removed and several smaller pieces attached

together with squiggle nails to become a complete box end. Cardboard boxes and paper bags were available but still regarded with much scepticism, and because of that, almost no one seemed to realize that the demise of the wooden box was just over the horizon. The 'corrugated invasion' would all but replace millions of locally-produced wooden boxes within a few years and as they became the fruit industry's container of choice, the standard wooden box and the box makers who had supplied the Okanagan's fruit and vegetable industry for the previous half century disappeared into history.

Interior Box Makers' Association promotional box measuring 2" x 3" (Courtesy of Don Sandberg)

Of organizations and Royal Commissions

During the 1940s, two organizations played a significant role in the Interior's lumber and box industries: the Interior Lumber Manufacturers' Association and the Interior Box Makers' Association. Okanagan lumber manufacturers had primarily supplied local markets with railway ties and bridge timbers, mine supports and outbuildings, and wooden boxes for the fruit and vegetable industries prior to World War II. Most mills also turned out enough dimension lumber for the local construction trade, but populations were small and few buildings were constructed during the Depression. But there was considerable demand from overseas markets that had to rely almost entirely on Canadian wood with the onset of the war. Coupled with Canada's own wartime mobilization, the burgeoning export market created an unprecedented demand for anything made of wood. Suddenly, Interior forestry companies had to cope with freight rates, forestry and licensing regulations, and industry grading standards that had previously been dealt with by each mill as needed. With the huge increase in demand, Interior mill owners felt that an organization that could address these issues on behalf of all of them would be more effective, and in August 1941 S. M. Simpson Ltd. joined with seven other Interior lumber companies[40] to form the Interior Lumber Manufacturers' Association (ILMA).

After the war, Interior lumber producers wanted to expand their markets but discovered that they were competing against quality control and lumber grading procedures established by other countries. With only a handful of the hundreds of mills in the area producing grade-stamped lumber and the U.S. Federal Housing Administration demanding a recognized standard, Interior lumber producers had to scramble to organize and set up an acceptable grading system. Following the Canadian Standards Association's (CSA) certification of the ILMA's new grade-stamping program, classes were set up throughout the Interior to train mill personnel in appropriate procedures. The immediate problems were solved, but it wasn't long before the U.S. market wanted greater uniformity and demanded a single grading standard for the whole country. With 90 per cent of Interior production heading to U.S. markets mills were forced to comply, but it took until 1970 before a uniform Canadian standard was finally adopted.[41]

The other organization to take an active interest in the Valley's lumber industry was the Interior Box Makers' Association. No records have survived to explain the role or mandate of the Association, though it likely came into existence during the early '20s. Fruit had been shipped out of the Okanagan and Kootenays since the turn of the previous century and until the mid-'50s, most of it was sent in wooden boxes made in Interior sawmills that included box factories and sometimes veneer plants. Disputes between box makers and the fruit industry were frequent when shook prices increased and the additional costs had to be passed along to the packinghouses or shippers, and the Association provided a voice for the area's box makers, including Sandler Box Ltd., S. M. Simpson Ltd., Summerland Box Co. Ltd., Vernon Box and Pine Lumber Co., Wynndel Box and Lumber Co. Ltd., Armstrong Sawmill Ltd., Grand Forks Sawmills Ltd., Gorman Bros. Lumber & Box Co., Oliver Sawmills Ltd., Penticton Sawmills Ltd., and Rutland Sawmills Ltd. The Association disappeared without much fanfare a few decades after it came into existence, and mill owners were left to fend for themselves.

The Valley's lumber industry was also greatly influenced by the B.C Royal Commission of 1945, one of many Commissions that have played a significant role in developing the province's forestry policies. Mr. Justice Gordon Sloan of the Appeal Court of B.C. was chosen to head up the 1945 commission to examine B.C.'s forests and forest industry, and make recommendations to the government about policy changes that would both enhance and support what had become the province's main source of revenue. Stan joined others from the fruit industry, irrigation districts, the local Board of Trade, the Water Rights Branch, and lumber industry in October 1944 to make presentations to the commission on the current state of affairs. As part of his presentation, he noted that

> I am speaking as an operator of over twenty years experience in this district and as a member of the Executive of the Interior Lumbermen's Association. The views I am about to express are my own and are the result of careful observation of developments in this area and the needs of the lumber industry and relative industries to make them a permanent part of our communities, and ... the imperative necessity of a continuing lumber industry in order to serve other basic industries in the Interior of the Province. It is proper to point out at the outset that in the Okanagan area from Kelowna south, the depletion of readily accessible timber has been carried to greater lengths that elsewhere in the Interior.[42]

Stan's presentation ran for 13 legal-sized pages and sounds as relevant today as it did then. It was his opinion that

- forests must be managed on a sustained yield basis;
- areas that have been burned over or otherwise depleted must be replanted;
- fire prevention and insect and pest control efforts must be stepped up;
- cutting permits must be allocated by a process other than competitive bidding;
- pine, the preferred species for box making, must be protected;
- because the Interior forests were substantially different from those on the Coast, (the primary focus of the province's Forest Act) a separate administrative unit should be set up for the Interior;
- a thorough inventory of all stands of timber should be undertaken to determine extent, species and volume ... by extensive aerial survey followed by thorough ground cruises.[43]

The recommendations of the Royal Commission and Sloan's findings were presented later that year. They addressed some of Stan's concerns, but Sloan admitted his "most vexing problem came with trying to formulate recommendations that would assist both the sawmills and the fruit industry."[44] It was an undeniable fact that yellow pine areas in the Interior had been over-cut, the species was rapidly disappearing, and remaining stands were insufficient to meet the fruit industry's future box requirements. While there was an obvious need to replant the species, this would only benefit fruit growers in 60 or 70 years when those stands reached maturity. A partial solution would have been to ensure that remaining stands be allocated to box shook manufacturers, but the Commission recognized that the same timber would bring higher prices as dimension lumber. Sloan acknowledged that future plans for Interior forest management needed to be geared toward the fruit industry and its dependency on wooden boxes, but no mention was made about a possible alternative to the traditional wooden fruit box, and no recommendations were subsequently made about ensuring an ongoing supply of wood for the box industry.

About the time Stan was reporting to the Royal Commission, the Kelowna Saw Mill burned to the ground and he again found opportunity in the midst of potential disaster.

A civic opportunity

The mid-'40s were an incredibly busy period for S. M.: his business was running flat out, wartime demands were huge, he was negotiating with the unions, making presentations to the Royal Commission, and one of his mills burned down, but he still seemed to find time to become more directly involved in his community. Kelowna's leading citizens had been advocating the purchase of land for a civic centre since the town was incorporated in 1905, and while discussions about the availability of the KSM site had taken place with David Lloyd-Jones nothing had ever materialized. Early in 1944, as the *Courier* was covering stories of local boys dying on European fronts and packinghouses were bemoaning the lack of wooden boxes, several prominent citizens met and insisted Kelowna City Council take charge of postwar planning for such a centre. A newly-formed citizens' committee suggested a variety of buildings that could be used for both "esthetic [*sic*] development and athletic pursuits" be constructed in park-like, well-landscaped surroundings. High on the committee's list of priorities were sports facilities – a skating rink, gymnasium, and indoor swimming pool, as well as a theatre or auditorium and possibly even a proper city hall instead of the second floor of a local hardware store that had been used for council meetings for years.

The Kelowna Saw Mill fire of 1944 left the land empty and provided council with the opportunity it had been looking for, and it wasn't long before Stan was approached to see if he was interested in selling the property. Negotiations progressed slowly, and S. M. voiced his frustration in a letter to Mayor McKay:

> This Company has made tentative postwar plans for the establishment of an up-to-date retail business for the purpose of providing an adequate service for this growing community. These plans call for the use of a site on the property at the foot of Pendozi [Pandosy] Street. In view of our response to the City's request for an offer on this particular site, it has prevented us with proceeding with any definite planning. Therefore, we would kindly ask that this Company be given a decision as early as possible.[45]

Stan knew the KSM was obsolete when he bought it, and was aware that its location adjacent to the town's expanding business district could be put to better use. He didn't want to let the KSM name disappear entirely, however. The mill was a well-established part of the community and recognized throughout the Valley, and Stan wanted to incorporate the KSM name and its historic site into his future plans. He had intended to expand his retail building supply business beyond the makeshift sheds at Manhattan Beach and had preliminary plans in place to build a large showroom and office building on the edge of the KSM property at the foot of Pendozi (Pandosy) Street (now the Bennett Clock) that would provide the his new retail outlet with the exposure he was looking for.

By December 1945, the *Courier* was reporting the pending sale and changes to the site:

Sawmill Property Is Considered For Civic Centre Site

(The Kelowna Courier, December 14, 1945)

The proposed purchase was a 7.52 acre parcel of land between Water and Ellis Streets, the lane south of Mill Street (now Queensway), and the extension of Doyle Avenue (which then stopped at Ellis Street), through to Water Street on the west. Stan and council agreed upon a sale price of $30,000 for the property, which, according to the *Courier*, was "considerably less than the actual value of the property. As a condition of sale, Mr. Simpson stipulated that the property must only be used only for community purposes."[46] The town council decided to hold a referendum in March 1945 to ensure Kelowna's residents approved of the purchase, which by then had expanded to include an additional 4.5 acres between Water Street and Okanagan Lake. Some members of the citizens' committee thought this was an "advantageous acquirement now rather than leaving it and finding out later that it should have been purchased,"[47] and Stan insisted the additional parcel, priced at $25,000, be covered by the same covenants that were attached to the initial acreage.

The war was drawing to a close in the spring of 1945 and as everyone awaited final word of the German surrender, civic leaders notified the town's that "as and when Victory in the European Theatre of War is declared, retail stores would be closed."[48] When the V-E Day[49] announcement was finally made on May 8, 1945, the town's response was one of sombre relief, likely tempered by the ongoing conflict in the South Pacific. Though world events continued to occupy much of the *Courier*'s front page, local events also took considerable space as Alderman W. B. Hughes-Games cautioned his fellow aldermen that a number of ratepayers would not be in favour of adding the second waterfront parcel and its increased cost to the civic centre site plan. While Kelowna's future growth was still somewhat uncertain, Hughes-Games' caution was countered by an air of optimism and a sense of urgency from many citizens who were concerned that the opportunity to acquire these properties might be lost. "An Appeal" was made by 38 community leaders in the *Courier* on May 10, the same day the referendum was held, to urge support for both a bylaw and a plebiscite – the bylaw approving the expenditure of $30,000 to purchase the original 7.52 acre and the plebiscite supporting the future purchase of the 4.5 acres of lakeshore property for $25,000. Mindful of the controversy, Stan made the decision easier for the town's residents:

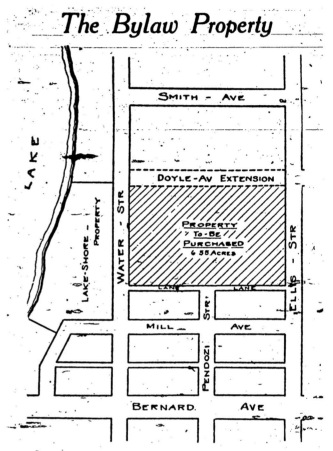

The Bylaw Property

In the map above, the shaded area represents that portion of the Kelowna Sawmill property, consisting of 7.55 acres, the purchase of which the ratepayers are asked to approve by voting "Yes" on the bylaw on May 10th. The property, it is proposed, will be used for civic buildings to be erected sometime in the future. The lakeshore property is also indicated above. Ratepayers are asked also to give their opinion as to whether or not the City should purchase this property in addition to the other site.

> If City Council, upon re-examining the situation after the passage of the bylaw and plebiscite, concludes that not all the bylaw area is required, I would be prepared to sell to the City the lakeshore area at the agreed price and a portion only of the land covered by the bylaw ... provided the portion left is a commercially desirable area and the matter is decided by June 30th of this year.[50]

The city could hardly loose and voters overwhelmingly approved the sale. As the Civic Centre Committee discussed various buildings that should be considered for the old KSM property, members expanded their plans and recommended the further purchase of the properties on the north side of

Mill Avenue (Queensway Avenue today) between Water Street and Ellis Street. Not wanting the unsightly backyards of the Kelowna Steam Laundry, Salvation Army, Orchard City Motors, and private landowners to be visible from the new civic centre, the Committee also recommended the purchase of eight additional lots at a fair market value of $60,000. The civic centre site was finally complete.[51]

Even after the public expressed its support for the plan, some councillors were still not convinced the city needed to purchase all the available property. Council decided to resolve the issue by hiring one of best-known town planning organizations on the continent, Harland Bartholomew, from St. Louis, Missouri.[52] The firm's consultant reported back to council that the additional property be included in a civic administration and recreational centre, and that a city the size of Kelowna, with healthy prospects for growth and development, deserved such an investment. Furthermore, he also recommended that the property between Water Street and the lake be cleared and turned into a park that would provide a clear view of the civic centre from the waterfront. With that report in hand, the City of Kelowna and S. M. finally signed an agreement to transfer the title of the property in January 1946. The land that had been the site of the area's earliest sawmill for half a century was about to be transformed into Kelowna's new civic centre. More importantly, Mayor Jim Pettigrew and his council agreed to the covenants Stan had insisted on, namely that the property only be used for "municipal purposes and that buildings should be of attractive design and set in park-like surroundings and, secondly, that the city would not at any time, sell or use the property for commercial or industrial purposes."[53]

In the end, the properties were sold for about what it cost Stan to remove the fire debris and remnants of the old Kelowna Saw Mill.

Before land became the valuable commodity it is today, many early pioneers found they possessed more land than cash and Kelowna has benefited substantially from the generosity of many of these early residents. Stan's motivation for making this land available to the city at such a generous price is unclear, but the decision to sell it likely came from his travels across the country and the influence of such frontier towns as Lethbridge, whose downtown civic square and abundant green spaces were noted as one of the finest features of that fast-growing community. He may also have felt an obligation to the town that had provided him with so many opportunities, and believed that by making this land available he was repaying some of that debt.

The first building erected on the Kelowna Civic Centre site was the Memorial Arena, paid for by public subscription and formally opened on November 11, 1948. A three-sheet curling rink was built in 1951, followed by the Okanagan Regional Library headquarters in 1955 and the South Okanagan Health Unit in 1952; all of these buildings, with the exception of the Arena, have since been demolished. The Centennial Museum, which was built in 1967 and added to in 1976 and 2001, temporarily housed the Kelowna Art Galley, but the gallery subsequently moved from the civic square in 1996. Other additions to the civic square include the Bennett Carillon Clock and reflecting pool, and the Kasugai Garden that was created in 1987 to commemorate Kelowna's sister-city relationship with Kasugai, Japan.

After a complicated land swap with the City in 1958, the provincial government built a new courthouse on waterlogged land across from City Hall. Many thought the reinforced concrete building would slowly sink into the marsh but it remained standing until 2001, when it was demolished amidst little controversy. Stan also made provision for The Kelowna Yacht Club to lease its lakefront land in perpetuity, in the mid-'40s. The Community Theatre, new Kelowna library, and RCMP building are also on property once owned by S. M. Simpson Ltd., and purchased by the City at a later date.

The kind of growth Kelowna has experienced over the past six decades since S. M. sold the land has surely exceeded the expectations of even the City's most optimistic community leaders in the 1940s, and their vision of a civic centre that would become a focal point for the future growth and development of Kelowna's downtown core has survived the more-recent exodus to the malls and strip developments. While there are still room for improvements to the civic centre property, Stan's vision of it being the heart of Kelowna's downtown has become a reality: it now anchors a new seven-story provincial courthouse, an art gallery, convention centre and hotel complex, multipurpose sports facility, a wine and orchard museum, and arts centre. The land to the north of the KSM property and previously occupied by the CNR marshalling yards and wharves, now called Brandt's Creek Crossing, rests between the civic centre and Stan's original sawmill, awaiting residential, commercial, and hotel development, and the entire area has recently been designated as Kelowna's Cultural Zone.

The terms of Stan's covenant have occasionally been challenged: in the mid-'50s, plans were in place to sell a portion of the waterfront for hotel construction. Stan, who was in hospital in Vancouver recovering from a stroke, wrote the mayor and expressed his distress and surprise that such a sale would be considered given the restrictions against either selling the property or its commercial use.[54] That deal fell through and with the recent demolition of the Provincial Court House, Kelowna has another opportunity to return to the original vision for the site – that the property be turned into a park and provide a clear view of the civic centre buildings and property from the lake.[55]

The land also boasts a number of natural features as well as development. A public walkway now traces the shoreline of Okanagan Lake from Mill Creek through City Park, past the old ferry wharf, in front of City Hall and the Kelowna Yacht Club where, inside, Stan's photo acknowledges his contribution to the club's existence. Beyond the Grand Hotel (once Whittup's Slough), the path's hard surface becomes a boardwalk – Simpson Walk – in recognition of S. M. and his contribution to the community. The hard surface returns as the path skirts Tugboat Bay, currently bereft of the historic boat it is named for, and on past the location of the old CNR wharves and shunting yards to the Brandt's Creek Bird Sanctuary. The walkway has become one of the city's premier outdoor attractions and exemplifies the potential civic leaders in the '40s saw for the area.

"Everything for Building"

S. M. was usually looking ahead and plans to expand the company's retail business and consolidate his other operations – custom cabinetry, windows and doors from the sash and door plant, a lucrative automobile windshield replacement business, dimension lumber and a growing range of other building materials – were already in the works in 1944 when Stan began negotiating the sale of the KSM property. Once the sale was complete, the company's first job was to bring it all under one roof in a more centrally located downtown site.

Stan moved his proposed retail operation and lumber yard from the foot of Pandosy Street to the corner of Ellis Street and Doyle Avenue, the land now occupied by the Kelowna library, RCMP offices, and Kelowna Community Theatre. The new retail outlet, using the familiar KSM name, was written up in *Hardware and Builder*, an independent trade journal, as "one of the outstanding retail lumber and building supply merchants in Western Canada."[56] The sash and door operation on Abbott Street moved to the Ellis Street site, where it continued to make a variety of custom building products that could now be displayed in the showrooms that proved to be the forerunner of today's mega-building supply centres.

The custom paint colours of General Paint, as well as louvered doors and sylvaply from MacMillan Bloedel & Powell River were on display. Perfection in Reflection became the motto of the glass division, which offered the new thermopane along with cathedral and figured glass, and the latest rage – glass blocks. Cement, plaster, wallboard, wood and asphalt shingles, insulation, custom moulding,

Stan's office in the KSM building was functional, and the two telephones gave him direct contact with the Manahattan Beach operation.

gypsum, and fibre wallboard were also in inventory. Orchard ladders ranging from 6 feet in height to the huge 16 footers, which had been made by Simpson's since its earliest days, were now produced in the millwork shop on the Ellis Street. With its large plate glass windows, the building soon became a landmark and Stan moved his office, the company's sales department, and the forestry division to the new location.[57] The two-story operation manufactured wooden doors and windows, ladders, and custom millwork on site, while a moulding shed, three warehouses, and a lumber storage area occupied the rest of the block. Terry Greenwood managed the KSM retail operation as well as Simpson's wholesale lumber sales, John Bottle was office manager and chief accountant for both companies, and Sandy Camozzi moved over from the Abbott Street sash and door operation to continue on as foreman.

The decade ends

If Stan had stopped long enough to reflect back on the past decade, he would have been struck by the fundamental changes that had taken place in his company. Its very survival had been put to the test during the Depression but when war was declared, he had to scramble to keep up with the enormous demands and still supply boxes to his long-time customers in the fruit industry. After the war, the tumultuous period of unionization challenged Stan and the way he did business, and though he didn't know it at the time, set the stage for labour negotiations for decades to come; his long-time employees and customers would also pay a price for those changes. He had represented his industry during the war, both locally and nationally, and was increasingly recognized as an innovative, hard-working leader in the lumber business. S. M.'s influence had grown far beyond his own community and the narrow confines of the Okanagan Valley.

S. M. Simpson Ltd. had become the largest sawmill in the Interior and provided Kelowna with its second largest payroll after the agricultural sector. The fruit industry had been exploring different types of fruit containers, but it still looked like the traditional wooden box – the mainstay of the Simpson's operation – would be the container of choice for some time to come:

> No satisfactory substitute has been found for the wooden container … as box shook, veneer boxes, flats, lugs, and baskets are all in demand and the greater percent age of the demand for the entire industry is turned out in Kelowna. The box shook cut

The Kelowna Saw Mill building supply
centre and warehouse at the corner of
Ellis Street and Doyle Avenue.

The company's retail operation sold "Everything
for building" – paint, doors and windows, insulation, glass, moulding, and more.

annually in Kelowna, if laid end to end, would reach from Kelowna to Winnipeg and back again.[58]

Not only was the company expanding, but so too was Kelowna. The city's population had grown to 8,500 during the decade, and another 3,000 people in adjacent areas already felt they were part of the town. With the opening of the new Hope-Princeton Highway in 1949, the Valley became more accessible to the outside world, and Kelowna's Board of Trade invited the world "to make Kelowna YOUR home. Life is good here and we want you to share it with us."[59] Things seemed equally bright for Stan's company when it received one of the new forest management licenses in 1949. The stage was set for S. M. Simpson Ltd.'s growth and expansion, and everyone was looking forward to what the '50s would bring.

Boards and boxes at the end of the '40s

Chapter **6**

Was It the Best or Worst of Times?– the 1950s

Simpson's sawdust trucks loading in the mill yard. Before the sawdust piles were ventilated, spontaneous combustion fires often broke out, and men were known to get buried if the piles collapsed.
(Kelowna Museum photo)

"King Winter," as the *Courier* noted, had the province firmly in its clutches at the beginning of the new decade, with Okanagan Lake freezing solid for an unusual second year in a row. Devastating floods had ravaged the area the previous spring, and now unbearably cold temperatures were adding to the misery and people were literally freezing to death. Cherry and peach trees split as the mercury dropped and at -38°C, even the hardier apples could not withstand the onslaught. When the Valley finally thawed, over 400,000 dead or dying fruit trees were wrenched out of its orchards. The ferries that were the only way for cars and people to cross the lake were immobilized during the coldest days, when huge chunks of ice jammed the zigzag channel that had been carved out for them. Coal and wood supplies were running low, isolated communities survived on sporadic power, and plumbing firms had to hire extra help to thaw the frozen pipes that were rupturing all over town. And it looked like things were getting worse:

Present Supply of Sawdust Will Last for Only 6 Days
The Arctic's Bunyan-barrelled onslaught on the Okanagan's "banana belt" continues without letup

(The Kelowna Courier, January 30, 1950)

As record-low temperatures continued unabated through January, Simpson's began running out of sawdust. The sawmill would ordinarily be closed on the coldest days, but now saws were kept running so they could produce much-needed fuel. Snowbound roads and frigid conditions made it almost impossible for people to get more sawdust from smaller rural mills on their own and it became Stan's mission to make up the shortfall.

S. M. announced he would try to acquire sawdust from more distant mills even if it meant Simpson's employees had to clear the roads themselves. Supplies were available from Mabel Lake, near Enderby to the north, but it took the driver over 20 hours on almost impassable roads to complete the 274 km round trip. More fuel was available from the Olinger mill in Carmi, near Beaverdell to the east,

S. M. Simpson Ltd. - early '50s.
(Bill Greenwood photo)

but the provincial public works department wouldn't guarantee that the roads would be passable, so Stan sent his own bulldozers out to clear enough of a track to get trucks there and back. Most supplies of dry wood had already been used up, coal was still rationed, grocery stores were running out of food, and the situation was becoming critical. Thankfully, train service was finally restored to the Valley a few days later, and tank cars of fuel oil took some of the pressure off those few households that had already converted their stoves and furnaces. Store shelves were gradually restocked, and life started to return to normal. Conditions had been unbelieveably harsh: where snow had been scraped away or compacted, the frost reached 42" down into the ground. Kelowna had been both isolated and extremely vulnerable, and there was virtually nothing anyone could have done.

The mill was having its own problems as well. Loggers couldn't get into the woods to re-supply the Manhattan Beach operation, and tugs couldn't haul booms from around the lake. Even booms already at the mill were a solidly frozen mass and had to be freed from their icy trap before any sawdust could be produced. Simpson's dynamite supply was stored in a powder magazine nearby on Knox Mountain, and explosives became the easiest and most readily available way to break up the ice encasing the logs. One morning, Andy Gaspardone, the boom man and scaler who started at the mill in 1936, stood on the wharf and lit the fuse on a stick of dynamite – but slipped as he flung it out onto the boom. In the same instant, he lost his footing and fell through the thinner ice surrounding the pilings. Those nearby described his subsequent departure from the water as one of the fastest exits ever witnessed in the annals of human history.

It was so cold that the men didn't want to stand outside, light the dynamite, wait to see if the fuse caught, and then throw it out onto the boom. Instead, they gathered in the meagre warmth of the lunchroom, lit the fuse, and raced outside to pitch the explosives as far out as they could – safety wasn't the first thing on their minds, and besides, it added a little adventure to their ordinary day.

A cherry picker in the Bear Creek Valley.

Stan discovered what was going on and put an end to the lunchroom staging area. The risk to his sawmill outweighed the cold and discomfort of a few employees.

A company snapshot

The Lumberman, a forest industry magazine, provided a unique overview of the S. M. Simpson Ltd. operation in the early '50s, noting it was the largest, fastest-growing, and most fully-integrated forest company in the Interior.[1] The article was lengthy and painted a detailed picture of an operating sawmill of the day: depending upon the season, the company employed between 400 to 500 people and its output averaged between 20 and 24 million board feet a year, including about 12 million feet of veneer. It noted that Stan had recognized early-on that the fruit industry was the major driving force behind the Okanagan economy, and would require an enormous number of boxes and other wooden containers annually. It also highlighted the fact that Stan developed a good working relationship with the fruit shippers and packinghouses, and then designed and integrated his sawmill, box factory, veneer plant, and planing mill to meet the needs of that industry. Simpson's shipped box shook from Osoyoos, near the U.S. border, to Kamloops in the north, and produced dimension lumber for local customers as well as the growing spruce markets in eastern Canadian and Midwestern U.S. – all of which was beyond the capacities of most other mills and box factories in the Valley.

The article went on to say that independent contractors did most of the company's logging in the hills to the west of Okanagan Lake, with Jack Seaton taking out most of the larger logs and Justin McCarthy, the jack pine. Titan power saws were used in the bush, while yarding was done with Caterpillar tractors, horses, and cherry pickers. About two dozen contractors owned the trucks that hauled logs from up to 50 km away, while the company owned the trailers and maintained them in its machine shop. The logs were either brought directly to the Manhattan Beach operation or off-loaded at booming grounds around the lake and transported to the mill by the *Manhattan* and the *Stanley M* tugs. The logs were then sorted into species: fir (50 per cent of the mill's cut), spruce (40 per cent), and pine (10 per cent), as only one species was processed at a time. Nimble boom men with pike poles steered the logs into the path of the drag saw, which cut them into block lengths for the veneer operation while they were still in the water. Logs were then fed onto the jack ladder and spray-washed to remove any debris before ending up on the shotgun carriage for sawing.

In a 1952 industrial display at the Kelowna Memorial Arena, Simpson's had a full range of its products on view.

About 80,000 feet of dimension lumber was produced per shift year-round, but during the six months between March and August, Simpson's focused on making fruit containers. About 10 to 12 million feet of box shook, or about 20,000 completed apple boxes, were produced each day. Slabs, the initial cut taken off the four sides of the log, were usually waste, though at Stan's initiative the

The machine shops took advantage of the natural light and were built on the west side of the mill yard.

The machine shop
(Jack Leier photo)

cuts were thicker than usual and sent directly to the planing mill to be converted into sides or ends for fruit boxes. Logs sent to the veneer plant were peeled into various thicknesses, cut to specified lengths, and then stapled together with cleats to become the tops and bottoms of the boxes and other containers manufactured in the box factory. Blythen unitizers produced 30,000 box lids per shift for the apples, peaches, pears, and other fruits, while another machine stitched the tops and bottoms of the tomato boxes, junior apple boxes, and display lugs. In total, 10 million unitized tops and bottoms of eight to 10 different sizes were produced annually, in addition to veneer berry-crates, tintops, and six-quart baskets. The article also observed that Simpson's did a substantial business selling veneer tops and bottoms to other box makers who didn't have the capacity to make veneer.

The mill yard housed three cross-circulation dry kilns, along with a 45-foot side loading kiln, two lumber stackers, and four lumber carriers. It was also noted that sawdust was a big part of the company's business, that a power plant built in the '30s provided all the 1,250 kilowatts of electricity the mill required, and 12 men worked in the machine shops doing equipment repairs and maintenance, improvising whatever couldn't be purchased. In conclusion, the article commented that at a time when many men would think of retiring, Stan, at 65 years of age, continued to oversee the day-to-day operations of his company and make significant improvements each year – in addition to serving as president of the recently founded Interior Lumber Manufacturers' Association and director of the Canadian Manufacturers' Association. *The Lumberman* provided a remarkably comprehensive picture of the business Stan had built in the 20 years since he had started the Manhattan Beach operation.

Forestry changes

The introduction of B.C.'s forest management licenses in the late 1940s and early '50s changed the way the province's forests were managed. The underlying premise of the license was that by allocating specific forest tenure to a private company, the manufacturing plants owned and operated by that company would have sufficient timber to keep them in business. Companies were also responsible for the long-term maintenance and productivity of their license areas, which served to split the burden of managing the province's forest resources between the government and the private sector. All planning and implementation, however, was to be carried out under forest ministry supervision.

When S. M. Simpson Ltd. was awarded Forest Management License #9 (FML#9) in 1951, Stan was required to hire a professional forester but there were few in the province at that time. His chance summer encounter with a man named Alan Moss, while on an overseas tour with a group of B.C. timber men, set the stage for the company's future development and focus. Alan was an Edinburgh

The checkpoint at the Bear Creek Road entrance to the forest management area.

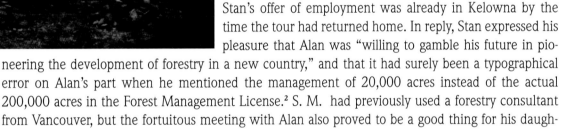

Early snowmobiles replaced sleighs and horse teams for winter logging.

University forestry graduate who had also worked in India, England, Scotland, and Scandinavia, and his letter accepting Stan's offer of employment was already in Kelowna by the time the tour had returned home. In reply, Stan expressed his pleasure that Alan was "willing to gamble his future in pioneering the development of forestry in a new country," and that it had surely been a typographical error on Alan's part when he mentioned the management of 20,000 acres instead of the actual 200,000 acres in the Forest Management License.[2] S. M. had previously used a forestry consultant from Vancouver, but the fortuitous meeting with Alan also proved to be a good thing for his daughter, Rhoda as well as Simpson's. She and Alan were married in Kelowna later that year.

Once on the job, Alan set up the company's forestry department and in the following two years, hired staff, built 16 km of main haul roads and 6 km of horse trails that linked to the main roads, and developed plans to increase both. He oversaw the cruising and mapping of more than 25,000 acres, equipped and organized a firefighting plan for the management area and fought four fires, cleaned and thinned 100 acres of bush, and introduced new ways of marking cutting permit areas. In preparing his first management plan – Working Circle Plan #1 – Alan set the stage for this license being recognized throughout the province as one of the Interior's best-managed tenures.[3]

A discontented workforce

During the '50s, S. M. Simpson Ltd.'s agenda was largely determined by its combative relationship with the fledgling IWA. The company was under enormous pressure from the fruit industry because of its yearly labour negotiations and the potential for a work stoppage; packinghouses didn't know if they would have enough boxes for the coming season or how much they would have to pay for them. Contentious negotiations began to consume more and more of Stan's time and energy as he travelled between Kelowna, Vancouver (where the ILMA offices were located), and Prince George, where northern operators, negotiating as the Northern Interior Lumber Association (NILA), were comparing and co-ordinating their negotiation strategies with Southern Interior operators.

This wasn't an easy time for mill employees either, as the IWA was still dealing with Communist dissidents as part of its attempt to establish a tighter grip on the province's forest industry. In an effort to strengthen its control of that sizeable workforce, IWA organizers sometimes used legally questionable tactics to achieve their objectives. Those who didn't want the union in their workplace felt

89

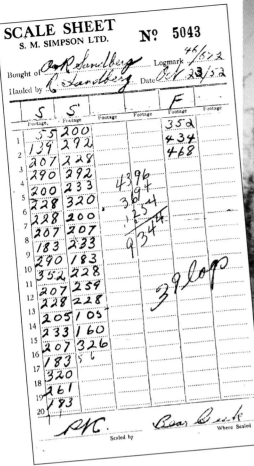

Scale sheet for the load – October 23, 1952. "If we hadn't loaded on that fir, we could have added a couple more good-sized spruce logs."
(Don Sandburg invoice)

Load restrictions didn't apply on private roads and this Sandburg load was the largest taken from the Interior at the time. The 10,000 board feet had been loaded by horses onto a single-axle International out of the Bear Creek area. Ken Graf on the right, Don Sanburg, middle, and Otto Sandburg on the left.
(Don Sandburg photo)

intimidated, angry, and fearful. Few people could withstand the pressure, and as negotiations dragged on, and threats, counter-threats, and accusations became everyday realities, S. M.'s older employees would telephone his home – often at suppertime – in great distress and apologize for betraying him, saying that for the sake of their families, they had no choice but to become union members. Stan wouldn't be intimidated, but he knew others were and it strengthened his resolve not to give in to the union's demands.

Labour troubles had started at Simpson's back in 1943, and they resurfaced again in 1946 when Stan had refused to accept what he saw as a vocal minority coming into the Valley and intimidating the majority of his employees into accepting the IWA as their bargaining agent. At that time, he had referred to it as "limiting their individual security," and as the 1940s gave way to the '50s, Stan remained committed to the principle that his employees should be free to make their own decisions, even as the collective voice was gaining more and more support. His refusal to be swayed from this point of view lead to a decade of unprecedented labour unrest at S. M. Simpson Ltd.

The legacy of 1946

The acrimony left over from the 1946 strike would not go away, and it set the tone for subsequent negotiations between S. M. and the union. One-year labour contracts were the norm at the time and the settlement of one contract was followed by negotiations for the next only a few months later. As a consequence, the disputes of the '50s seemed constant and relentless. The union started out the decade by demanding a 17¢-per-hour, across-the-board wage increase, settling for 12¢; shook prices increased 3¢ a box and lumber, $10 per thousand feet. But there was no strike. In 1951, the demand was for a 30¢ across-the-board wage increase plus a cost-of-living clause, a closed union shop, a 40-hour week, increased vacation allowances, and changes in the contract expiry date. When the two sides couldn't agree, the contract was sent to a arbitration board for its recommendation. A local

90

radio station revealed that a large percentage of the Simpson workforce favoured further attempts at conciliation; the union was furious and denied the outcome. Unlike the secrecy surrounding present-day labour negotiations, both sides used local newspapers and radio stations to state their case: a quarter-page ad placed in the *Courier* by mill owners confirmed the ILMA offer of a 20¢-an-hour increase and claimed the real problem was the IWA's demand for a closed shop:

THE ISSUE IS NOT WAGES!

> The issue appears to be whether or not the employers can be forced into signing a contract whereby they would have to fire any employee who didn't pay dues to the IWA, whether a member or not. This compulsory dues payment as a condition of continued employment is not in keeping with democratic principles and the operators will not accept the responsibility for implementing it.[4]

If Stan didn't write the ad himself, his voice certainly formed the Association's position as it too officially supported his belief that individual employees should be able to choose whether or not they wanted to join the union and pay its dues.

Stan refused to be muzzled and reserved what he saw as his right to speak to his own employees. On November 1, 1951, he sent "A Letter to our Employees," saying that he had been asked by some to give up-to-date information on current negotiations. Reiterating that Southern Interior employers were prepared to give a 20¢-an-hour increase, he repeated his 1946 position:

> It is our opinion that to be compelled to pay money to any individual or organization apart from that required by government statute, is contrary to the right and freedom of any individual and is not in keeping with our democratic system and Canadian way of life.[5]

S. M. also rejected the union claim that employers were negotiating in bad faith, and offered to meet with any individual employee or groups of employees, and personally signed the letter.[6] In other letters to his employees, Stan noted that wage rates in the B.C. forest industry were the highest in Canada, and that secondary woodworking industries such as furniture and box making could not survive if these kind of excessive demands continued. Stan was becoming increasingly aware that the orchard industry was finding alternatives to the traditional wooden box, and since many Valley box makers had already gone out of business, he felt it was important to remind his employees in another letter that that S. M. Simpson Ltd. was the last major Okanagan box factory still certified by the IWA:

> You have no doubt read in the local press of the efforts being made to provide a cheaper container for the products of the Valley's fruit industry, and even today, used boxes are being returned from Prairie and Coastal points for re-use as shipping containers. We would ask that you once again consider very carefully all the factors in connection with the present negotiations before you make your own decision and then mark your ballot according to your own judgment.[7]

Less than half of Simpson's 400 employees belonged to the IWA in late 1951, but the 150 who wanted to go out on strike could force the majority out with them. A small anti-strike group formed that weekend, but few employees wanted to be identified with it and it soon disappeared. Although no agreement had been reached by the November 21 strike deadline, employees showed up for work and then, in a well-orchestrated move, walked off their jobs for an hour-and-a-half 'rest period' before returning to work. Tom McKenzie, secretary of the IWA district negotiating committee, said this was not a strike, simply a rest period, and several more were likely to be called over the next few days. Resting employees consumed large amounts of coffee and carried on heated games of horseshoes while negotiations continued in Vancouver for another three months. The eventual settlement included the originally agreed upon 20¢-an-hour increase retroactive to the August 31 contract expiry date, which became an unexpected Christmas bonus for the employees, and the thorny issue of the compulsory check-off of union dues disappeared – least for the time being.

The other big issue

Labour negotiations were only one of the issues facing mill owners. There was much talk but no resolution during the early '50s to the challenging problem of finding a more readily available and cheaper replacement for traditional wooden fruit boxes. Interior box factories continued to produce millions of the boxes, often with imported lumber, and the costs kept increasing.[8] Local packinghouses had become unionized by this time and their regular wage increases, coupled with those of the lumber industry, were adding to the final retail price of a box of apples. Shook prices escalated from 36.6¢ a box to 39.3¢ in 1951 and then, a few months later, to 44¢ a box.

In an attempt to deal with price hikes, the BCFGA funded the BC Research Council to come up with a suitable cardboard container that was lightweight, rigid enough to withstand handling and stacking, low cost, but also attractive and convenient enough to display the Valley's produce in grocery stores. Growers and packinghouses even began recycling their old boxes as a cost-cutting measure, having them returned from the Prairies, cleaned up, and reused again – an unprecedented move for an industry that had previously insisted it would only use clean, new boxes for shipping crops to market. The fruit industry's determination to move away from traditional wooden boxes would soon become a very real concern for S. M. Simpson Ltd.

Outside influences

In June 1952, 30,000 Coastal woodworkers refused to work without a contract and walked off the job. The strike was illegal but it lasted for 45 days and opened the door for what was about to happen in the Interior. Stan's contract wasn't due to expire until the end of August, but he was in Prince George in July trying to develop a unified strategy with Northern operators for upcoming contract negotiations in the face of preliminary IWA demands for a 35¢ across-the-board wage increase, nine statutory holidays, improved vacations, employer-paid health and welfare plans, and once again, a union shop.[9] Mill operators wanted the previous year's contract extended, though a conciliation board recommended a 3¢ pay increase and three paid statutory holidays. Believing the Kelowna local members were inexperienced in the finer points of organizing and maintaining a strike, IWA headquarters in Vancouver sent district officials, international reps, and all possible personnel to the Interior to help achieve a satisfactory settlement.[10] Negotiations carried on for several months, but as the *Courier* reported, the outside support didn't achieve much:

Mill Workers Oppose Strike
72% Turn Back Union Demand for Strike Action

(The Kelowna Courier, November 27, 1952)

When the strike deadline passed without anything happening, Stan said it was because his employees wanted to extend the previous year's contract; IWA officials in Vancouver disagreed. Stan warned that if there was no agreement, the mill would be closed down for an indefinite period and all employees covered by IWA certification would be laid off. This direct challenge was not Stan's usual style, but he wanted to support his employees who had voted against a strike. The union countered, saying, "repeated attempts by the operators to decertify [i.e. remove the union as bargaining agent] the IWA in a number of operations were beaten back by the employees' vote of confidence in the IWA."[11] Stan was not bluffing and by December 4, the boilers were drained and the mill shut down.

Union officials seemed surprised that Stan had closed his plant, and rumours began to circulate that

WORKERS!

- The IWA strike in the Interior lumber industry is now a fight for the right to organize and bargain collectively.
- The employers intend to break the strike by the use of strike-breakers, and throw the IWA strikers on the bread line.

THE FACTS ARE:—

1. For two years, Conciliation Boards have recommended better contract terms as necessary and possible. These have been rejected by the employers.

2. The employers threatened lock-outs to force the lumber workers to accept the 1951 contract terms, with a base rate $1.52 a day less than is paid at the coast.

3. The employers have refused to mediate the strike issues, hoping to starve the strikers into surrender.

Back the Strikers

- The IWA can and will finance its picket lines for another six months, if necessary.
- The entire trade union movement in Canada is behind the strike. Get in step.

Don't be a Scab

- Workers are warned against accepting employment offers as strike-breakers.
- Strike-breakers will be named throughout the unions in the Canadian West as "scabs".
- A victory for the IWA strikers is a victory for all the Interior workers.

SCABS KEEP AWAY

IWA Strike Committee   45 Kingsway, Vancouver, B.C.

The threat of hiring replacement workers was always a possibility, although it is unlikely Stan would have chosen that route over closing the mill. This did not stop the IWA from using the threat to organize a "scab-herding blockade" throughout the Interior, however. They ringed the strike-bound area with a publicity picket to offset any danger of an organized migration of strike-breakers from outside points, and all transportation routes into the Interior by rail, bus, or highway were picketed and placarded with this information. The Kelowna Courier, November 30, 1953.

the union was hoping to work without a contract for the next few months so that it would be in a stronger position when negotiations resumed, presumably in the spring, since companies would be gearing up for their critical box shook season. Some employees circulated a petition to decertify the IWA, but they did not get the necessary 50 per cent support and the lockout continued. Finally, the union – perhaps realizing it didn't have as tight a grip on Stan's employees as it originally thought – capitulated and extended the previous year's contract. Just a week before Christmas, 175 employees returned to work and the town's merchants heaved a sign of relief, knowing the holiday shopping season wouldn't be a total loss. The 1952 contract dispute had started in early July and ended just before Christmas – six months of strife just so the previous year's contract could be extended. Stan had forced the union's hand by closing his mill, but the uncertainty and conflict had everyone on edge and cast a shadow over their Christmas celebrations. In spite of all that had gone on, Stan still delivered the company's usual gift of turkeys to his employees on Christmas Eve.

The sawmill battleground

Following the events of the 1952 lockout, the IWA saw that it didn't have the solid support of Simpson's employees. The non-union group was encouraged when Stan locked out IWA members, and some felt empowered enough to try to decertify the IWA. Their enthusiasm was short-lived, however, when union organizers descended on Kelowna and intensified their efforts to sign up dissidents who were not yet union members. The negotiations that followed in 1953 became among the toughest, most contentious in IWA history.

That year's contract demands would affect about 8,000 woodworkers in the Northern and Southern Interior, but the mill owners' industry associations had agreed to a unified stand on several issues. The union demanded the usual wage increase (18¢ across-the-board), a full union shop, which meant life-time union membership within the industry for all present and future employees, and the compulsory check-off of dues for all employees, whether they were union members or not. There were also demands for increased statutory holidays and the standard change in the contract expiry date from the end of August to the beginning of June. Given current unfavourable market conditions, Stan called the demands "utterly fantastic,"[12] and said he and the other operators would only settle for the extension of the previous year's contract, which had actually been an extension of the 1950 contract.

The dispute was sent to a conciliation board in mid-July, with the majority recommending a 3¢-per-hour increase versus the minority recommendation of 10¢, three statutory holidays, and the check-off of union dues. In the Northern Interior, 900 union members voted to strike and took another 4,000 employees out with them. In the Southern Interior, Stan again used the *Courier* to argue his case:

> The IWA demand a collective agreement for our employees equal to the contract at the Coast, which would mean our employees would receive an increase of 18¢ per hour and other benefits. An equivalent agreement would be satisfactory IF all other conditions were equal.

The ad went on to explain the difference between the Coastal and Interior forest industries, stating why the Interior companies could not agree to the union demands:

> If our employees vote in favour of strike action on October 15, 1953, the Union's own secretary, George Mitchell, has said "it will be a long strike." Kelowna and

93

District will also be the losers as well as our employees and ourselves. We hope for the sake of all concerned that our employees will use their own best judgment when voting.[13]

In spite of the ILMA negotiating on behalf of Southern mill owners, Stan knew his mill was being targeted by the IWA. He had successfully called the union on its demands the previous year and locked IWA members out, and there were enough Simpson employees who didn't belong to the union to cause the IWA trouble. S. M. didn't wait for the ILMA to argue his case and put an ad in the newspaper himself. It had almost become Stan's trademark to end by urging his employees to make up their own minds when casting their ballot and, though it was left unsaid, not be intimidated by others to vote against their conscience.

S. M.'s son Horace, who was by now the company manager, made a last minute plea to employees to stay on the job. If they chose not to, he said, it could be a long while before the mill reopened since the uncertainty surrounding the Korean War had sent the Canadian economy into a tailspin and building starts in the past couple of years had slowed dramatically. He also reminded them that more and more packinghouses were using cardboard boxes and polyethylene bags, and that Simpson's veneer plant had cut production to 60 per cent of capacity and the box factory to 40 per cent.[14] Today, old-timers can still recall the signs of an impending strike: the loggers stopped hauling, the boilers and pipes were drained, the tugs called back in from various parts of the lake, and any pending deliveries rushed out.

When the strike votes for the Southern Interior were tallied, it was – astoundingly – a tie. 795 employees had voted in favour of going on strike and 795 against, with 25 spoiled ballots. George Mitchell, the IWA district secretary, went on the radio and declared, "the over-all results of the voting … indicate that the majority of the lumber workers prefer strike action … No other interpretation can possibly be placed on the balloting results." The *Courier* challenged his math,[15] and Horace said it was business as usual until the mill was forced to shut down.

On the recommendation of the Vancouver union executive, 2,500 mill employees in the Southern Interior – including those at S. M. Simpson Ltd. – walked out on October 22, 1953.[16] Picket squads were set up and no one crossed the picket lines, although both the IWA and Simpson's agreed to continue local sawdust deliveries. Stan had a meeting with the union in Vancouver and ended up negotiating with four IWA reps from Vancouver and two from Portland, Oregon, which supported his earlier claim that the Kelowna IWA local was being run by outsiders, and that given "their demands, there does not seem to be any basis for further negotiations."[17] Stan ran another ad in the *Courier*.

> For the information of the public I am giving some facts respecting the question of lumber production and the present labour situation … In the Kamloops Forest District [which included the Kelowna mill] 22 mills voted on the question of strike action (out of a total of 578 different types of sawmills in the district). Of the 17 mills, 12 voted not to strike and 5 to strike … At the present time only three mills where employees voted, are on strike and are picketed by the IWA, namely Osoyoos Sawmills Ltd., Kamloops Lumber Co., and S. M. Simpson Ltd.[18]

Stan further noted that "before the strike vote, special attention was given to the employees at the S. M. Simpson Ltd. mill by the head officials of the IWA." The union had changed its priorities over the course of negotiations, with compulsory dues check-off and the maintenance of membership now being of greatest importance, and contract termination dates and wages being relegated to second place; Stan felt his employees had been mislead because that had not been the union's earlier position. S. M. didn't think there was any reason to reopen negotiations with the union, and ran another ad, signing it "S. M. Simpson" with no mention of the ILMA – it was Stan speaking directly to his employees and the public.

Tensions mounted on both sides. Union drivers stopped delivering sawdust to local homeowners and businesses, so mill supervisory staff got behind the wheel to continue the service. During the fifth week of the strike, picketers ripped the side off a truck driven by Spen Price, an East Kelowna orchardist, who had crossed the picket line to pick up a load of sawdust. When Price realized he couldn't load the damaged truck, he crossed back through the picketers, who then tore the other side off his truck. These issues, along with another incident of a packinghouse employee being chased off the property when he came to pick up a load of lath for bracing boxes in the rail cars, led Simpson's to apply for a court injunction, which was granted three days later. The IWA executive "in their representative capacity" and 17 local members in their "individual capacities" were cited and barred "from watching or besetting ... or causing a nuisance adjacent to or in the vicinity of the mill property for the next 10 days."[19] Violation of the terms would result in charges of contempt against the union members and possible jail sentences. Soon, injunctions became a common, although not always successful, tool in keeping warring mill owners and union members apart.

At this same time, the ongoing strike in the Northern Interior was proclaimed to be "the messiest strike in Western Canada." It lasted 100 days and saw 27 injunctions, and in the end, 5¢ was all that was gained. A disinformation campaign started in the newspapers and then moved on to union head-quarters, where rumours about who did what to whom were rampant. It became a total war of the goon squads from both sides, involving the RCMP and dirty tricks that never made the newspapers. Prince George was known as "the toughest town north of Tijuana," and both management and labour were full of men who would fight as soon as spit. Most of the mill owners had started as woodworkers and come damnation and hellfire, there was no way they were going to give up any of what they'd fought so hard to get. Management was accused of hiring ex-Pinkerton Detective Agency employees who were "pros – they knew how to beat a man unconscious without leaving a mark on him." Companies applied for injunctions whenever the going got too tough, and by the time the contract was signed, the town was on its last legs.[20]

The Southern Interior Lumber Association proposed a three-year contract and a 3¢-an-hour increase, but the IWA stuck to its demands for a full union shop in spite of the employers' refusal to deduct union dues for non-members. The union countered that because everyone benefited from its negoti-ations, everyone should have to pay, and wage demands remained at 18¢ an hour. The provincial government appointed a judge to investigate the dispute in the Southern Interior, but given that it was the same judge who had just conducted a similar investigation of the northern strike and report-ed that "it is impossible to suggest ... that this is a responsible union, entitled to a compulsory check-off or union shop,"[21] it was understandable that the IWA was not happy with the appointment.[22]

The strike was two months old when Christmas 1953 rolled around and celebrations were leaner for the whole town. The union held its usual Christmas party for 120 children and provided a little extra money for families in dire circumstances. Those still on picket duty were taken back when S. M. drove up to where they were warming themselves around a burning oil drum, walked down the picket line, and shook hands with everyone, wishing them a Merry Christmas while he handed out turkeys.[23]

The Southern Interior strike finally ended in January, 103 days after it began. The two sides agreed to the first-ever three-year contract, set to expire on August 31, 1956 (the north had settled for a one-year contract again), a 10¢-per-hour wage increase to be spread over those three years, and three paid statutory holidays: Dominion Day / July1, Labour Day, and Christmas Day – one for each year of the contract. The union gained an industry-wide maintenance of membership, which meant once an IWA member, always an IWA member, but the thorny issues of compulsory membership and employer-deducted union dues were again removed from the negotiating table. The big plus for everyone was the three-year duration of the contract, which allowed for relative labour peace in the Southern Interior for the next two-and-a-half years. When the strike began in October, Simpson's had already moved into a slower season and only about 175 to 200 people were still working. Things were even quieter when the boilers were fired up again in January, and only 80 to 100 men returned to the plant.

Grow or perish

The history of British Columbia's forest industry has always been characterized by boom times followed by periods of consolidation and shrinkage. Sawmills closed or were bought out by larger companies that needed to grow to survive. Mills were often purchased for their timber leases or cutting rights, and once the assets were transferred to the new owner, they were shut down. Some of these sales were as a result of the province's changing forest policy, while others were because of the evolving marketplace, and operations at S. M. Simpson Ltd. typified much of what was going on during the 1950s.

From the mid-'20s onwards, when Stan expanded his sash and door business and began to manufacture boxes, sufficient timber resources were always an issue. S. M. built his early sawmills in the middle of the forest, and when all the suitable trees within a 5 km radius had been cut, he moved again. By the time the Manhattan Beach sawmill began operating in the early '30s, improved roads and trucks meant logs could be hauled from further away. While S. M. Simpson Ltd. owned a small amount of land, leased more, acquired FML#9, attended timber auctions, and purchased cutting rights, the company never stopped looking for additional timber. Stan really had no choice but to start buying other sawmills if he wanted to continue growing Simpson's. If their products weren't a good fit with the larger Kelowna operation, the new acquisitions were closed and their timber assets incorporated into the company's development plans.

Obtaining more timber rights didn't solve every problem, however, as the Interior supply of yellow pine was substantially depleted by the mid-'50s and its slow regeneration would not help Simpson's in the foreseeable future. Pine logs had been shipped in from other parts of the province for several years and although this had enabled the Valley's box factories to keep producing, it added considerably to the end-cost of shook. The shortage of timber and increasing labour costs in both the packinghouses and box factories, coupled with the uncertainty of union disputes, made the demise of the wooden fruit box inevitable and ushered in what those in the box business in the early '50s referred to as 'the corrugated invasion.'

S. M. Simpson Ltd. was still the largest box maker in the Valley, and while Stan was aware of the move towards cardboard boxes and polyethylene bags, he had spent so much time dealing with labour problems over the previous decade that he had little left to develop a long-term plan to handle the potential loss of his company's major product line. But the lengthy '53 strike, along with the fruit industry's concerted efforts to find an alternative to heavy, costly, and possibly unavailable wooden boxes forced Stan to face the reality that his once-thriving box business was disappearing. He was going to have to find alternative products if his company was going to survive. Production of dimension lumber had been increasing, but cyclical timber markets and an increasing dependence upon the U.S. housing industry left Interior sawmills very vulnerable to outside forces. 1953, 1954, and 1955 were fairly lean years for S. M. Simpson Ltd., but one of the few positives during this time was the relative labour peace that allowed Stan and Horace to explore some of the options available for their company, and do some concrete planning.

There is no written record of what the father and son team wanted Simpson's future to look like, but in 1955, the first steps of a plan were implemented when they purchased the Trautman and Garraway sawmill in Peachland,[24] and four months later, the Peachland Box and Sawmill Ltd. The two companies annually cut about two million feet of dimension lumber for U.S. markets, which was a good fit with what Simpson's was producing at the time, and neither was a union operation. It wasn't until 1956, however, that the full extent of Horace and Stan's plans for the company became apparent.

A quiet calamity

At a time when the local newspaper reported a child falling off a bicycle and a rushed trip to the hospital, no word ever appeared in print to tell anyone that Stan suffered a severe stroke in July 1955. The attack was serious enough that he was quickly and quietly transferred to Vancouver General Hospital, and he remained away from Kelowna for most of the following year. There is no doubt that Mayor J. J. Ladd and the editor of *The Kelowna Courier*, R. P. McLean, knew what had befallen their friend, but Stan was a very private man and this was considered a family matter, so news of his misfortune never appeared in the paper.

Elsie and Bud Newick (on the left) and Horace and Joan Simpson at a company Safety Dinner.

Stan was 69 years old at the time of his stroke and if he thought about slowing down, he had never found time to actually do it. S. M. had been under considerable pressure for years: the Depression had almost destroyed his business; he had dealt with huge wartime demands and the challenges of supplying his longstanding packinghouse customers with boxes; and travelling around the province and across the country many times, both before and during the stress of yearly union negotiations, had been exhausting. In the midst of all this, his traditional business was in transition and Stan knew he had to come up with a viable plan to ensure Simpson's survival. It all took a cumulative toll, and finally forced him to slow down.

Another transition

Between his stroke and the implementation of the next phase of the company's long-term plan, Stan stepped down as president of the company that bore his name, and Horace Birch Simpson assumed the presidency. As a small boy, H. B. (as he was commonly known) spent most weekends at the mill with his dad and by the late '50s was very comfortable with every part of its operations and the employees who worked there. All Horace ever wanted to do was work at the mill and once he finished high school, he started working there full-time. It was as much in his blood as in his father's.

There were no breaks for being the boss' son, however. S. M. was a tough taskmaster and Horace had started at the bottom and done it all, including the worst of what needed to be done. H. B. once commented that he quickly learned not to fudge an answer to his father's questions as there would be heck to pay if he did. Horace became assistant general manager in the '40s before being named general manager, so his transition to president was relatively seamless and his biggest challenge became finding a new role for his father. As Horace began implementing the plan he and S. M. had been working on prior to Stan's stroke, the older man could be seen out in the yard with his usual stubby pencil and scrap of paper, planning a new bucking plant or configuring machinery layouts. He had done little else in his life but work, and while his capacity to do so was somewhat diminished by the stroke, Stan remained a familiar figure at the Manhattan Beach plant until his death.

The plan is implemented

It was left to Horace to put the company's long-term plan into action, and an in-depth study was commissioned to determine if the production of particle board or plywood would be the best use of local timber. H. B. and some mill staff visited a number of plywood plants in the Pacific Northwest and then decided to have a feasibility study done to see if a plywood plant was a viable addition to the

Manhattan Beach operation. Quesnel, in central B.C., had the only plywood plant operating in the Interior but it used Douglas fir, and problems had arisen with the glue bond used to make plywood when the plant had experimented with spruce. Since Simpson's wood supply was only about 22 per cent fir and the rest was primarily spruce (little use was made of the area's lodgepole pine forests), an acceptable glue had to be found before the company could proceed. Eventually, Monsanto Chemical Company was able come up with an adhesive that suited the fibre characteristics of spruce, and the *Courier* carried the good news:

S. M. Simpson Ltd. plans huge expansion program

(The Kelowna Courier, March 29, 1956*)*

> A major change in company policy and a $2,000,000 plant expansion which will give employment to 150 additional people was announced ... by H. B. Simpson, president of S. M. Simpson Ltd. The change in policy involves the retirement of the company from the retail business field and the devoting of all its energies to the manufacturing field.[25]

The plan Stan and Horace had been working on was becoming a reality. Not only would a plywood plant guarantee S. M. Simpson Ltd.'s survival, but it would also strengthen the economic life of the community and enhance the company's standing as the largest year-round employer in town. Simpson's retail arm – the KSM – would be replaced by a wholesale operation that would continue to provide local building supply firms with the company's in-house products as well as the usual line of MacMillan Bloedel and JohnsManville building materials.

According to H. B. "This is a major step for our company ... We are leaving the retail field simply because we feel that we should confine our energies to the manufacturing field. We will concentrate on one thing and not spread our energies too thinly by engaging in too many activities."[26]

He also noted that the company would proceed immediately with the construction of a sheathing-grade plywood plant and upon completion of this plant, would build a second operation for particle board.

When the KSM closed its retail outlet in 1957, the sales, forestry, and management offices that had been in the building on the corner of Doyle Avenue and Ellis Street were moved to Manhattan Beach.

The plywood building pilings with the floor and building above.

The bow-string trusses waiting to be raised to the roof though the floor still had not been completed. The trusses were built on-site.

The crane hoisting the bow-string trusses into place.

The finished plywood plant.

Building on the bog

The $1.5 million plywood plant (the balance of the funds noted in the announcement were earmarked for the particle board plant) proved to be both a building nightmare and a construction achievement. Pressure was on to get the project up and running as soon as possible, and an in-house crew with Bill Buss as project manager, Dan Hill as mechanical supervisor, and Bill Marshall as construction supervisor,[27] managed to complete construction and have the machinery operational 13 months after ground was broken.

The first obstacle they had to contend with was the water-logged and swampy Manhattan Beach property, which was difficult to build on at the best of times and almost impossible during heavy rainstorms or when Okanagan Lake flooded. The land had been filled with slabs, wood, bark, and whatever waste was available and then covered with dirt, rocks, and shale, but logging trucks and other heavy machinery still got so stuck in the bog that only the D9 Cats could drag them out.[28] The entire two-acre building, which would house hundreds of tons of machinery and additional tons of wood, had to be built on top of 3,500 pilings, each 12" to 14" in diameter and driven 20' to 40' into the waterlogged soil until they hit bedrock, leaving about 4' of the piling above ground to support the floor. The building was constructed with two rows of 125' laminated bowstring trusses, constructed on-site; they were the largest-known plywood trusses built in Canada at the time. More generating power was needed to handle the substantially increased energy requirements for the plant, so Simpson's installed three new generators and a transformer that could have met all the electrical needs of Kelowna. Larry Gorby, the mill's chief electrician, noted that if electrical wires in the plant were strung out in one long piece, they would encircle the whole town.[29]

The new plywood operation turned out three carloads of plywood daily – or a million 1/16" veneers a day – according to Bill Crooks, the manager who had been recruited from MacMillan Bloedel's Port Alberni plywood plant. The finished product was unsanded sheathing or unsanded underlay,[30] in 4' x 8' panels from 5/16" to 3/4" thick, both of which were much in demand by the construction industry.

The Kelowna Courier reported that "comely lassies, vintage 1957, in slacks and work shirts" worked at various jobs in the plant, including on the Raimann Patcher, a piece of equipment that repaired knot holes in the sheets of plywood. Since its function was seen to be similar to that of a sewing machine, the reporter apparently felt it was an appropriate place for the women to work. "If you have a hole in the set of your pants, your wife patches it. If there is a hole in the plywood veneer, the pretty young miss on the machine patches it." The story went on to say that the "young ladies can be as feminine as they like, as the company provides her with a looking glass. However, according to the manager, its main use was for the girls to watch the boys heaving heavy sheets of plywood." The new plant employed approximately 150 workers, about 10 per cent of whom were women, and while women had worked in the box factory since the '30s, the reporter seemed intrigued they could also manage the challenges of working in a plywood plant.[31]

The S&K saga

Although construction of the plywood plant proceeded quickly, serious staffing problems occurred before it even began turning out sheets of plywood. The IWA was adamant that S. M. Simpson Ltd. employees with the highest seniority should be able to transfer over to the new operation. Bill Crooks was equally adamant that he would not hire from the parent company's seniority list, especially since those with the highest seniority were also the oldest employees.[32] There was a standoff and battle lines were drawn when Simpson's management decided to resurrect an inactive company – S&K Ltd. – and make it their plywood operation. S&K, which stood for Simpson and Kelowna Sawmill, was originally created as a logging company by Charlie Stuart, Terry Greenwood, and Stan Simpson. While never an operating company, S. M.

The original S&K office.

Simpson Ltd. had always maintained its corporate registration so it was immediately available when the decision was made to have the plywood plant operate as a separate corporate entity, with Horace as its president. The IWA quickly charged S. M. Simpson Ltd. with setting up a phoney company in order to get around the law and the existing contract.[33]

Both sides felt they were right: the new company didn't want to be limited to hiring from Simpson's seniority list, as it wanted employees who already had or could quickly learn the different skills needed in the plywood plant, and the union wanted its existing members to have the higher-paying plywood jobs. By November 1956, the IWA Information Bulletin characterized its relationship with S. M. Simpson Ltd. as a "running battle":

> Many obstacles and stumbling blocks were placed in the way of the Union, in an effort by Management to establish a heresy unequalled anywhere in the Valley. To those of you who know this Company, this will come as no surprise; for we have

The official invitation to the opening of the plywood plant.

A sample of plywood of various species and a key were given to each guest as a memento of the occasion. No one can remember why the key was included.

here in our midst an employer who, in this day and age, still believes in feudalistic iron-fist tradition. Here is an empire controlled by one man who believes himself Lord and Master of all he surveys. His words and his decisions are so tremendous that the serfs must bow with humility to his will. NO ONE DARE CHALLENGE HIS WORDS.[34]

If the "Lord and Master" referred to Stan, which it almost certainly did, few employees would have thought it truthfully described the man. His involvement in the company was minimal by this time and the union's rhetoric spoke more to his stature in the industry than to his role in the negotiations.

As word of the new plywood plant spread throughout the province, men began arriving from the MacMillan Bloedel & Powell River plant in Port Alberni, on Vancouver Island, and B.C. Forest Products in Victoria, and became the start-up crew and core of the new plant's workforce.[35] Meanwhile, the seniority dispute continued as each side accused the other of being underhanded. The IWA said the new employees were parachuted in and given seniority over Simpson's employees, while S&K denied it and still refused to hire from Simpson's seniority list. Finally, a compromise was reached: any Simpson employee could apply for a job in the plywood plant, and if they were hired, they had to quit their job at the mill on the Friday prior to the plywood plant start-up before being hired by S&K Ltd. on the Monday. Employee seniority at the plywood plant began the first day on the job, though benefits carried over from S. M. Simpson Ltd. Despite assurances, many people were uncertain because this was only a verbal deal and nothing was written down: "It was a 'good faith' thing. I talked to Horace, who said the deal was as it had been explained, and I would have a job on the Monday. Horace was good on his word. Still, there was a bit of apprehension."[36] The dispute was finally resolved, but once again the battle between the union and Simpson's management had again been acrimonious. And its legacy would resurface a few years later.

The new plywood plant's opening was a major event and attracted considerable attention:

Horace Simpson on the right showing dignitaries the intricacies of plywood production. Mayor Ladd on the left of the group, Sharron Simpson and Joan Simpson, Mrs. Bennett and Premier W. A. C. Bennett.

Premier will open S&K Plywood plant

(The Kelowna Courier, April 29, 1957)

Premier W. A. C. Bennett joined Kelowna businessmen, civic dignitaries, government representatives and industrial leaders from outside points for a glimpse of a new million dollar industry in the Okanagan … Close to 200 invited guests went on a personally conducted tour of the mammoth plant, and saw first-hand how plywood is manufactured by the most modern machinery available. For the majority, it was an education in itself … The fabulous plant … was officially opened by Premier W. A. C. Bennett, who a few hours earlier, made a first-hand inspection of the site where materials are being harnessed for the Okanagan Lake bridge.[38]

In addition to opening the plywood plant, S. M. was recognized a few days later for his contributions to the community:

S. M. made Freeman

(The Kelowna Courier, May 2, 1957)

Stan was very much part of the official plywood plant opening on May 5, 1957. Building it had been the centrepiece of the plan he and Horace put together some years earlier, and he wouldn't have missed it. With Premier Bennett on hand to cut the ribbon and Reverend Leitch giving the benediction, invited guests were taken on a VIP tour of the state-of-the-art facility. The eventful day culminated in a Board of Trade reception and dinner, where local businessmen were part of a guest list that was a who's who of the forest industry Stan had been part of for most of his life.[39] The evening's highlight was Mayor Ladd's presentation of the Freedom of the City[40] to Stan "as a token of our appreciation of the services he has rendered in the advancement of our City."[41] Ladd gave a few highlights of Stan's life as part of his presentation, including his memory of meeting Stan as he stepped off the

Mayor Jack Ladd in his robes of office, congratulating Stan on being awarded Freedom of the City. Dr. Billy Knox is in the background.

SS *Okanagan* with his new partner in 1913. The mayor also recalled the old days, "when S. M. had a horse and cart to carry away his mill refuse, and the days when his only truck was an old Gray Dort touring car with the back seat cut off and replaced with a rack the size of what a three-ton truck would use today." Ladd also noted that the city was very grateful to S. M. for selling the Kelowna Saw Mill property "at a very nominal price, enabling us to plan and build the most modern civic centre in British Columbia. I should also mention … that S. M. has been a wonderful citizen – very keen for the betterment of Kelowna, particularly in town planning." From those humble beginnings, Stan's business had grown into a $10 million operation that culminated in the opening of the new plywood plant.[42]

It was a grand day for Stan. Being acknowledged and feted by his peers was probably the greatest tribute that could have been given to this unassuming man. His business was now soundly established on a new course, his community had acknowledged his vision and contribution, and he was still healthy enough to enjoy the celebration. Stan's letter of thanks to the mayor reflected his sentiments:

> Your award has filled me with a sense of humble gratitude … the small part that I have contributed to the growth of Kelowna during the past forty-four years has been

done with a feeling of pride in our community and confidence in the future. I am at a loss to understand why I should be chosen to be the recipient of this high honour. However, in doing so, may I express my sincere appreciation of your action, which I will treasure as one of my most cherished possessions ... we look forward to further building a permanent industry ... and we trust when the trees we planted this spring in our Forest Management License are being harvested about the year 2080, this Company will still be contributing to the economic welfare of the Province of British Columbia and to a better standard of living for the citizens of the Okanagan Valley.[43]

Labour – more of the same

The three-year 1953 labour contract between the IWA and the Southern Interior mill owners expired while the plywood plant was being planned, but the time had allowed the union to regroup and Simpson's to get on with its expansion. The 1956 contract was settled for a two-year term and saw a 13¢ across-the-board wage increase, and finally, the compulsory check-off of union dues. S. M. had adamantly refused to deduct union dues from employees who did not want to join the union when he had been directly involved in negotiations, but he was no longer at the table and Horace, likely hoping for a smooth start-up at the new plywood plant, wanted to remove at least one of the contentious contract demands from the union's list. It wasn't long before other mill owners also agreed to the IWA's demand and began deducting union dues off their employees' paycheques. These same employees were back on the picket lines in 1959 for another ten weeks, amidst what the *Courier* called "bitter and caustic comments," although the paper also noted that this time, "there was a noticeable lack of disorder or violence of any kind."[44] The settlement was agreed to by the majority of employees from the 32 Southern Interior mills, including S. M. Simpson Ltd. employees, but the animosity of the S&K hiring dispute lingered and the overwhelming majority of those employees rejected the new contract. Settlements and picket lines were no longer based on the voting results at individual mills by the mid-'50s, and S&K employees were forced to go along when other Southern Interior woodworkers accepted the deal.

The '50s were a time of relentless labour / management confrontation and unrest in the B.C. forest industry with the IWA in what it saw as a life-and-death struggle for the right to organize and bargain collectively. It fought every contract and bullied those who didn't want to become union members; the battle was aggressive and militant, and the union gave little ground. Employers resented the IWA trying to run the businesses that existed because of their sweat, determination, and capital. They felt entitled to call the shots and believed they ran good operations, treated their workers with respect, and paid what the market would bear. Whether they were good employers or not was irrelevant, and the IWA tried to unionize mill workers across the province. Most employers didn't think their employees needed a union, and the IWA acknowledged in one of its own editorials that a union was an anathema to the entrepreneurs who ran the companies they were trying to organize,[45] leading to what was undoubtedly the most challenging decade in the forest industry's labour history for both sides of the negotiating table.

More and more wood

When Simpson's was awarded FML#9 in 1949, along with its mandate to make better use of the area's forest resources, the company began looking at different ways to utilize the trees within its license area. As had been the case so often in past, Simpson's management realized that any substantial expansion project would require more timber than the company had available. Just as Stan guaranteed his timber supply in the mid-'20s buy purchasing more mills, he did the same in the mid '50s, with the purchases of Trautman Garraway Ltd. and Peachland Lumber and Box. S.M. Simpson Ltd. embarked on another major sawmill acquisition program that would ensure the new plywood plant and sawmill could continue growing as the company's holdings spread throughout the Southern Interior.

In 1957, Simpson's purchased McLean Sawmills in Malakwa, about 113 km north of Lumby, with

103

The 25 bushel bulk bin has many advantages over the one bushel picking box. It can be handled easier, it can be stored higher due to its rugged construction, and it requires less storage space. One tier of eight bulk bins contains more fruit than the entire stack of 192 one bushel boxes shown piled beside the bulk bins.

The picture at the right tells the story. The two bulk bins with their 50 bushel capacity occupy less storage space as compared to the 48 bushels of apples in the one bushel boxes. It is suggested that storage space savings of 33% can be effected by using the bulk bins in preference to the smaller one bushel boxes, not to mention the ease of handling, absence of damaged fruit and maintenance of smaller boxes.

THE 1959 BULK PLYWOOD BINS OFFER GREATER STRENGTH AND EASE OF HANDLING

The popular 25 Bushel bulk fruit handling plywood bin has proved itself to be invaluable in fruit harvesting operations.

Considerable thought has been given to improvements. The addition of bolted corners, as illustrated in sketch overleaf, will overcome any weakness at these points and increase the general stability of the container.

During the past season, many thousands of units have been successfully used by fruit growers and packing houses and are proving the new method of fruit handling by bulk plywood bins is an economical labour saving, space saving, innovation that will increase to greater proportions as the bulk handling method is generally accepted.

Greater profits can be expected as the hours of back-breaking manual labour are reduced and fruit grades are maintained with a minimum of handling and bruising.

Plywood Bulk fruit bins are a product of Kelowna and are distributed ready for assembly, complete with metal angles, straps, rivets and bolts, supplied by:

S. M. SIMPSON LIMITED, KELOWNA, BRITISH COLUMBIA
Manufacturers of Pine, Spruce, Fir, Box Shook, Veneer and Fruit Containers.

S. M. Simpson Ltd.'s promotional material on the merits of switching from traditional apple boxes to the new bulk bin.

cutting rights in the Eagle Valley, north of Sicamous; its peeler logs[46] were sent by rail to the plywood plant in Kelowna. When Simpson's bought Lumby Timber Co. in 1959, the Malakawa mill was closed and the balance of its logs shipped to Lumby, which in turn compensated that operation for the peeler logs it was also sending to the Kelowna plywood plant. On November 1, 1961, Lumby Timber's main sawmill burned to the ground. The loss was estimated at $300,000,[47] but the mill had been modernized and electricity brought in 10 years earlier, and the actual cost to rebuild was closer to $400,000.[48] During the following four years, S. M. Simpson Ltd. also bought Ferguson Brother Lumber (1962), Stave Lumber (1962), Eagle Pass Lumber (1963), and R. & L. Timber (1964). These were buoyant, expansionist times for Simpson's and the company was carried along with the same optimism that pervaded the rest of the industry during its profitable good times. No one imagined that the boom would ever end.

Back to the fruit business

By the late '50s, Valley packinghouses and fruit shippers had solved most of the design and structural problems with cardboard boxes and had, for the most part, stopped using wooden boxes to ship their fruit and vegetables to market. Neither Simpson's box factory nor the veneer plant closed completely, but production was severely curtailed and both operations were primarily processing wood that

Simpson's advertisement in the B.C. Orchardist *magazine, November 1959.*

was not viable for other uses. For a few years, it looked like the company's long affiliation with the fruit industry was over. But a 1954 visit to New Zealand by Dr. James Marshall from the Summerland Experimental Research Station introduced the idea of bulk fruit handling to the Okanagan, and it wasn't long before an industry delegation recommended that B.C. growers move from the traditional 40 lb. apple boxes to a larger, more efficient bulk bin.

S. M. Simpson Ltd. began experimenting with the box dimensions (48" x 43" x 24")[49] suggested by an industry committee, and by 1957, the company was supplying over 4,000 bulk bins that each held the equivalent of 25 bushels (or 25, 40 lb. boxes) to 37 growers who were shipping to six area packinghouses. The new bins proved so popular the following year that over 25,000 were used by several hundred growers shipping to packinghouses from Osoyoos to Vernon.[50] Bins could be filled two or three times during a season, but growers had to acquire a forklift to both lift the bins from the truck that delivered them and reload them once they had been filled. The bins were emptied at the packinghouses, initially by dumping the apples onto a conveyor, which caused considerable bruising. To alleviate that problem, the bins were immersed in a tank of water, causing the apples to float to the surface where they were pushed towards a conveyor belt for grading and finally packed in cardboard boxes. By 1960, enough adaptations had been made to the bulk bin that a patent was granted to Horace, on behalf of the company[52]

S&K Ltd. initially made the component bin parts and the bins were assembled by packinghouse staff in the off-season, but after 1963 S. M. Simpson Ltd. took over the assembly of bins at the former KSM millwork plant. The first bins were dipped in different-coloured preservatives to identify the packinghouse they belonged to, but that procedure became too labour intensive and instead all bins were stained the same colour, with the name of the packinghouse and the year of manufacture stencilled on the end panel.[51]

As the bins grew more popular in B.C., Washington State apple growers became more interested in them and Simpson's developed a substantial U.S. clientele, against the better judgement of Terry Greenwood, the company's lumber sales manager. Greenwood was concerned that exporting a large number of bins to the U.S. might adversely affect the sawmill's trade agreements with its largest customer – the U.S. housing market. Negotiations soon cleared the way for bins to be exported as 'agricultural implements' and the apple-growing areas of Washington became the company's major market, as hundreds of semi-trailer loads of partially assembled bulk bins headed across the border each year.[53]

Gorman Bros. Lumber and Box Company in Westbank also began purchasing plywood from various suppliers in the late '50s and making its own bulk bins for the American market. The increased number of bins being sent to Washington from British Columbia alarmed protectionists in the U.S., and it wasn't long before the same trade tariffs that plague the industry today became a fact of life for both Simpson's and Gorman's. The two companies hired lawyers to appeal the 20 per cent tariff slapped on bulk bins, but it took a year for the original agricultural implements designation to be reinstated.[54]

After the collapse of its traditional box market, Simpson's was able to re-establish its relationship with the fruit industry by supplying growers and packinghouses with a significantly different product. New markets continued to open up for the company as bulk fruit handling became more universal, and MacMillan Bloedel & Powell River, a longstanding Simpson's product partner, became sales agents for

105

the patented bins and took over distribution in Alberta and Ontario. Bill Buss, who with his wife Sybil had immigrated to Canada in the late '40s and been instrumental in many facets of the company's business, returned home to England to set up a bin assembly and distribution plant in Herefordshire, while Seaboard Sales, the overseas sales arm of the MacMillan organization, managed European sales. Seaboard also made contacts in France and Italy, but import duties and excessive shipping costs made any potential move to the Continent unfeasible.

Growers found new uses for the plywood bins beyond apples and pears, and bin sizes were reduced so soft fruits such as peaches, plums, and apricots, as well as grapes and a variety of vegetables, could be put into bins. But they weren't just used for fruit and produce. Frozen foods, fish, fertilizers, and seeds were also shipped in the containers; crates were made for White Trucks, the precursor to Western Star, for shipping truck parts to Australia; large collapsible containers were made for shipping and storing furniture; and the bins have even been used as coffins.

Stan and his company

S. M. spent less and less time at the mill as the impact of his stroke began to take its toll, though he still visited and could be seen out in the yard sizing up the latest piece of equipment or checking out changes in the plant. The stamina and energy that had sustained him for so many years was beginning to disappear, and he was even known to take an occasional afternoon nap. But given his 73 years and the pace of events during the previous two decades, he allowed himself that indulgence. Stan continued on as chairman of S. M. Simpson Ltd., and while he was no longer involved in the day-to-day activities of the company, he made the transition to a less active role reluctantly.

Early in 1959, four years after his stroke, Stan and his sister Ruth sailed out of Vancouver to Australia and New Zealand to fulfill his life-long wish to see their forest industries in action. Six weeks into the trip, Stan died suddenly of a heart attack in Melbourne, Australia. The demise of this gentle man, who was unquestionably a leader and standard-setter through some of his industry's most turbulent times, came as a shock to everyone who knew him. He was survived by his wife Blanche, sons Horace and Bob, his daughter Rhoda, eight grandchildren, brothers George and Vern, and sisters Ruth and Ann. He had been predeceased by his sister Norma and brother Alf some years before.

Stan had maintained a low profile in the years preceding his death, and most of the people who had arrived in Kelowna during that time did not know him. But those who had lived in the same town as Stan during the 45 years before his death knew he had provided the community with its largest year-round payroll, that he had constantly expanded the boundaries of his industry and experimented with ways to improve his own operations, and that S. M. Simpson Ltd. continued to "served as a monument to the man."[55] A newspaper editorial published upon his death acknowledged that S. M. never liked the spotlight of publicity, and many of his little acts of kindness were unknown to other than the recipient. He often told the newspaper to "play down" his personal parts in a story that "normally would have given the average man self-satisfaction and pride."[56] In acknowledging Stan's problems and disputes with organized labour, the *Courier* noted that many of his employees, especially those old-timers who had been with him through the company's "dark years," had a very real personal affection for him. The editorial recognized S. M.'s generosity in selling the Civic Centre site "for a nominal sum, which was less than 'nominal' if such be possible."[57] It went on to say:

> Kelowna mourns his passing but in the minds of those who know his story and his contribution to the life and growth of this city; his memory will be ever green. For those who are less familiar with the background there are two concrete evidences, the company he built and the Civic Centre site, to remind them of a man who during his lifetime certainly demonstrated that in this country, the free enterprise system does permit a man to build an enterprise giving employment to hundreds of his fel-

Stanley Merriam Simpson.

low citizens and at the same time make a substantial contribution to the welfare and happiness of the whole community. In a quiet, self-effacing way, S. M. Simpson was one of Kelowna's major builders. His memory should never be forgotten.[58]

The memorial service at First United Church was filled to overflowing as many friends and business associates from around the province came to pay their respects. Stan's old friend, Premier Bennett, was among the honorary pallbearers but it was long-time mill employee Mike Paly – Klondike Mike – standing outside the doors of the church in his red-and-black chequered work shirt who best embodied Stan's relationship with those he worked with. Mike may not have felt comfortable inside with the prominent guests, but he came to pay his last respects to the man he had worked for through good times and bad. Stan had respected Mike as a loyal employee and hard worker, and Mike respected Stan for sticking to his principles and never asking anyone to do a job that he wasn't prepared to do himself.

The two men recognized in each other the tough reality of their early pioneer years, though their lives had taken different paths. Stan never lost his belief that hard work built the character that was so essential to one's survival, which is likely why he respected a man like Mike, who lived year-round in a tent on the side of Knox Mountain and rowed a small boat to work every day. And respected him regardless of how cantankerous the old-timer might have been. Stan and Mike both came from the old school where a man's word was all that was needed and loyalty was the strongest bond of all. In many ways, the men had been cut from the same cloth many years before, and by chance, they spent many of their working years with the same company. In the end, the fact that one owned the company and one worked there didn't seem to matter much.

For some, it was the best of times

Many people who grew up in the still-small town of Kelowna during the '50s look back on the period fondly, but some of those who worked at S. M. Simpson Ltd., S&K Ltd., and the other companies that became part of the Simpson group during that time found those years to be the most difficult and personally challenging they would ever face. The city itself has grown to nearly 13,000 people and it looked as though Kelowna would continue to enjoy relative prosperity, thanks in no small part to the lumber industry. And while S. M. Simpson Ltd. had also grown and prospered during the '50s, the decade had been filled with strife and change; both the IWA and former Simpson's employees remember the 1953 strike as one of the most contentious and difficult in their collective histories.

In hindsight, the demise of the wooden fruit box was a forgone conclusion but it seems that most of the box makers still in business in the early '50s were caught off guard and had done little planning to find alternative products that would keep their mills operating. Smaller box makers, who had been scattered throughout the Valley for years, simply closed their shops and went on to something else, while larger companies were forced to redefine themselves. As some parts of its traditional business came to an end, Simpson's was able to re-invent itself and move into the 1960s with its new plywood plant and bulk bin. The company remained one of the few family-owned lumber companies in the Interior, and Horace took the original expansion plan beyond Kelowna to include sawmills further a field in the Lumby and Salmon Arm areas. The newly configured company's future looked promising at the end of the decade, but it wasn't long before things changed once again.

107

Chapter 7

The Inevitable Change
– 1960 to 1965

(Clare Holford photo)

Horace Simpson on the wind screen of the first chip car to leave Kelowna on May 1, 1963.

The pace of change in the lumber industry increased dramatically in the years following Stan's death. New government policies required more wood be recovered from the province's forests, which in turn forced loggers and sawmills to retool their operations if they were going to stay in business. This was particularly evident in the Interior: many smaller mills were simply closed when faced with the high costs of new equipment, while others were absorbed by multinational corporations that could better afford the new technology and re-training it required. New cutting specifications also meant loggers had to cut to 6" stump diameters and 4" tops, which pushed the Southern Interior operators into the large stands of lodgepole pine covering the area's dry hillsides. Previously considered a weed species, the pine was so abundant that it provided a new source of timber for mills; it remains the economic backbone of the Interior forest industry.

Optimism and good markets

The U.S. housing market saw spectacular growth in 1959 and with the resulting spike in lumber prices, Simpson's sent more shipments across the border that year than ever before. The company entered the '60s full of optimism: production was up 30 per cent, and for the first three months of the new decade, the sawmill ran double shifts to keep up with the demand. Although the box factory and veneer plant were no longer great profit centres now that the fruit industry had switched to cardboard, some specialty boxes were still being manufactured and the plants made use of timber that would otherwise have become waste. Bulk bins were used beyond the fruit industry, and while they didn't bring in the same profits as the 4' x 8' plywood sheathing panels, there was enough volume to make their production a valuable component of the company's balance sheet.

Simpson's wasn't the only company that was benefiting from the forest industry boom. Foreign capital was attracted by Premier Bennett's 'open for business' economic policy and began to develop forest and mineral resources. As money flowed into B.C., pulp mills were built to take advantage of the increasing amounts of wood fibre generated as a direct result of the revamped forestry regulations. The first of the new mills was built in the Prince George area, and it wasn't long before they also appeared in the Kootenays, where Celgar consolidated its sawmill operation and opened a pulp mill in Castlegar in 1960. Several Kamloops-area sawmill operators started talking about sending their waste residues to pulp mills on the Coast about the same time, but realized that a pulp mill closer to home would be a better solution. Initial contact was made with Crown Zellerbach (CZ), a large U.S. pulp and paper company that had operations in several parts of B.C., including the Elk Falls Company on Vancouver Island, but the company was unwilling to run a mill that was totally dependent upon sawmill waste. As CZ hesitated, another major U.S. forest company, Weyerhaeuser, saw an opportunity and built the pulp mill that it continues to operate in Kamloops today. With the advent of pulp mills that were either wholly or substantially dependent upon sawmill waste for fibre, Simpson's and the Interior's traditional sawmills were pushed into changing their production methods and diversifying their product line to include pulp-grade chips.

Bennett's optimism about B.C.'s future continued, in spite of growing economic restraint in the countries that had begun to invest in the province. The premier's vision wasn't enough, however, and B.C.'s buoyant economy began to fail. The demand for construction-grade lumber dropped abruptly and plywood prices plummeted. Both loggers and sawmills were having difficulty cutting and processing the smaller-diameter timber, and even the strong bulk bin market declined as several small fruit-crop years saturated the market with surplus bins and significantly reduced the demand for new ones. Profits dropped and retained earnings became a thing of the past. For many in the industry, the radical changes brought about by the new forest policy and abruptly disappearing markets made it feel like they had to start all over again.[1]

The downturn

The economic cycles of the forest industry are like a roller coaster, and during the early '60s, companies went from the heady optimism of the first part of the decade into a sudden market downturn. The slowdown made headlines:

Lumber Industry Weakens in B.C.

(The Kelowna Daily Courier, April 28, 1960*)*

Then – as now – the euphoria of the boom or despair of the bust seems to grip as if it will never let go. Overseas exports were about one-eighth of what they had been a few years earlier, as the United Kingdom returned to its traditional pre-war suppliers. In an era before trucks transported much of the country's freight, railway rate increases also added to the impact of the general economic malaise. Lumber sales in western Canada dropped by 66 per cent, and 38 per cent in the east. At the same time, the U.S. was moving to protect its own forest industry and began introducing new tariffs and duties. With about 90 per cent of the Interior's lumber products heading across the border,[2] the future looked increasingly uncertain for Valley sawmill operators.

Against this backdrop, Simpson's cut production. Other plywood plants around B.C. cut prices in hopes of encouraging sales, and when that didn't work shutdowns and layoffs became inevitable:

> The bottom fell out of the market and this is the worst it has been in 20 years. No one anticipated things would be so sluggish. Prices for unsanded sheathing – Simpson's bread-and-butter products – were cut five times in the previous five months.[3]

Horace dropped plywood production down to a single shift, four days a week. The company fortunately still had the bulk bin business to sustain its plywood plant during the downturn, but there was little cause for optimism even in that sector. The sluggish North American economy and the drop in new housing starts reduced the demand for dimension lumber as well, and not wanting to build up any substantial inventory, Simpson's also cut the sawmill operation back to a single shift, four days a week. It was at this time that the U.S. levied a 16 2/3 per cent tariff on the bulk bins that S. M.

110

Simpson Ltd. and Gorman Bros. Lumber in Westbank were shipping across the border, which further impacted both companies' plywood operations. They were able to successfully appeal the ruling, but not before suffering serious financial setbacks.

The sawdust era ends

In order to stay afloat, Simpson's had to cut costs, which involved making some difficult decisions. One of those impacted a decades-old business:

Simpson's Ends Fuel Trade To Start On Pulp Chips

(The Kelowna Daily Courier, February 26, 1963)

Forced to deal with shrinking lumber and plywood markets, increasing overhead, plants burning down and being rebuilt, and declining production, Simpson's decided to cease operating the waste wood business that had been an integral part of the operation since the beginning. Swamps throughout Kelowna's downtown had dried up and become usable only when filled with Simpson's sawmill waste. Sawdust had insulated in the town's early homes when nothing else was available, and most people had burned sawdust in their kitchen stoves and furnaces for years. It wasn't waste in the beginning and for 45 years, revenue from the sale of sawdust, shavings, and slabs had been a steady source of income for the company. Natural gas had arrived in the Valley in the early '60s, and when combined with the already-available fuel oil and coal, the demand for sawdust disappeared and Simpson's actually began having to pay to dispose of it. Many loads went to the company-owned property on Knox Mountain, where it was dumped over the bank into a perpetual fire – much to the disgust of neighbours. The pollution-spewing beehive burners that were a fact of life in many mill towns were never built in Kelowna, although the Knox Mountain burn wasn't much better and the company started exploring the possibility of diverting some of its waste to the province's growing pulp industry.

Chips to the rescue

At the outset, the cost benefit of turning waste into chips was marginal, but it seemed to be a better option than burning it, and Horace began searching for a market for what he hoped could become a new company product. Although Simpson's had been a long-standing partner of MacMillan Bloedel & Powell River Company,[4] H. B. entered discussions with Crown Zellerbach Canada Ltd. (CZ), which had been purchasing wood chips from Kamloops-area sawmills. The S. M. Simpson Ltd. and CZ deal was announced in the fall of 1962:

Pulp Firm at Coast to Buy Kelowna Mill Wood Chips

(The Kelowna Daily Courier, October 2, 1962)

This agreement marked the first time sawmill waste from the Okanagan would be used for pulp production on the Coast, and there were some logistical hurdles to overcome. Rail cars would be loaded at Simpson's Manhattan Beach plant, sent to the Coast, unloaded onto chip barges at Port Moody, and hauled by CZ tugs to the company's pulp mill on Vancouver Island. According to the *Courier*:

> The sale of chips will be a marginal operation as the price paid at Kelowna together with the cost of freight to the Coast must be equivalent to the value of chips obtained at the Coast. It was only considered economically feasible to embark on the pulp chip process by savings resulting from using certain equipment already in the plant and by eliminating the cost of dumping surplus waste wood.[5]

Simpson's existing machinery wasn't capable of producing chips to meet the demanding specifications of the pulp industry – all bark had to be removed and the chips had to be a certain length and thickness – so the company set about retooling its operation. One of the newest pieces of equipment available on the market was the Chip N'Saw, which could cut small logs into dimension lumber and at the same time convert the slabs and edgings into chips. Developed in Vancouver by the Canadian Car (Pacific) Division of Hawker Siddley Canada, an experimental model was sent to Quesnel in 1960, where a number of Simpson's staff checked it out. A test load of different-sized logs was also sent to Vancouver for processing and while it was not without some glitches, the results were satisfactory enough for the first production model Chip N'Saw to be shipped up to Kelowna. Once on-site, Dan Hill, who looked after the company's engineering needs, quickly realized the equipment was not ready to go into production and it took several months and much effort to make the necessary modifications.

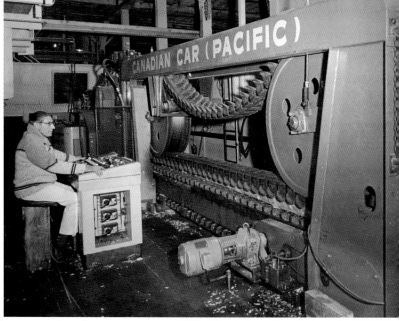
The Chip N'Saw

Although it was expensive and initially unreliable, industry people came from all over North America to see the Chip N'Saw in operation.

S. M. Simpson Ltd. was the first Southern Interior sawmill to install this new type of equipment with the clear objective of taking advantage of the changing marketplace. Smaller mills couldn't afford such expensive technology, however, and while they had been adapting existing equipment or cobbling together what they needed for years, these operations now found the high-tech equipment financially and technically beyond them. Many were faced with two options: either cease to operate, or sell out to larger companies that might also close them down but would be interested in acquiring their timber assets. Inevitably, another wave of consolidation began and in the Southern Interior, Northwood, the lumber arm of Canadian conglomerate Noranda, bought small, older sawmills in Greenwood, Princeton, Osoyoos, Keremeos, Penticton, Summerland, and Beaverdell, and closed them. Soon after, new mills were built in Princeton and Okanagan Falls and later sold to Weyerhaeuser. With these far-reaching changes to the industry, the uncertainty faced by smaller operators began to spread to mid-sized companies, many of which were still family-owned businesses. These family mills didn't have the deep pockets of the multi-nationals and for many, the risks associated with arranging financing and retooling their operations were unacceptable, even if it had been possible.[6] S. M. Simpson Ltd. was among the mid-sized companies that found itself having to deal with that dilemma.

To sell or not to sell

In the spring of 1964, S. M. Simpson Ltd.'s Vancouver accountant, Bill Anderson, quietly approached Bob Rogers, President of Crown Zellerbach Canada Ltd., to see if CZ would be interested in buying Lumby Timber, and the Trautmann and Garraway operations from Simpson's. Rogers wasn't, but said CZ might consider purchasing S. M. Simpson Ltd., and if the other companies were still available, they could be part of the deal. In CZ's view, Simpson's timber holdings, which had grown significantly during the '50s, were a bonus and the primary reason for purchasing the company. Discussions continued in the "strictest confidence," visits were made, appraisals provided, and negotiations for the sale of S. M. Simpson Ltd. began in 1964.[7] Horace and the accountant carried out talks in such secrecy that some Simpson family members didn't know they were going on until an agreement was finally reached a year later.

It is unlikely H. B. was thinking of selling his entire company when Anderson made contact with CZ. He was only 48 years old and all he had ever wanted to do was work in his family's sawmill business. There is little doubt that the preceding years had been difficult, and with the high costs of change and the relatively small nature of the company, he was abundantly aware his family's future was at stake if anything should happen to the company. The Simpson name had been on the bank loans that had enabled the company to grow and modernize since its earliest days, but with the costs of buying several mills during the latter part of the '50s, the new plywood plant, rebuilding burned-out sawmills, and the new high-tech equipment, Horace likely wondered how much more the family could – or should – take on. S. M. Simpson Ltd. needed bank financing to grow and keep up with changes in the lumber business, but the risk to family members increased with each new purchase or expansion. Stan's admonitions about the perils of debt likely also resonated throughout the family, even though he was no longer around and the world had become a substantially different place in only a few years.

Added value

Horace knew his company could offer a lot to a potential purchaser: a new plywood plant had been built and was profitable, Lumby Timber had recently been rebuilt to state-of-the-art specifications, and the Trautman and Garraway mill in Peachland had also been rebuilt after a fire and continued as Simpson's back-up, non-union operation. The Chip N'Saw was operational, timber inventories were good, and by converting the company's waste into chips, another revenue stream was possible.

The major downside Horace would have to deal with if he didn't accept CZ's purchase offer was that Simpson's Kelowna operation and the Manhattan Beach sawmill had become so obsolete that the company would require a major cash infusion to bring them up to industry standards. The veneer plant and box factory were also outdated and needed to be replaced with a more productive operation. With the poor markets and the uncertainty of the previous four years, Simpson's earnings had been minimal and any future improvements would require additional financing.

On the plus side, Crown Zellerbach was promising a $60 to $80 million infusion of capital over the next few years, which would ensure Simpson's survival. Beyond the physical plant, employees would be offered CZ's generous pension and benefit packages and would be well-looked after, few personnel changes were expected, and employees would be able to access new career opportunities within the larger company. Qualified staff, including engineering and technical specialists, was available through CZ and employees would get the training and upgrading needed to operate the new equipment. Most of all, the family company would become part of a multi-national organization and benefit from its marketing skills and deeper pockets that could carry S. M. Simpson Ltd. through the economic downturns.

H. B. recognized the vulnerability inherent in owning a mid-sized, family-based forest products company: markets could evolve in a matter of months; new forest policies were impacting the way business was done; new and costly equipment had to be purchased; the workforce needed retraining; and the marketplace wanted standardized products and didn't need his company's wooden apple boxes, veneer berry baskets, or sawdust any more. Changes to the forest industry were so significant, so expensive, and it was evolving at such a rapid pace that many of the Interior's smaller sawmill and bush mill operators shut down during these years.[8] Given the circumstances, Simpson's was also in danger of disappearing.

There were few choices for Horace other than to sell his company, and it seemed to be an all-or-nothing deal – CZ wanted the main Manhattan Beach operation, as well as Forest Management License #9 and the timber leases that went along with it, and would include the smaller operations, but only if S. M. Simpson Ltd. was part of the deal. H. B. might have considered taking the company public as a way of raising the needed funds, but that wasn't as easy in the early '60s as it is now. The intensely private nature of the man would have also made him very uncomfortable disclosing information about the company's finances, and it is unlikely he would have even considered that as a viable option. By selling S. M. Simpson Ltd. to Crown Zellerbach, Horace knew the company would stay

113

intact, employees would be well-looked after and get to keep their jobs, and the plant would continue to operate in Kelowna. He also had the option of staying on for the next 12 months to provide continuity during the transition, and longer if he chose to.

But why sell to Crown Zellerbach? Had Horace discussed the sale of some – or all – of S. M. Simpson Ltd.'s assets with its long-standing partner, MacMillan Bloedel? He certainly noted that the share price and dividend yield of M & B and CZ were similar,[9] but other than that, there is no record of any approaches being made to the Coastal giant. What does remain is an account of the turmoil resulting from the recent 'marriage' between M & B and its great newsprint rival, The Powell River Company, in the early '60s. A magazine article from the time characterized H. R. MacMillan as a "buccaneer," to which the usually humourless H. R. responded, "That's me, a buccaneer. I sink 'em without a trace!" The article went on to recount the clashes that erupted when the MacMillan group apparently acted contrary to the understandings of the merger agreement and large numbers of Powell River executives were either fired or forced to resign.[10] If the huge Powell River Company couldn't survive within the tightly-controlled MacMillan organization, it was highly unlikely that a small player like Simpson's would have been able to, and Horace didn't want to risk seeing the company disappear.

The decision
By the spring of 1945, the writing was on the wall for S. M. Simpson Ltd.:

Simpson Sawmill Joins the Crown Zellerbach Group
(The Kelowna Daily Courier, April 12, 1965)

This wasn't a simple transaction involving two independent companies. Crown Zellerbach Corporation, the parent company of Crown Zellerbach Canada, had a long and convoluted history of mergers, acquisitions, subsidiaries, and sales that involved over 184 companies during its lifetime. Crown Zellerbach Canada was launched in 1928 and its numerous companies, partnerships, and acquisitions included some of the key players in the province's forest industry: Vancouver Pacific Paper Co., Elk Falls Co. Ltd., Fraser Mills, Comox Logging & Railway Co., Northwood Pulp, and Norsk Pacific Steamship Co. The world-wide multi-national remained in B.C. for relatively few years, however, and its eventual demise perhaps foretold what was to become of B.C.'s forest industry as a whole in subsequent years.[11] CZ purchased assets throughout the province until its Canadian operations were sold to Fletcher Challenge Canada in 1982. The parent company was then sold to the James River Corporation, a leader in the packaged goods industry, in 1985. The James River Corporation was subsequently sold to Georgia Pacific in 2000; the new owner continues to be one of the world's leading distributors of tissue, paper packaging, building products, pulp, and related chemicals.[12]

But there was no way H. B. could have known what lay ahead for CZ in the decades to come when he accepted the company's offer to purchase S. M. Simpson Ltd. The *Courier* noted that Horace described the transaction as, "not a takeover and not a purchase," while Bob Rogers, President of Crown Zellerbach Canada Ltd., commented: "As a public company we are interested in the development of our resources everywhere. We have been doing business with Simpson's for three years[13] and a mutual interest developed over many months."[14] Rogers also added that his company felt the future potential for the Okanagan lumber business was "most spectacular" and that prospects for the B.C. forest industry as a whole were greatest in the Interior.[15] Because S. M. Simpson Ltd. was privately owned by family members, with a few long-time employees holding a small number of additional shares, the terms of the sale were never disclosed. In fact, the settlement consisted of a modest cash payout to the primary shareholders with the balance of the payment in the form of CZ shares that couldn't be sold for three years. Whether the agreement was seen as positively by the shareholders three years after it was signed as it was in April 1965, is unknown.

All the shares, assets – including the 300 acre Bear Creek Ranch (now Bear Creek Provincial Park) and 102 acres on Knox Mountain – and liabilities of S. M. Simpson Ltd. were either purchased or assumed by Crown Zellerbach Canada Ltd. After more than five decades in the lumber and forestry business, Simpson's finally succumbed to the economic pressures of the day and joined a long list of forest companies that had been caught in the familiar pattern of expansion and consolidation.

The company had experienced both ends of the cycle – it had bought a number of small sawmills and logging companies, and as circumstances and conditions changed, had itself been bought out. There was almost an ebb and flow to the process: the era of the small independent bush mill operators, the risk-taking entrepreneurs, and the family-owned companies was coming to an end and being replaced by conglomerates with deep pockets and high-tech solutions. None of that, however, could change the fact that S. M. Simpson Ltd. had left an indelible mark on Kelowna.

For a few years following the sale, the company was known as the S. M. Simpson Ltd. Division of Crown Zellerbach Canada Ltd., before eventually being absorbed into the CZ corporation. The company disappeared and so too did the story of its founder, Stanley Merriam Simpson – until now.

S. M. SIMPSON *Limited*

LUMBER – PLYWOOD – SHOOK

SPRUCE – PINE – FIR

TELEPHONE 762-3411
P. O. BOX 220 – KELOWNA, B.C.

April 12, 1965.

TO ALL EMPLOYEES AND THEIR FAMILIES:

It has been announced that the S. M. Simpson organization has today joined forces with Crown Zellerbach Canada Limited.

After fifty-two years of operation as a "family" business, I am sure you will realize that the decision of the shareholders of S. M. Simpson Limited was reached only after careful consideration of the substantial advantages to the employees, their families, the communities in which we operate and the entire Okanagan Valley which will result from this merger.

Access to the research facilities, engineering services and marketing organization of this leader in the forest products field will ensure a continuation of the progress and development which has characterized the growth of the S.M. Simpson group in the past.

Crown Zellerbach Canada Limited are most desirous that the organization which has been built up will continue to function as a part of a larger unit. I have agreed to remain with the operation and feel that the opportunities for all are enhanced by this amalgamation. Crown Zellerbach Canada Limited has undertaken that as soon as possible, its Retirement Plan and its Retirement Plan for Salaried Employees will be made available to the hourly paid and salaried employees of the Simpson organization.

I would like to express, on behalf of the Simpson family, our sincere appreciation to you for your loyalty to the Companies over the years, and to ask your continued support as the Company moves forward under its new owners.

Yours sincerely,

R. H. Simpson

S. M. SIMPSON LIMITED
DIVISION OF CROWN ZELLERBACH CANADA LIMITED
P.O. BOX 220 – KELOWNA, B.C.

Chapter 8

The Intermediate Years
– 1965 to 2003

The Industry Today - A Fellerbuncher – one piece of equipment now delimbs, measures, cuts, stacks, and transports logs while the operator sits in an air-conditioned cab.

The transition from S. M. Simpson Ltd. to Crown Zellerbach Canada Ltd. went relatively smoothly, with Horace staying on as general manager for a year before taking on a long-term planning role and Bill Beaton becoming Interior general manager. Some things improved with the change in ownership, but others didn't as the relationship between CZ and the IWA was impacted by CZ's Coastal operations and the union's demand for wage parity between the Interior and the Coast. When negotiations for the 1967 contract began, Horace became chairman of the negotiating committee for the Southern Interior Forest Labour Relations Association. The union didn't approve of the appointment, accusing H. B. of being a mouthpiece for the new owners and saying he shouldn't be involved in negotiations because he no longer owned the mill.

Talks soon broke down and the ensuing seven-and-a-half month strike surpassed all earlier job actions to became the longest and one of the most bitter in the Interior's history. As the stalemate continued, mill operators tried to get Premier Bennett to step in and order their employees back to work, but he refused. The IWA and Northern Interior operators settled their dispute in five weeks, while the South was still on strike five months later because the union insisted that Southern Interior workers should have wage parity with the Coast. With no resolution in sight, Bennett finally ordered the two sides into the same room, where they were to stay until a settlement was reached. Negotiators had little choice and did as they were told, but sometimes sat in total silence. Other times, they played crib, and when that became tiresome, they talked about the weather, or a hockey game, or whatever came to mind – anything but the contract.[1]

The battle was so acrimonious and took so long to settle that it was hard for either side to claim victory. The IWA managed to change the contract expiry date, which had been an issue for years, but it still didn't get the wage parity it had been so adamant about. The strategy of the Interior union executive was eventually vindicated,[2] but negotiators for the Southern Interior operators paid an enormous price for their part in the lengthy dispute: one year after the settlement was reached, three of the five industry negotiators were dead, one from natural causes and two from suicide.[3] Another left the lumber business and moved away. Shortly after the strike was settled, Horace also bid farewell to the industry he had grown up with.

Soon after CZ took over Simpson's, it brought efficiency experts into all its B.C. operations, which likely created significant issues for H. B. and affirmed his decision to leave after the strike. As part the sale agreement, Horace had agreed not to become involved in another forest company for five years, and once away from the industry he changed his focus to the broader business community, becoming a director of B.C. Telephone, Brenda Mines, and Inland Gas, as well as chair of the Kelowna Hospital Board and a variety of fund raising and community service initiatives. Although he was no longer directly involved in the sawmill business, H. B. kept in touch with company old-timers and when they passed on, he went to every one's funeral. When Horace died in 1994, the employees who were left came to his funeral, and many took a few minutes to share some of their stories with his family. Horace had very few options in 1965 other than to sell S. M. Simpson Ltd. but the sawdust that still runs through the veins and lungs of old-timers never left him, and he remained keenly interested in the lumber industry until the end.

Crown Zellerbach carries on

The Simpson name disappeared not long after the Manhattan Beach operation became part of Crown Zellerbach's Interior operations. A few years later, CZ opened a corrugated cardboard container plant in Kelowna to supply the local fruit industry with boxes, and in 1972 embarked on the company's largest capital project in a decade – a $25 million modernization and centralization of the sawmill and plywood operations in Kelowna, Armstrong, and Lumby. Upon its completion, the *Courier* announced:

Crown Zellerbach Opens Door For New Era In Lumber

(The Kelowna Daily Courier, July 17, 1974)

At the same time, CZ closed five obsolete operations in Armstrong,[4] Enderby, Vernon, Falkland, and Monte Lake, and replaced Simpson's old box factory, veneer plant, and sawmill with a stud mill and new planer operation. As part of these consolidations, CZ also combined three tree farm licenses (the earlier Forest Management Licenses) in the area to expand and enhance its forest tenure.

The cycle continues

CZ operated its mills in the Southern Interior for the next half-decade, but in the same ebb and flow that saw the end of S. M. Simpson Ltd., the early '80s found Crown Zellerbach struggling to survive the deepest North American recession since the 1930s. CZ sold its Interior operations to Fletcher Challenge of New Zealand in 1982, and the company became known as Crown Forest Industries. The prevailing sentiment among industry-watchers in the Valley at the time was the company's holdings were sold "for a pittance" to service a sizeable debt. That assessment might well have been true, as Crown Zellerbach, the American parent company, was acquired by the James River Corporation in 1985 and ceased to exist. In the confusing pattern of sales and mergers that characterizes B.C.'s forest industry, Crown Forest Industries merged with B.C. Forest Products in 1988 and changed its name to Fletcher Challenge Canada, Ltd. That company, in turn, lasted for another five years before selling 51 per cent of its shares to TimberWest from Vancouver Island. The balance of Fletcher Challenge stock was acquired by Norske Skog Canada (NorskeCanada), a Norwegian pulp and paper company that currently operates pulp mills on Vancouver Island. In 1993, Riverside Forest Products purchased Fletcher Challenge's operations in B.C.'s Southern Interior, and the old Manhattan Beach operation became Riverside's Kelowna operation. All vestiges of Simpson's were finally gone.

Simpson's old box factory – 1972
(Jack Leier photo)

*Large timbers removed from
original box factory*
(Jack Leier photo)

Demolished.
(Jack Leier photo)

A new era

Riverside was not quite the story of the 'mouse swallowing the elephant' when it bought out Fletcher Challenge, but almost. Riverside became a publicly-traded company in the early '90s in order to fund the original purchase, as well as modernize and expand its operations. The company is now the largest producer of softwood plywood in Canada, and operates four stud mills, a dimension lumber sawmill, veneer plant, a re-manufacturing facility, a whole-log chipping plant, a railway tie treatment and processing facility, and a seedling nursery in the Interior. It has also become one of the top 10 tenure holders and lumber producers in British Columbia, and is only missing a pulp mill to become a truly integrated forestry operation.

But what's to stop Riverside from following the same pattern as so many of the province's other forest companies? Gordon Steele, Riverside's President and CEO, characterizes his company as a mid-sized operation that is "swift on its feet."[5] Even with its highly efficient and competitive operations, the current marketplace is tough and to remain successful Riverside will have to remain vigilant and adapt accordingly. Many things have changed in the years since Stan ran his sawmill, and issues he would never have thought of now impact the forest industry on a daily basis: lumber markets are global and face increasing competition from Third World countries; tight government regulations put huge bur-

119

dens on forest companies; export tariffs and duties are imposed, challenged, and seem to lack a logical resolution; land use and resource-sharing negotiations with First Nations are ongoing; and the often-radical tactics of environmentalists have all added to today's challenge of staying in business.

The lumber industry in the Okanagan continues to survive, however, and Stan left Riverside with a legacy of good planning and innovation. Riverside has improved on Simpson's first plywood plant, but it was S. M. Simpson Ltd.'s introduction of a unique glue to bond the spruce veneer that has enabled Riverside to solidify its position as the largest softwood plywood producer in Canada.

When he chose to build his sawmill in Kelowna's north end, S. M. had the foresight to buy more land than he actually needed at the time and add to it when adjacent properties became available.[6] Riverside uses most of that land today, and the mill's neighbours would likely object if the company tried to expand its Manhattan operation any further. Soon after Stan built his sawmill, Canadian National Railways extended its tracks to the mill site. It continues as an essential link in delivering the company's various products to market, just as it was for Simpson's lumber, box shook, and chips, even though rail service throughout the country has been scaled back in the last two decades, and the line has new owners.

Perhaps the most valuable contribution was S. M.'s decision to built his first permanent sawmill on the waterfront. He chose that location at a time when both logging trucks and the roads they travelled on were in their infancy, and Okanagan Lake was the Valley's main transportation route. The company's booming grounds around the lake enabled contractors to deliver their loads closer to the logging sites and tugs to pick up the booms and haul them to the mill. It was an efficient and cost-effective plan in the '30s, and it remains so today as the *Stanley M* still hauls logs up and down the lake, avoiding bridge traffic and highway congestion.

The IWA also changes

Considerable changes have also taken place in the IWA in the years following the sale of S. M. Simpson Ltd. Its 50 year affiliation with the original International Woodworkers of America ended in 1987 when the organization became the IWA – Canada, and refocused its efforts to what was happening in Canada. By 1994, however, membership from the forest sector had declined substantially and the union was forced to recruit workers from other industries. Along with that came a name change to the Industrial, Wood and Allied Workers of Canada (IWA – Canada). While the IWA continues to speak for the province's forest workers, it now also bargains for the service industry, the public sector, and in manufacturing industries far removed from the forests, and the acronym 'IWA' represents a far more diverse workforce that it did in the early days.

In the '40s and '50s, the guys at the mill were young, new union members, and were out to change the workplace come hell or high water – and usually it was some of both. From the '60s through to the '80s, union leaders came off the shop floor, were street smart, learned on the job, fought for their principles, and stood their ground. By the '90s, most of the tough stuff had been accomplished. Today's union workforce is smarter, better educated, more independent, and doesn't have the same kind of loyalty to the IWA that many of the old-timers had, but neither do those employees have the same kind of loyalty to their employer. The workplace has changed on all fronts,[7] and when times are good, the IWA looks like the big companies it negotiates with – it has its own market analysts, economists, historians, and lawyers. But when things get tough, those employees get laid off as well.

The negotiations themselves have also changed, as the days of yelling matches and storming out are largely gone. So too are the outrageous demands, the stonewalling, and negotiation by exhaustion. Both sides realize that B.C.'s forestry workers are among the best paid in the world and that there isn't much manoeuvring room if the province's industry is to remain competitive.[8] Most of the turf battles within the IWA organization have been resolved, and now the forest industry and the IWA

120

carry out a single set of negotiations, although there are still three separate contracts: one for the Coast, and one each for the Northern and Southern Interior. Long-gone as well are the days when an individual operator – such as Stan – would go it alone, send letters to his employees during a strike, and fight his battle through the newspapers.

The future?

B.C.'s forest industry has gone through several restructurings, amalgamations, and closures since S. M. Simpson Ltd. was sold in the mid-'60s. The Coastal forest industry, once thought to be invincible, is struggling with aging plants, tough markets, and declining wood supplies. Bob Rogers, the former CZ company president, forecast in 1965 that the future of the province's forest industry would be found in the Interior, and with about 70 per cent of B.C.'s lumber products coming from the Northern and Southern Interior today, his assessment has proven to be correct. Both time and history have shown, however, that for many sawmills, the distance between being the best in the business and non-existent isn't a very long journey – whether it was S. M. Simpson Ltd, Crown Zellerbach, or Fletcher Challenge. With the pace of change, uncertainty in the marketplace, shifting government policy, and international competition, even being "swift on your feet," as Riverside's Gordon Steele noted, doesn't guarantee survival.

In Stan's 1957 letter to the City of Kelowna, acknowledging the honour of the Freedom of the City he noted:

> We look forward to the building of a permanent industry that will make for the greatest possible use of the wood that is grown in this part of the province. We trust, when the trees we have planted this spring on our Forest Management License are harvested, this company will still be contributing to the economic welfare of the province and to a better standard of living for the citizens of the Okanagan Valley.[9]

Stan's comments were echoed nearly 45 years later by Steele, who commented, "We're planning to be here for the next hundred years, too." With luck some luck, careful planning, and the hard work needed to stay on top, Riverside might just be. But if history tells us anything, it is that nothing lasts forever in the British Columbia forest industry. Stan and Horace Simpson knew that better than most.

Chapter 9

Of Stories and Storytellers

Everyone loves a good story and when former Simpson employees gather, whether it's at their informal lunches, a reunion, or maybe even on a street corner, the stories flow. Every story will be a bit different because that's the way our memory works – each of us experience things differently and in most cases, there is no 'correct' version of the tale. The following are only a sampling of the many stories that were told, written, or recorded during the past four years it has taken to write this book. They add colour, humour, and details that can never be found in newspaper clippings, libraries, or company documents, and they are a valuable and unique part of S. M. Simpson Ltd.'s history.

Every effort has been made to verify the factual information in *Boards, Boxes, and Bins* but these stories from employees, their wives, sons, or daughters have been included here as they were told. Many have characterized their years working with Stan and Horace as "the best years of my life." Others said it was a time when many treated their jobs almost like it was a contest to see who could work the hardest. In looking back, others say it was mostly 'bull work' – tough, hard work, especially when you look at how mills operate today. There were bad times, problems, grudges, and disagreements, but our memories are selective and we forget unpleasant things and remember only the best and the funniest. These are only a few of the many stories that could be told.

About Stan

Mary and John Olinger had a mill at Carmi, south-east of Kelowna, and later owned Rutland Sawmills. John wasn't much of a mechanic, so when Stan had a bit of time, he would drive Les McDonald, his sometimes mechanic, over to Carmi. When Les went up the hill to work on the machinery, Stan and Mary would have a cup of tea and visit. Things were pretty slim when John and Mary were starting out, so she and Stan would sit on the stumps that doubled as chairs and pull them up to the table for tea and homemade bread.

The jack ladder

Mary said she was so ashamed, but Stan didn't notice and seemed glad to have someone to talk to who knew about the business. She remembers him talking about getting started in the business, telling her, "Just hang in, it's going to be tough, you'll have ups and downs and lumber prices will go up and down and back up again, but don't get discouraged." He also talked about the banks and how difficult it was to get them to believe he needed money, but he also told her that if one bank would-n't help, then go an find another that would. (The advice would serve her well later when the couple bought Rutland Sawmills.) – Mary Olinger

▲ ▲ ▲

In the '40s and '50s employees worked hard, the hours were long, and it was heavy physical labour, but S. M. and Horace knew everyone by name and there was a respect there for them. Behind their backs, we called them 'old Stanley M' and 'young Horace.' Stan Simpson would walk around the mill in his suit and if you were behind on your job, he would take off his jacket and help you get caught up, and then say to you, "Okay, now let's see you keep up." – Ray Ottenbreit

▲ ▲ ▲

There was a young man who had come from Italy and used to say to me, "You remind me of my dead wife," and he began to stalk me at work and uptown, which I found very unnerving. He cir-cled the dry kiln when I was working in it and I said to the girls, "I'm going to take a handful of slats and hit him with it when he comes around again." So I was ready with the slats in the air when I heard footsteps. However, this time it was Mr. S. and when he asked me what I intended to do, I told him and he said he'd attend to it. And he did, he let the man go. – Gwen Campbell

▲ ▲ ▲

Sometimes employees were building houses but couldn't afford to buy the lumber, so it was okay with Stan if they got it from the mill when they needed it and paid it off $20 a paycheque. – Jack Leier

▲ ▲ ▲

In March or early April of 1950, I went to the mill office for a job application. On the walk back up to town, a big Oldsmobile pulled over and an older gentleman asked if I wanted a ride. I learned later that it was S. M. The Olds and S. M. became familiar figures for a few years after I started work at the planer mill on May 9, 1950. When I first started working at the mill, I ran the old Berlin resaw. I was on the afternoon shift one week and the day shift fellow on the resaw forgot to shut the water off that cooled the saw. The water had wet the sawdust in the pit and plugged the sawdust pipe.

Keith Menzies

I was in the pit cleaning it up so I could start to work. The other fellows were supposed to be clean-ing up and I was trying to get the pipes together, and I said, "Hand down that *#%&* bar!" Down came the bar to me in the pit and the pipe went together. I came out of the pit and it was S. M. that had passed the bar down to me. My fellow workers were nowhere to be seen. S. M. didn't like swearing, and away he went. – Keith Menzies

▲ ▲ ▲

We were stopped for a planer break-down one day and we were all supposed to clean up. We were, but we were doing a lot of horsing around. Someone broke a couple of good stripper sticks that could have been used again and threw them in the waste box. Sure enough, there was S. M. and he saw everything. He went to the fellow and said, "You know, that could be the difference between profit and loss." – Keith Menzies

▲ ▲ ▲

One day, a small bundle of lumber was returned to the mill from either eastern Canada or the U.S. – it was about 1949. That's when Mr. Simpson called a meeting of all the sawmill and planing mill employees, and told them all to go to the truck shop. That lumber had gone through the planer and

124

lumber grader and been loaded into a box car and sent all the way there, and then a bundle of three or four reject pieces was sent back. That was like an insult to Mr. Simpson and he made sure every one of his employees knew about it. That really smartened up some people. – Arthur Marty

♦ ♦ ♦

S. M. spent a lot of time thinking. Usually, he never said very much. I remember when they were building the plywood plant and we were hauling logs from Whiteman's Creek and Charlesworth, the head scaling inspector from Kamloops told S. M. he was being cheated when the logs were scaled on the truck. So Stan came down to the dock where the trucks were unloading and he stood there every day for two weeks just looking at what was going on.

Well, when you had the owner of the sawmill watching everything you were doing, you kind of wondered what was going on. He stood there on the catwalk so still that a mink came along and sniffed his pant cuff before carrying on. Stan had the logs unloaded from the truck and spread over the dock and had them measured and scaled. When he had it all figured out, he designed a new bucking plant for the plywood operation in such a way that it would pretty well eliminate any underhanded scaling. – Arthur Marty

♦ ♦ ♦

Mr. Simpson was always working. He came down to the office one the morning, down to Manhattan, and something happened to the steering of his car. It just ran off the road into the marsh where the frogs use to crawl across the road when they were migrating from the marsh across to the lake in the spring [now the area around The Grand Hotel]. I guess he just left his car there and was going to get some of the fellows at the garage to pick it up and fix it. But he came into the office and went on with whatever he had on his mind and then he came to me at noon and said, "Evelyn, have you seen my car around?" and I said, "No, but I hadn't been looking for it." Then it dawned on him that it had run off the road earlier that morning and he hadn't remembered to tell anyone about it. – Evelyn Radomski, who was Stan's secretary for many years

♦ ♦ ♦

In front of the Abbott Street sash and door factory. Evelyn Radomski, front right

My father delivered a load of logs to Mr. Simpson's mill and was paid for them. But when they were taken out of the water a year later, the value of the logs had gone up and Mr. Simpson sent my dad another cheque for the difference. – Unknown

♦ ♦ ♦

I think Mr. Simpson just lived for the mill, and he knew everything that went on there. Whenever he had plans, he drew what he wanted on pieces of paper and took them in to Dan Hill, who could build anything. He would just walk through the mill and know who was on the job and who was off … he was very observant. He must have had a computer brain, as he stored everything. It just amazed me sometimes what he came up with. – Evelyn Radomski

♦ ♦ ♦

There was a mutual respect. I think if you talked to any of the old people they respected S. M. and H. B. for who they were because they were, what do you call it – square shooters – honest, you know. You had to work hard and everything like that, but there was always that mutual respect there because they were good people. Some of the people that worked with them sometimes weren't too great but they, themselves, were good.

When we [were sold] to the bigger corporations, a lot of the guys used to say we lost that [feeling] because the bigger corporations didn't care. They didn't know who you were, they'd never even say Merry Christmas at Christmas time or anything. That all disappeared and that's something that with the private ownership was never lost. I was on the union side for 44 years but there was always that mutual respect and I knew H. B. as good guy I worked with. You know, Stanley M. was a good guy, too. He always had that serious look on his face, but deep down inside he was a pretty good guy. – Ray Ottenbreit

⧫ ⧫ ⧫

Mr. Simpson was a man that walked around the mill most of the time. When he saw someone doing something wrong, he would not talk to the employee about it but would go to the foreman and let him know. – Arthur Marty

In the office

I was just amazed when I first started at Abbott Street [the sash and door plant]. S. M. was a terrible speller, but he never worried about his spelling – it was the meaning that he got so clear. I had changed a letter around just to make it a little more readable and y'know, he was very kind and he told me that was not quite what he wanted … I had changed the meaning of the letter and he knew exactly what he wanted.

I was just amazed what he could do in his head. I always said we didn't need any calculators with him around. He could look at a boom of logs and guestimate what was there within a few hundred board feet. Charlie Stuart was very good at that, too. Yes, maybe Stan's spelling wasn't very good but he certainly knew the English language very well and knew exactly what he wanted to say. – Evelyn Radomski

⧫ ⧫ ⧫

In the office around noon one day, everything suddenly became very quiet. Mr. Simpson had come in and gone out again, and I really didn't know where he was. Mrs. Simpson came tearing in all dressed up like she was going somewhere and asked, "Where's Stanley?" I didn't know but said I would phone around and see if I could find him. He was down at the mill and what happened was that he was supposed to just check something out quickly and then come right home, as they were to go to Vernon for some do. S. M. had totally forgotten about the event as he became involved in some problem at the mill. Mrs. Simpson looked at me and said, "I should have married a buzz saw!" – Evelyn Radomski

Stan and his wife, Blanche. 1957

Fighting forest fires

Stan would shut the mill when there was a forest fire, and we would be get shovels and axes loaded into the back of sawdust trucks or whatever trucks were available. We were off at the Blue Grouse fire for about a week and had to patrol the fire break during the night to make sure the fire didn't leap across. In the early morning light, when we were walking down to the camp for breakfast, we realized that the fire break was covered with rattlesnakes who were trying to escape the fire. We had been walking over them all night. I don't know who was more scared – them or us. – Leonard Campbell

Blue Grouse Mountain fire – August 1952. Flames could be seen for several miles and hundreds of holidayers watched in amazement as the fire race up the hillside. Strong winds hampered firefighting efforts as experienced loggers joined with men from the sawmill in a struggle to get the flames under control. About 1,500 acres of timber burned while company bulldozers hacked out a fire guard, which helped to control the blaze. S. M. Simpson Ltd. leased the timber rights on the mountain and had been logging in the area for a number of years. As Stan walked around the site, he was dismayed to see the good second-growth timber being destroyed in the blaze. (The Kelowna Courier, August 14, 1952)

Don Sandburg

"We had a good laugh now and then"

It didn't take new employees long to figure out how the place worked, but until they did, they were fair game and everyone was in on it. In the shook plant, if one of the boards came out too short, the new kid would be sent over to shops to get a board stretcher, which of course didn't exist. So they sent him off to another place and another, until someone finally took pity on the kid and clued him in. The same thing happened in the power house when the pressure dropped in the boilers. The new kid would be sent off to the shop to get a couple of buckets of steam to get things fired up again. It never failed and it likely only happened once. You had to be a quick learner to survive. – Don Sandburg

🌲 🌲 🌲

The old Lancaster boiler in the powerhouse had an opening in the front of it so you could crawl into it and clean it out. Ol' Tscharke, who worked there, was a pretty stocky guy. He could barely get through that hole, but he finally made it. His legs were just sticking out and Tony, the welder, took the sledge hammer and hit the barrel. Well – Tscharke's legs flung up in the air and he was vibrating for a week! – Anonymous

🌲 🌲 🌲

40 years ago, I installed the very first turbine in the power house. I welded my name and birth date on it. It's still there in the front of the pit, and they still give me a bad time about it. – Evert Does

The lunchroom was a little shack that hung out over the water, and you had lunch whenever you could fit it into what you were doing. We use to watch the mink come out of the water through the floor slats. Porcupines also ate the axe handles, and bob cats came in with the loads of logs.

A few years later, a number of the guys would get over to the area behind the machine shop and we would play horseshoes while we ate our lunch. Another favourite thing at lunchtime was to draw a circle on the floor and throw pennies up against the wall and try to get them to bounce back. The one closest to the circle would take all the pot that day. That used to be a favourite game in those days. – Various sources

127

Bill Sinclair could make the best equipment, like peavey hooks and tongs. He did a lot of work for the loggers and the stuff he made never broke. Bill wasn't necessarily the ringleader of the antics that went on in the machine shop and the lunch room, but he certainly seemed to be there much of the time. One time, somebody made sort of a home-made bomb – it was just a plastic pail filled with acetylene. We put it under the lunchroom table and then there was this spark plug and a piece of wire that melted when we plugged it into the wall … and, well, it set the bomb off. That thing went off like an atomic bomb and we all jumped about this high, and ol' Bill was doubled up he was laughing so hard." – Anonymous

♦ ♦ ♦

The day before S&K Plywood was to have its big official opening, the fire marshal refused to issue an occupancy permit because the sprinkler system hadn't been connected. This put the company in a really embarrassing situation, because a lot of invitations had already been sent out for the opening. To ensure that the plant opened in time, a section of pipe had to be installed to complete the hook-up to the sprinkler. Bob Springer was the area representative for Transite Pipe, a successful sideline that the company had taken on. Bob and Len Smith were given the job of installing the pipe the night before the opening so the plant could continue on with the ceremony. A ditch had been dug, and Bob and I were standing in water with knee-high rubber boots on, and Bob, being the practical joker he was, told me to grab one end of the ten-foot pipe that was in the water while he picked up the other end. As the pipe was waist high, Bob tilted his end up so that the water in the pipe ran down to my end and completely filled my rubber boots. – Len Smith's notes

♦ ♦ ♦

There was a lot of BS going on in the lunchroom at dinner time so I had a tape recorder and I decided I'm going to pick it all up. The shop had pipes that ran under it to heat the place up, but it wasn't cold so I put the tape recorder on the pipes and I let it start so I could pick up all the baloney that was going on. So anyway, when it was all over I went out to get my tape recorder but someone had switched the heat on, and that thing was like bubble gum … there was my tape recorder all melted. Bill Sinclair was smoking a cigar – he almost swallowed it he was laughing so hard. – Anonymous

♦ ♦ ♦

One year, the weather was so wet that many acres of onions, which were a big crop in this area and normally dried in fields or packinghouses, were still too wet to put in storage, and no one knew what to do with them. So we made an arrangement to try and dry out hundreds of tons of wet onions in our dry kilns. When the truck delivering the onions stopped at the end of the yard and asked where they should unload, it took awhile but the baffled employee eventually sent them over to the mill office. As the onions dried, their skins became loose and they could be seen escaping through the dry kiln vents and flying all over the yard – accompanied by the strong smell of partially-cooked onions. The experiment was not very successful. – Horace Simpson's notes

When CHBC - TV was starting up, locally-produced shows filled much of its air time. One of its more popular game shows had teams from different clubs and businesses competing for fur coats, Toro lawn movers, Bulova watches, Black Cat Cosmetic Kits, and chaise lounges. Simpson's office staff had two successful teams, known as Wood Ticks One and Wood Ticks Two.

Willie Schumaker

When contract negotia-tions became tense, Willie Schumaker was often able to defused the situation by capturing the scene in one of his drawings – in this case, B.C. labour legend Jack Munro.

The Union

There were very few stories passed along about what was happening during the strikes, but there is little doubt that these were really tough times for everyone. Taps blew off machinery or parts became loose, and while there was no proof that anything was intentional, it was suspicious. No one got shot but all the trees on someone's property were cut down one night and the message was pretty clear. People in the mill office often kept working during a strike, but would have to face cat-calls from strikers on the picket line. – Various anonymous sources

🔺 🔺 🔺

When I started, we worked six days a week and they were 10 hours days. When the contract first came in, it changed to five, 10 hour days a week and four on Saturday, and then we eventually dropped the Saturdays. It stayed at 10 hours for awhile and then dropped down to eight hours. Boy, those 10-hour days were killers. We were paid twice a month after the Saturday shift to make sure we came to work that day. No banks were open on Saturday, so both Safeway and SuperValu kept extra cash on hand to cash our cheques. The guys today don't know what good is. I've been quite involved with the union and we used to tell a lot of the young guys in there, "Y'know, you guys don't know how good you've got it – it's the guys ahead of you that broke the ground and got it the way it is today." – Ray Ottenbreit

🔺 🔺 🔺

Once during the '50s, we were on strike and I was parked by the old box factory with three other fellows in my car, close to the Simpson property. I looked in the mirror and I said, "We are in trouble. Here comes S. M.!" He pulled in front of me and stopped and got out of his car. As he approached, I rolled the window down and and he said "Merry Christmas," as he shook hands all around before heading off. – Keith Menzies

Ray Ottenbreit

Generations

When I first started working at the mill in the early days, which is pretty typical of being a smaller town, the guys used to kid each other because they were either a Welder, a Redlick, a Rasky, or a Bouvette, because between these families there used to be about 30 or 40 of them [working there] including their wives and girlfriends and everyone else. I worked with a grandpa, a son, with a grand-son, and a great-grandson before I left. – Ray Ottenbreit

🔺 🔺 🔺

129

The mill was a great place to work in the summer and the sons of the supervisory staff often got hired on. The money wasn't bad and at some point, most of them talked about quitting school. There are a number of stories, but they all sound more or less the same.

I was thinking of quitting school and my dad said he could get me a job at the mill. I thought this sounded easy, so I agreed. What I didn't know was that he went to the foreman and said if they had a job that was messy or unpleasant and they didn't know who to give it to, then get my son to do it. It cured me very quickly, as I ended up working night shift that summer and cleaning out conveyor belts and working at some of the most boring jobs possible. Then I went back to university. – Dale Gregory

Dale Gregory and his mother, Sadie Gregory

In and around the mill

Log booms were towed in by the *Manhattan* or brought in by truck and dumped in the lake at the east end of Simpson's booming grounds. Don Poole had driven a lot of piles into the lake in 1947, forming a sorting circle and five pockets – there would be different species in each pocket. One day, Mr. Simpson came down to the sorting circle where we were sorting logs and just watched us sorting. Some of the logs that came in from the West Side [of Okanagan Lake] were long logs and had to be cut. One of his best ideas was that the logs should be high-graded into peeler logs or saw logs. The peeler logs were sent to the plywood plant and the saw logs were sent down a race-way, where they floated toward the sorting circle. This was a real good idea.

Another time, Mr. Simpson came right into where I was operating this 84" saw and asked if it would be too much trouble to have counters to get some record of how many logs of each species was coming into the plant. We started with three counters. These was the second time Mr. Simpson and I ever had a lengthy talk. From this bucking plant and sorting circle a lot of other improvements were made. – Arthur Marty

🌲 🌲 🌲

The last summer I worked at the mill – 1956 – I had broken my wrist so I couldn't work in the box factory as I had done other summers. I could drive a truck, so I was given the job of taking sawdust from the mill out to the yard and dumping it in a hopper to stockpile it. The hopper had a very steep ramp that you had to gun the truck up and then stop the truck very quickly once it dropped over the chocks before you hit the front bumpers and bounced back over the chocks. If you did that, you slid all the way down the ramp and had to start over.

When you were backing down the ramp, you had to back down blind. To overcome this there was a mark on the steering wheel that you set at a particular angle in order to back down straight. On one occasion, I did this and backed over the side and almost turned the truck over. It turned out that the steering linkage had broken. Sawdust was everywhere and I got so much of it down my cast that it almost drove me crazy. – Dale Gregory

🌲 🌲 🌲

S. M. was brought up to make do with what was available and not waste anything, but when the mill was sold, the new owners brought in a bunch of efficiency experts and if they didn't need it any more, they just knocked it down or blew it up. They brought in Fred Kitsch one Saturday morning and took nine sticks of dynamite and some grease and blew up the wharf. He did such a good job, not even one dead fish came up to the surface. – Unknown

🌲 🌲 🌲

130

There was a suggestion or idea box that was available to anyone who had an idea how to make a piece of equipment work better. Everything was considered and if changes were made as a result of the suggestion, the person who made it was given 10 per cent of the savings that resulted. Sometimes this ended up to be quite a lot of money, and lots of guys suggested changes. – Ray Ottenbreit

♣ ♣ ♣

When we were thinking of starting up a plywood plant we knew we would have to use spruce although almost all mills at the time were using fir. The problem with spruce was the glue bond. We talked with Monsanto and sent some spruce blocks to a Vancouver plywood plant for peeling and testing, and Monsanto was able to develop a specific glue formula to suit the fibre characteristics of spruce. From the knowledge we had gained in the veneer plant, we knew that in order to achieve a smooth veneer from the lathe, the blocks would have to be heated by steam or immersed in hot water prior to peeling. Otherwise, the grain distortion around the knots would create voids and cause a problem in glue bonding. – Horace Simpson's notes

♣ ♣ ♣

Lumber Carrier (straddle truck)

When the first glue used to get shipped up to the plywood plant, a rubber container [filled with glue] would be strapped onto a flat bed and if the weather was fine, unloading would be relatively easy. But if the weather was cold, the glue would gel and have to be heated with steam to liquefy before being poured out of the rubber tube. Often, it was too difficult to remove it and a lot would be left inside. – Ray Ottenbreit

♣ ♣ ♣

When a new lumber carrier would arrive, there was almost a ceremony to hand it over. The old ones had a lifting bracket on the bottom that was run by hydraulics, and if the lumber wasn't stacked perfectly, the brackets that were shaped like two Ls facing each other would bang shut and then bang back open. Sometimes it would only catch part of the load and would leave a trail of lumber strewn all over the road behind it. – Ray Ottenbreit

♣ ♣ ♣

I started working at the Simpson mill in March of 1942. My first job was as a tail sawyer and the buzz lasted in my ears for two or three days, even when I wasn't on the job. Then I rode the saw carriage as the dogger for a month or two before moving down to the jack ladder, where I had to keep feeding the logs onto the winch to be hauled up into the mill. I remember how some of the edgings were saved to make cleats for the box tops and the 2" slabs were made into laths, and the other waste went over to the power plant for fuel for the boilers. Some of the better logs were sent to the veneer plant. I think of all the jobs that were created. It's sure different today. – Arthur Marty

♣ ♣ ♣

When I returned from the war in '46, I went back to the mill and my first job was to unload two box cars of yellow pine – 2" x 6"s, 2" x 8"s, 2" x 10"s, and 2" x 12"s – I thought my arms would fall off. My next job was in the mill yard with Jack Colton, where they were hauling shale from the foot of Knox Mountain. They were putting about 12" of shale all over that yard and about every 100 feet, clay tile to drain the yard. Then big pieces of slate would be dumped in the yard and we were

131

supposed to try and break it up with a big hammer. Mr. Simpson was never afraid of hard work and would take that big hammer, stand there and study that rock for a minute, and hammer away at it. Chips of rock didn't bother him or his glasses. He would lend a hand at anything. – Arthur Marty

⚇ ⚇ ⚇

I started in the box factory in 1934, and aside from a year in the army during the war, I worked for the company until 1980, when I retired. An extra shift was added to the mill, so I got a chance to become a helper saw filer working with Joe Marty, who was the head filer. It was his job to look after the large band saw used for cutting the logs, as well as oversee the helpers. The number of saws to be sharpened daily were 28 gang saws, six edger saws, 12 cleat saws, 10 lathe saws, plus one to two slasher and trim saws per week. So we were busy all day. Joe Marty left to go to Midway and was replaced by Omar Gravelle, who got sick after a few years and was replaced by Roy Hawkes. Both these filers came from the large mill at New Westminster – Fraser Mills. I was fortunate to train under experienced filers such as these. In the early '50s, Ray left and Horace asked if I would like the head saw-filer's position. I said yes and was the head saw filer 'til retiring in 1980. – Leonard Campbell

⚇ ⚇ ⚇

In the saw-filing room, there was an automatic band saw sharpener. Normally, the band saws were changed every four hours, oftener if they hit rocks or dirt in the logs. It took about one hour to sharpen these saws. Every so often, these saws were taken to a levelling bench to be re-tensioned and the lumps taken out of the blades. *Len Campbell* About 14 at a time were changed every four hours. They also had to be levelled and tensioned at a separate bench. Then we had a post grinder for the circular blades. It was used to keep the circular saws round and to keep the tooth gullets at the proper depth. We also had an acetylene welding torch to weld cracks on the band saws or to replace broken teeth on the bands when they hit a nail in the logs. – Leonard Campbell

⚇ ⚇ ⚇

S. M. started up the old veneer plant so he could make strawberry crates and raspberry crates to go into competition with the ones coming up from the Coast. The lathe operation in the veneer plant used to bring the log up out of the lake and they took a chainsaw and cut it to the length they wanted, which was usually about four or five feet. Then they put two hooks on it with a chain attached and they lifted it up – they had one of those little electric motors and you pulled it by hand – and dropped it down on the lathe. They had two spindles that they brought in on the sides, which would hold it on the lathe. Then they'd start turning it and they had a great big arm – it was probably five feet long – and it had little claws on it and that was the barker. A guy used to lean on it – sometimes the logs were so big and the bark was so rough that this guy would be sitting on there with all his weight riding it, going back and forth trying to knock all this bark off. In a lot of cases, they couldn't get it all off but it was enough to get the rocks and stuff off so they didn't hurt the knife too much.

⚇ ⚇ ⚇

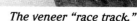
The veneer "race track."

I worked for three or four months on the veneer section because they always wanted the younger guys that could run. When the lathe operator turned the log to get a sheet of veneer coming off, two guys used to grab it – one on either side – and then we'd run 40 or 50 feet. At the other end, there'd be another two guys and they would hit it with their hands to break the sheet and then it would drop to the floor. Meanwhile, two other guys would grab the next sheet coming off the lathe, and then we'd run back to grab the next sheet. When the logs were being barked, you'd have your break but we used to always be laughing and you'd have to wear your running shoes to be on the race track. Then the veneer would be steamed a bit before the gals would cut it or bend it to make the tintops. – Ray Ottenbreit

Dan Hill and his treasure house. If you were sent down to the shed for some piece of discarded equipment or a piece of scrap, you had better return with it because Dan knew exactly what was there.

Sawdust and box cuttings

S. M. Simpson Ltd. produced massive amounts of shaving, edgings, sawdust, and box ends, which most sawmills disposed of in beehive burners that spewed cinders and dark, heavy smoke over neighbouring towns. Stan filled swamps all over Kelowna with sawdust before he began to sell it – along with box cuttings – for fuel. Slabs, created when a round log was squared before being cut into boards, were sent to the box factory and used for making lath, as well as to fire up the boilers in the mill's power house. It wasn't until the early '60s that these sawmill by-products truly became waste and were dumped into a perpetual fire on the side of Knox Mountain.

Both Stan and Horace – and most other people in town – heated their homes with sawdust, and Horace kept track of every load delivered into his basement sawdust bin. Was it dry or wet? Fir or spruce? Did it

The Kelowna Courier, *May 14, 1953*

The Kelowna Courier, *April 13, 1951*

burn well or not? Sometimes it jammed in the hopper and had to be loosened by shoving an ever-handy stick down into the plugged-up mass. Other times the sawdust smothered the flames and had to be cleaned out and the fire relit again. The whole hopper could even catch on fire. Because it was such a significant part of Simpson's business, many stories remain, including those about collapsing sawdust piles and men getting trapped by a wall of cascading sawdust.

I remember working on the sawdust trucks as a kid and we'd usually have to start about 7:30 in the morning. We'd get there about 7 to go through all the orders for sawdust because some of them were the pits to fill and you'd never wanted a bad one. If you delivered to the restaurants, they used to give you a piece of pie or something like that. There was a lady that used to live at the corner of Ethel and Harvey, and any time you took a load of sawdust to her you had to come in and have a glass of wine. You used to always be looking for that order when you went through the pile of them. – Ray Ottenbreit

🌲 🌲 🌲

I can remember one time this fellow came into the office with a gunny sack over his shoulder and he emptied it all out and yelled, "You call this fuel?!" I can still remember this great big, frozen lump of wet sawdust. – Evelyn Radomski

🌲 🌲 🌲

We used to live on the corner of Harvey Avenue and Water Street, and there used to be a three-story apartment building across the street from us. The winter of '49 was so cold I can still remember sawdust trucks pulling up to that building three or four times a day to make sure they could keep their furnace going. The lake was frozen and they couldn't keep the mill open, so they had to go to Lumby to get the sawdust. – Hillas Francis

Christmas turkeys

Horace and some of the mill supervisors would deliver turkeys to the employees on Christmas Eve. There was a ritual to the occasion, as they were usually invited in for a chat and a bit of 'Christmas cheer.' They drove from house to house throughout the evening, visiting and drinking, and eventually arrived back home long after Santa had filled their kids' stockings. They had to drive because they had had far too much Christmas cheer to walk. – Various sources

🌲 🌲 🌲

We really appreciated the turkeys given to us. Times were tough and the turkeys sure helped to make Christmas happy times. The Christmas parties with famous people entertaining were also appreciated. – Min Mori

🌲 🌲 🌲

I was the union plant chairman at the plywood plant for probably 30 years and I remember I was on the picket line – we were on strike against all the lumber companies that were part of that lumber association [the ILMA]. It was the day before Christmas and S. M. comes driving down the picket line with his car and he had it all full of turkeys in the back, and he came up and he shook hands with every guy on the picket line and gave us all a turkey. I'll never forget that because we were on strike against him at the time. Turkeys eventually became vouchers that could be turned in at the grocery stores. – Ray Ottenbreit

The loggers and their camps

When we bought McLean sawmills at Malakawa, just north of Sicamous, all the logging was done by contract. The first thing the loggers wanted to see was a written contract. They couldn't believe

134

it when we told them that we didn't have written agreements, so we gave them the names of the contractors that had been successful working for us so they could talk to them. They did and we continued working that way. I think that was a great period in our history and a great way of operating.
– Horace Simpson's notes

🌲 🌲 🌲

Charlie Stuart was my mentor at Simpson's. He was an imposing presence with his large craggy face, big broad shoulders, and a belly to match. You couldn't miss him. Beneath his rather gruff, old-time logger persona, however, was pure gold. An astute, honest, thoroughly decent man whose integrity was of the highest standard and whose common sense was the best I'd ever seen, then and now. Stan Simpson used to entrust Charlie with large sums of cash with which to buy logs. I've heard that one such amount was $30,000, which was a pretty substantial amount given that Charlie was likely earning about $4,000 a year at the time. – David Jeffrey

David Jeffrey (third from the left) and Charlie Stuart (third from the right).

🌲 🌲 🌲

In the mid-'50s, Saturday was a regular working day. The loggers (mainly contractors and truck owners) used to come into the office to shoot the breeze and negotiate with Charlie. He would stand behind a large counter that served as his desk, and with his elbow resting on the top, appeared to be relaxed as he listened to their stories. The conversations took the same pattern: lots of general chat and laughter and then, when the logger felt at ease, a few minutes of intense negotiating. With his eyes half closed, Charlie would listen intently, concentrating on the conversation, and everyone knew it was foolish and futile to be less than frank with Charlie. Many thousands of Simpson's dollars were guaranteed by Charlie at these Saturday sessions – no contracts, no formal handshakes, no witnesses – just Charlie's simple "yes." It was amazing to behold. – David Jeffrey

🌲 🌲 🌲

In the early days, all the wood was high-graded. If there was a knot the size of your fingernail in the box end, it would be chucked out. With the big trees, we'd cut them up to the branches because all we wanted was straight and clear [wood]. Even if there was another ten to twelve feet that was good, we'd leave it. – Don Sandburg

🌲 🌲 🌲

Andy Gaspardone scaled the logs on the trucks until they built the log cut-up and he could scale them in the yard. Andy lived not far from the mill, and if the loaded trucks came in after 5:00 they went over to his house so he could scale them there and then they could be unloaded. Well, one day Billy

Schneider came in and parked his truck on Roanoke Street, near Gaspardone's house and waited for a while for Andy to come out of his house. When he got tired of waiting, he went to the door and was met by Mrs. Gaspardone. Billy said he was waiting for Andy to come out and scale his load, and was told he would have to wait until Andy finished his supper. Billy didn't like that idea and the talk got kind of hot, and that carried on for awhile until Mrs. Gaspardone got so fed up she called Mr. Simpson to come down and sort the mess out. I think scaling on the street stopped after that. – Arthur Marty

🌲 🌲 🌲

When the plywood plant started up in '57, the plant managers set the specifications of the logs they needed – minimum diameter, preferred lengths, restricted defects, and so on. I was to communicate these new requirements to the loggers. After spending a few days watching the plywood operation, I set off to talk to the loggers. My first day I spent with O&R Sandberg and Peterson Logging, who were working in the Bear Creek area. I though everyone understood what was needed but went back to check a few days later. Peterson was not a happy camper, and told me, "We need more money if we're manufacturing logs for the plywood plant." We went to the job site so he could show me the problem. Peterson had taken it upon himself to describe the logs destined for the plywood plant as *peeled* logs and two of his crew had spent all afternoon chipping the bark off six or seven logs destined for the plywood plant using an axe and hand turning each log with a peavey. No wonder Peterson thought there was no money to be made in plywood logs. – David Jeffrey

'Bunny' Wills' 1941 International

🌲 🌲 🌲

Mike Paly was working at the input end of the jack ladder. I was on sales and the prices for Douglas fir were very good, so I wanted to book all I could but did not want to oversell, as my customers would be extremely upset. The mill was cutting fir and I asked both Vic Gregory and Dick Hartwick how much longer the logs would last. They both gave me answers that were probably pretty accurate, but I've since forgotten them. I went to look at the boom myself and watched Mike with his pike pole feeding the logs up the jack ladder so I asked him what he thought. He looked out at the remaining logs and said, "Fir logs will last to about 3:00 tomorrow afternoon." I remember that they lasted to within half an hour of his estimation. I booked the orders and we filled them exactly. – Bill Greenwood

🌲 🌲 🌲

Jack Seaton's camp was in the valley bottom and they logged several thousand feet up the valley sides. Access to the logging was by way of steep, narrow roads with tight switchbacks. Going up in winter was especially tricky because snow and ice made the roads so treacherous. I admired the skill and courage of the logging truck drivers as they inched fully loaded trucks down those bobsled runs. Bunny Wills, one of the drivers, was frequently – by his own admission – in a cold sweat by the time he reached the valley bottom during winter logging. And he made three round trips a day. Like many of the other truck drivers, Bunny was an owner/operator and he had a huge bank loan to deal with and felt he had to keep going because his family depended on him. – David Jeffrey

🌲 🌲 🌲

It was a real treat to stay at Jack Seaton's camp at Whiteman's Creek. It was a great set-up. Portable generators supplied the camp with electricity. Everyone slept in warm huts, four to a building. I particularly remember the cookhouse. There were about 40 men in camp, and we ate our meals at two long tables in the cookhouse. The food was great – all you could possibly want. What was weird was that aside from "pass the potatoes or pass the steaks," we all ate in silence. Like monks in a monastery. Jack was an old army guy and didn't want the possibility of tired and maybe frustrated men getting into an argument at meal times and risking havoc in the cookhouse. If you had a beef, you had to save it 'til later. – David Jeffrey

136

Jack Seaton's logging camp. (Bob Murdin photo)

At times, the camps were plagued by hungry bears hanging around the cookhouse looking for scraps. On one occasion, Billy Schneider, a logging contractor, decided to shoot a bear in the hopes of scaring off the others. After supper, a number of loggers gathered at the bottom of a shale slide behind the cookhouse to watch Billy do his stuff. A black bear appeared at the top of the ridge and Billy took a quick shot. The animal fell wounded, then curled in a ball, rolled down the slope right into the group of loggers. It was like a scene in a bowling alley. Yelling men scattering in every direction while Billy kept his cool – after all, he had the gun – and all he had to do was wait for the opportune time to dispatch the poor bear. – David Jeffrey

When we were up timber cruising, life in the camps was pretty basic. Sometimes we slept in tents and other times we luxuriated in small shacks. After the evening meal there wasn't much to do. You dried out your clothing as best possible, chatted with your colleagues, read a book by the dim light of a Coleman lamp, or listened to CKOV on the portable radio. Earl Murdin, one of the bulldozer drivers,

Coffee break. From the left: Charlie Stuart, Janet Power, Bill Greenwood, Len Smith, Norma Morrison, Fred Kitsch, Ian Dunlop, David Jeffrey, Harry Chaplin. (Bill Greenwood photo)

stayed in camp while building roads for future logging operations and he used to enjoy going out in the evening and building roads on his own time. The 'dozer headlights and, if you were lucky, the moonlight, were all the light available. This was strictly voluntary. No one got paid any overtime, as we were all on monthly salary. No one talked about this outside the camp. It might have been therapeutic for the guy driving the machine, but for those of us trying to get some sleep, it sure wasn't. – David Jeffrey

I had just arrived in Kelowna from Scotland, and Alan Moss was explaining my duties as the new forester on the job when he suddenly stopped and asked if I played cricket. When I answered that I did, he seemed relieved: "Great! There is a Vancouver touring team playing in Kelowna this afternoon and we're a man short, so you're on the team" I thought, "Wow, Simpson's is sure a great place to work." Alan was a real professional and a great organizer. What was even more amazing was that he followed his plan to the letter. Alan was the first forester in the Interior to recognize the value of aerial photography in the practice of good forest management, and had the entire 200,000 acres of TFL #9 photographed in 1954. These photos were an invaluable tool in our daily operations. – David Jeffrey

Alan Moss

When the first load of bulk bins went out, we weren't sure what the orchardists wanted. And then they all came back because they had tiny knot holes in them the size of a fingernail, which would bruise the fruit. So we had to upgrade our veneer but in the meantime we had all these boxes and we had to patch the knot holes, so we went all over town buying putty and putty knives and we got all the crew together and we patched 24 hours a day. Once we finished one lot, we'd send it back and get another. – Bob Bain

The plywood foremen 1959-1961: Jack Duckworth, Bob Bain, and Len Rivold.
(Bob Christie photo)

Selling the wood

Terry Greenwood arrived in Kelowna in 1936 or '37 from Saskatchewan, where he had worked in the lumber industry. He and Stan were a good pair as he knew about selling lumber and Stan knew about producing it – and neither of them talked very much. When he retired just before S. M. Simpson Ltd was sold, Terry said he had enjoyed working for the company, though he hadn't always agreed with the decisions made by management. Bill, Terry's son, began working for Simpson's full-time in 1951.

During the 50's, the company was shipping to lumber brokers in Vancouver, Edmonton, and Detroit, Michigan. Then one of the brokers wintered in Florida and found buyers for Simpson's lumber there. As the American housing market expanded, wholesalers were desperate to supply their markets and would come through the area in a steady stream looking for every tiny little mill they could buy from. It wasn't expensive at this time to get into the lumber business, but the mill owners still had to pay for the logs and then their payroll before they even began shipping, so the wholesaler or rep calling on the smaller mills would make them a loan and the mill became obligated to them. Soon, the wholesaler was telling the mill what to cut, which may not have been the best for the mill, but by that time, they didn't have much choice. – Bill Greenwood

♣ ♣ ♣

Terry had to be a bit of a gambler, but he read the papers. If it was a bad winter in Prince George, there might be a shortage of logs. If it was a wet spring, prices would go up, while rising interest rates impacted housing markets. He'd read the wholesalers' ads in the newspapers and trade journals to see what they were looking for, and he had to know who wanted what. – Bill Greenwood

♣ ♣ ♣

85 per cent of Simpson's production was going to the U.S. before the company was sold. But the Prairies wanted green fir, and though they would accept dry they wouldn't pay more for it, even with the U.S. paying $10 extra for dry fir. The best money was in spruce boards sent to the U.S. Midwest – Michigan and Iowa. Before the plywood plant went in in 1957, logs weren't sorted for grade. Since plywood needed good big logs, the sawmill often got left with some inferior stuff. Simpson's had dry kilns early on, which enabled them to compete in markets that wouldn't otherwise have been available. They could also ship in the winter when lumber couldn't air dry. In summer, the lumber could dry in anywhere between four days and two weeks, but if it dried too fast it would be hard on the outside but still green inside, which caused splitting, twisting, and the knots to fall out. If it was dried in a kiln, the heat and steam would dry it slowly ensuring straight, good-quality lumber. – Bill Greenwood

♣ ♣ ♣

Terry had to tell the mill what the market needed – 2" x 10"s were a perennial favourite. They were great for flooring when houses were smaller, but 2" x 10"s and 2" x 14"s were the most popular – the wider the width, the greater the premium. Logs were bigger then and the sawyer didn't have the high-tech lasers to do his work for him. He would eyeball the log, decide how to put it on the carriage, and cut what the market needed. Terry also knew that just because you had a product didn't mean you could sell it, and sometimes he had to hustle to sell what the mill was producing. Today's market is far more standardized than it used to be then. – Bill Greenwood

⚓ ⚓ ⚓

The mill produced a lot of lath and a couple of guys would sit in a dark corner – like the Dark Ages – putting it into bundles of 50. These were pre-gyprock and drywall days when houses were finished with lath and plaster. It was also used in surveying and for snow fences. Simpson's shipped truckloads of lath across the U.S. border, and one day a call came into the office from one of the truck drivers who had run into a new customs guy who was green behind the ears. He was insisting that each product going into the U.S. had to be stamped with its country of origin – Made in Canada.

The truck was loaded with thousands of pieces of lath and it was just before a long weekend, so we told the guy to stay put, had Len Leathley at Kelowna Printers make up a stamp with "Canada" on it and hoped it would be okay, and rushed it down to the waiting trucker. He spent the next several hours stamping the end of thousands and thousands of pieces of lath with "Canada" before he could proceed. Any time another truck when through that same checkpoint, we had to make sure each piece was stamped. – Bill Greenwood

The tugs

I think the *Stanley M* was built in New Westminster and shipped via the Kettle Valley Railway to Penticton, and Fred Kitsch went down to pick it up. It was shipped up in two parts and the CPR crane and crew were supposed to get it in the water. Then they needed a man to splice together a couple of slings, and of course, he had to be called out. I can see Fred walking up and down that wharf, and he had smoke coming out his ears. Finally they got the hull in the water and then lifted the cabin on top of it. Then the steering and hydraulic line to the rudder. It took Fred about seven hours to run it up the lake.

The tug was parked at the wharf beside Sutherland Park for a while, then it was moved nearer the mill so the woodwork in the cabin could be done. Dan Hill had some cement put into the hull for ballast, but then it was discovered that the tug had been lying on a sunken log and that's why it hadn't been sitting in the water properly. By that time, it was too late to take the cement out so they just left it that way. That put the bow down so low in the water that it made the steering real bad. The *Stanley M* is still in use but the hull has been changed and the cement removed. The original D7 Caterpillar engine has also been changed. – Arthur Marty

⚓ ⚓ ⚓

This is a story from about 1947, when Kay Kawahara (who used to work at the Kelowna Saw Mill and seemed to know the lake like the back of his hand) and I were up at Whiteman's Creek. I took off from the mill about 7:00 a.m., picked up 41 boom sticks, and headed straight up the lake, watching the weather as we went. If the weather was not good, we would stay on the west side, point-to-point. We would get up to Whiteman's log dump about 2 or 2:30 p.m., open up the guard boom, and round up the logs with our boom sticks and take out what we thought was 200,000 board feet of logs. Then we'd close up the guard boom and shape the logs by spreading them out and putting rope across the logs, every two or three boom sticks. We would push this mass of logs onto the shore and tie them up, and then we would start pulling all the logs beside each other until our raft was about 50 feet wide. Then we would put a rope across each boom stick. We would have about 20 boom sticks, and we made it narrow at the front end and that's where we attached the tow rope.

139

This afternoon, we had put the mass of logs on the shore and started rafting until dark and I thought we would leave the tug tied to the boom. We had gone to bed and during the night, the wind started to blow from the north and the tug was rocking to the point that old Kay couldn't sleep, so he woke me up and suggested we go across the lake to get out of the wind. By this time, it was dark out and while I started the D6 engine down below, Kay untied the bow line and the stern line and was supposed to come back near me at the wheel. I started out with the cabin light still on but Kay was not at my side by the time I had pulled away from the boom at about half throttle, and I was wondering where he was – I though he had gone over-board. I stood there wondering what to do. I had put the cabin light out to see where I was going when I turned my head to the stern deck and there, at my side, was Kay. I just about kissed him right there and then, as I thought for sure I had lost him in the lake in the dark! – Arthur Marty

▲ ▲ ▲

They used to use the tugs to break up the ice in the lake when we had really cold winters. The tugs – the big one and the other little one that ran around pushing logs – and they used to drive them back and forth in order to keep the booms open. I think it was '51 or '52 when the lake froze. They even went so far as to have the powder man who worked up in the hills with the guys who did the roadwork come down and blow the ice up every once in a while so they could get the logs to the mill. – Ray Ottenbreit

▲ ▲ ▲

My worst tug boat story – this was about 1953 or '54, and a real cold day. Sigge Kawahara and Bill Nikon went up to Chaplin Bay to tow a boom down to the mill. They should have seen the clouds moving in, but they got the boom out, tied up the guard boom, and then hooked the cable onto the boom. Coming around Rocky Point at the south end of the booming ground was bad enough, and then out in open water and the waves were pretty bad and then sometimes there was a current to boot. They had gone out a fair distance when the boom stick broke, and trying to get it back together again was something else. By this time, they had drifted farther out into open water. They had nicely got towing again and the boom stick, or maybe it was the boom chain, broke again. The boom was pretty well out into the middle of the lake by this time but they managed to get it back together and on the tow line. Then it broke for a third time.

Arthur Marty

Jim Carpentier came over to the sorting circle and asked me to get the Manhattan tug started and go out and give them a hand. The Manhattan had been tied up and drained for the winter, so I put all the drain plugs back in the motor and tried to start it by using the starting motor, and that took some time. I finally got it started and headed out on my own, though I didn't know how I would be able to manage putting a tow line on the boom chain when everything would be moving up and down. Well, I went out toward Kidson's house and the waves out in the open water were pretty high, and I noticed the boat seemed to be wallowing in the water, so I looked down to the floor near the motor and saw there was water everywhere. I opened the trap door just behind me at the wheel and I had forgotten a half-inch plug where the water was supposed to go out the side of the hull, so in fact, the water was being pumped into the hull. I ran the boat around the south end of the guard boom and luckily I had a barrel pump to pump the water out. By this time, the wind had gone down, and Shigge and Bill were well on their way back to the mill. I was pretty mad about it all. – Arthur Marty

▲ ▲ ▲

The new plywood needed Canadian Standards Association (CSA) approval before the finished product could be used in home construction, and since the samples had to be randomly taken off the production line, the company could either shut down and wait for approval or continue operating and hope for the best. Not wanting to lose valuable time, production continued and when the approvals finally came, over 30 carloads of plywood had to be unstacked and each piece individually stamped CSA/CMHC Approved.

Mike Paly's map for Charlie Stuart

When I started at the mill, I was about 14 years old and I worked on school holidays. Likely at S. M.'s instructions, I did some of almost every job there was to do, I had been a shipper, a truck loader, and a driver by the time I was 17. I'm quite sure no favours were accorded me, and the worst thing I could do when asked a question by my father was to guess the answer. I learned most aspects of the business by doing jobs myself rather than watching others do them. I rose through most jobs as plant superintendent, manager, manager and vice president, to President and CEO and Chairman of the Board. – Horace Simpson's notes

H. B. Simpson

Epilogue

If Stan Simpson were somehow able to return to Kelowna more than four decades after his death, he would recognize his old Manhattan Beach property where Riverside Forest Products now runs a stud mill, chip operation, and plywood plant. His namesake, the tug *Stanley M*, continues to haul log booms up and down the lake, and while those booms and the plywood plant are still in their original location, little else would be familiar. He would be surprised at how few men were working in the stud mill that replaced his veneer plant and box factory, and wonder why they were encased in a glass booth, pushing buttons on a curious-looking keyboard. The red laser beam scanning the log that had just been hauled up from the lake on a new version of the old jack ladder would catch his attention, and he would watch with some amazement as an automatic saw cut the log into random lengths and carried them away on conveyor belts. The degree of mechanization, the noise, and speed of the operation that could produce so much lumber with so few people would astound him. Stan had been innovative, but he would never have imagined his sawmill could change so dramatically.

Both Kelowna and the Okanagan Valley have also grown significantly since Stan and his company disappeared over 40 years ago. With the influx of newcomers, the community has no collective memory of its early days nor of the individuals and businesses that made it what it is today.

Arriving in 1913 when Kelowna's population was about 1,800, Stan created a company, started a family, and survived two world wars and the Great Depression. His one-man operation grew to become the largest year-round employer in the Valley, and a leader in its field. S. M. was recognized for his generosity to his adopted home town and publicly honoured by being made Freeman of the City, and he continues to have a quiet presence in Kelowna today. The boardwalk at Waterfront Park is The Simpson Walk and a plaque explains his involvement in the community. A small park on the corner of Water Street and Doyle Avenue tells of Stan's generosity in selling the civic centre property to the city for a "very reasonable consideration." At the summit of nearby Knox Mountain, a new Pioneer Pavilion, substantially funded by a trust fund established by S. M. upon his death, replaces the previous Stanley M. Simpson Nature Pavilion and acknowledges Stan as one of the area's pioneers.

S. M. was a quiet, unassuming, gentle man who wouldn't have expected the city to acknowledge him or his gifts, but the plaques and storyboards give area residents an important glimpse of earlier times and the people who helped make Kelowna what it is today.

Boards, Boxes, and Bins – Stanley M. Simpson and the Okanagan Lumber Industry offers some insight into the Valley's history through the story of Stan Simpson and the business he created. Changes in the community and the lumber industry provide a backdrop for S. M.'s life, and in doing so tell part of the story of how Kelowna grew into the bustling, optimistic city it is today. Those wanting to learn more about the Okanagan will hopefully be inspired by this book to search out additional information, and doing so, decide to write about their own families and their unique stories.

*Manhattan Beach and Kelowna"s north end –
Circa 1970.*

Endnotes

INTRODUCTION

1 The conveyor for carrying boards from the saw mill to the yard for sorting and stacking.

CHAPTER ONE

1 Unpublished Simpson family correspondence.

2 The origins of the United Empire Loyalists (UEL) date back to 1775, when Britain attempted to tax and control its American colonies. Two groups emerged after protests broke out: those who objected to British interference and wanted their independence, and those who remained faithful to the Crown and wished to remain in the New World. About 50,000 people who chose the latter option fled across the border into Quebec, Ontario, and Nova Scotia, leaving their land and most of their possessions behind. They struggled to survive in an inhospitable isolated wilderness, and those who survived did so because of their determination, resourcefulness, and hard work in appallingly difficult circumstances.

3 Unpublished Simpson family files.

4 A quart of whiskey was cheaper than a quart of milk at the end of the 1800s, and often easier to come by. The Women's Christian Temperance Union actively lobbied in the Owen Sound area against the evils of drinking and its potentially ruinous impact upon the family.

5 The fire burned for two days – April 19 and 20, 1904 – before finally being extinguished.

6 Stan was young and new to the big city ways of doing business, but he learned quickly and as he did, his earnings increased. Job advertisements in *The Toronto Star* of the day noted that some contractors would pay $12 a week, while a waitress earned $5 a week and a "plain cook" $20 a month. An office assistant was paid $15 a month, and labourers who would enlarge a cellar were offered $1 a day. The ads told as much about the times as they did about wage rates. Servants were in great demand, especially those who would accompany a family to the cottage for the summer. Boys between 14 and 17 were needed for factory work, a restaurant was trying to hire 26 coloured cooks and waiters, a smart boy with a bicycle, and three active men to act as liquor detectives were required at once.

7 Locals joked that the requirements really meant that the government was betting $10 that the new homesteader couldn't live on the land for six months in each of three years, and make improvements without starving to death. *Gleanings Along the Way*, p. 325.

8 Little is known about Vern's 30-plus years as a Prairie farmer but there is little doubt that his was a harsh and in that he never married, lonely life. Vern stayed on his homestead throughout the Dirty '30s and finally joined his family in Kelowna in the early '40s.

9 Stories of those who settled the Prairies and lived through the hardships have been captured by Barry Broadfoot in his book *The Pioneer Years 1895 - 1914: Memories of Settlers Who Opened The West*.

10 Homestead documents, Unpublished Simpson family files.

11 Barry Broadfoot, *The Pioneer Years*.

CHAPTER TWO

1 *The Penticton Herald*, December 23, 1911.

2 Ibid., July 19, 1913.

3 Okanagan Telephone Company Directory, March 1916.

4 *The Penticton Herald*, October 21, 1937.

5 The Jubilee Edition of *The Kelowna Courier*, May 5, 1955. From 1908 City Council meeting.

6 Ibid.

7 *Courier* advertisements from 1913 offer a snapshot of the various activities going on in town. Veterinary surgeons, lawyers, and in the English tradition, both barristers and solicitors were available, as were civil engineers, architects, land surveyors, chartered accountants, undertakers and embalmers, real estate, insurance and loan companies, harness makers and jewellers. S. M. advertised extensively in the Courier, and the ads provide insight into the evolution of his business.

8 *The Kelowna Daily Courier*, through various incarnations, has been in continuous publication for over 100 years.

9 British remittance men – usually the second or the ne'er-do-well sons – headed to the colonies between 1880 and 1914 by the thousands, often arriving with tea sets, tennis rackets, tweed suits, rugs, and portable bath tubs for a life they were totally unprepared for. As they tried to recreate the aura of the landed gentry they left behind, they added a degree of sophistication and culture to the remote communities of the West. With the outbreak of World War I, many simply walked away from their shacks dotted all over the Valley's hillsides, returned to Britain and never came back to Canada.

10 *The Kelowna Courier and Okanagan Orchardist*, January 23, 1913.

11 By 1913, three large, well-established land development companies were aggressively marketing their acreages, 31 fruit ranchers had crops to sell, and two canneries and three packinghouses were processing all the locally grown fruits and vegetables available. The initial capital investment had paid off, and accomplished much more that just get the orchard industry on its feet.

12 The SS *Aberdeen* was in service from May 1893 until 1907, when it was replaced by the SS *Okanagan*, which was subsequently dismantled about 1938. The most luxurious of the Okanagan's sternwheelers was the SS *Sicamous*, which was launched in 1914 and tied up in 1936; the boat is back in service in Penticton.

13 Lequime had a number of other business interests in addition to the sawmill and general store, including a large cattle ranch, but he was also involved in developing the Kelowna town site and named its main thoroughfare, Bernard Avenue, after himself.

14 *The Kelowna Courier*, December 17, 1942.

15 Chutes could be several miles long and were usually made from long, large poles lashed together to form a

concave trough. Logs would be loaded into the chute and given a shove to start them down the hill. By the time they would hit the lake, they would be going in excess of 95 km/h and trailing a plume of smoke. A man would be posted beside a flume if it crossed a road, sometimes with a bugle, to warn travellers of the danger posed by the speeding logs.

16 Which curiously had a meat safe for sale that Stan had probably taken in lieu of cash from another customer.

17 The Frasers' small cannery was among the first in town to preserve fruit delivered by sternwheeler to the CPR wharf, only a short block away from their Abbott Street factory. Japanese farmers in the area also grew large quantities of tomatoes, loaded them into horse-drawn carts, and hauled them to the cannery where pigtailed Chinese men peeled and processed them in two, five, and ten pounds cans for shipment to Kettle Valley Railway construction camps. Tins of the Frasers' "Okanagan Brand" and "Standard of the Empire" tomatoes, packed in the small Abbott Street cannery, were also a common sight on cookhouse shelves in the Kootenay mining camps. The cannery, which was renamed Western Canners Ltd., fell into receivership in 1923 and went out of business.

18 Many years later, Horace Simpson recounted that "about ten years after moving into this building it was necessary to check and repair the foundation. Amongst all the debris under the floor, two cases of canned peaches were found. They must have gone through the floor during the fire. The cans had very little rust on them and the peaches were found to be in excellent condition, however my mother decided we shouldn't sample, let alone eat them." Unpublished Simpson family files.

19 *The Kelowna Courier and Orchardist*, October 23, 1913.

20 Little is known of the John Birch family, but two of his daughters, Daisy and Lillian, are well into their 90s and live in the Penticton Retirement Centre at the time of writing.

21 "Birch, Bertha; Dressmaker, Bernard Ave." was one of the few women listed in The Vernon and Okanagan Telephone Directory of 1913.

22 *The Kelowna Courier and Okanagan Orchardist*, February 19, 1914.

23 *The Kelowna Courier and Okanagan Orchardist*, May 11, 1916.

24 *The Kelowna Record*, April 12, 1917.

25 *Wrigley's Provincial Directory* for 1919. Henderson's and later, Wrigley's provincial gazetteer and directories were compiled in B.C. between 1905 and 1948. They were also prepared for Alberta and Saskatchewan and are an invaluable inventory business and personal inventory of the time.

26 *The Kelowna Courier and Okanagan Orchardist*, October 2, 1919.

CHAPTER THREE

1 The 1920 apple crop totalled 1,317,000 boxes. Only one year later, the crop size had grown to 2,769,000 boxes – but growth was never certain and crop sizes changed each year.

2 At the same time, a fruit rancher's testimonial as to the merits of growing apples in British Columbia noted:

"(1) British Columbia produces some of the very finest apples grown anywhere in the world. (2) Fruit growing can be, and is, carried on successfully as a commercial enterprise. (3) The life is interesting, pleasant, and, after the first year or so, easy. (4) The fruit ranch affords a satisfactory escape from the stress and strain of city life, and gives the added dignity and freedom to one's sense of individuality." J.T. Bealby, Adam and Charles Black, *Fruit Ranching in British Columbia*, p. 154.

3 *The Kelowna Courier and Okanagan Orchardist*, June 22, 1917.

4 Kelowna's substantial Chinatown was directly across the street from the curling rink, and one morning an S. M. Simpson Ltd. employee went into the curling rink to find an old Chinese man hanging from the rafters. The desperation and loneliness of the poor man's circumstances finally became too much for him, and he ended his life amid the stored piles of shook. Unpublished Simpson family files.

5 Bob Demara, an early resident of the area, vividly remembers adventures in the early '30s when he and his buddies built trenches and dug tunnels in the sawdust and spent hours in noisy battles. In hindsight, he was amazed the sawdust didn't collapse and bury them all. He also remembered taking his skates several blocks in from the lakeshore and skating on the swamps to the hospital. If area residents dig deep enough in their gardens or around their house foundations today, they can often find well-preserved compacted sawdust.

6 In theory, "the fruit grower consigned, or sometimes sold, his fruit to the local shipper, who was also usually the packer. The shipper put this fruit in the hands of a broker, who arranged to sell it at the best possible price to the jobber or wholesaler. The broker then remitted the returns, less his costs and commission, to the shipper, who made a similar deduction and finally paid the grower. The jobber, meanwhile, sold the fruit to the retail outlets who supplied the eventual consumer." Hugh Dendy, *A Fruitful Century*, p. 35.

7 While fruit and vegetable growers have kept on producing, marketing issues have caused so much dissent over time that almost every organization that has tried to enforce its co-operative principles on the industry has failed.

8 *The Kelowna Courier and Okanagan Orchardist*, May 13, 1926.

9 Ibid., April 19, 1928.

10 Unpublished Simpson family files.

11 Named after the Kelowna Land and Orchard Company, which originally subdivided many acres of land on the benches to the southeast of Kelowna.

12 The dusty trail that ran behind the summer cottages located along the west and north-facing beaches north of Kelowna's town centre was originally known as Camp Road. Lou Knowles, wife of the jeweller J. B. Knowles and a seasonal resident of the area, did not think this was a sufficiently elegant designation for her neighbourhood and petitioned her neighbours to change the name of the road to Manhattan Beach Drive.

13 Unpublished S. M. Simpson Ltd. records. The equivalent in 2003 dollars would be more than $86,000.

CHAPTER FOUR

1 Pierre Burton. *The Great Depression 1929-1939.* p.11.

2 "During the Depression, there was a camp . . . called "The Jungle," Many men who were riding the freight trains would camp there. They would go up to town and offer to do chores to get a meal. It was a black era in our history and controversy would flare as to whether the trees should be cut down to discourage the men from staying there. However, I remember them giving us little or no trouble." C. W. Knowles, *According to Bill – The Times and Tales of C.W. (Bill) Knowles*, p. 30.

3 Pierre Berton, *The Great Depression 1929 – 1939*, p. 86.

4 Cedric Boyer, "Thirty-three Years in the Fruit Industry," *Okanagan Historical Society - 48th Annual Report*, 1984. p. 28-45.

5 Unpublished Simpson family files.

6 Hugh Dendy, *A Fruitful Century*, p. 68.

7 Rowcliffe later charged he was "forced to sign" in an attempt to reclaim stabilization levies he had been coerced into paying at the time of this incident. *The Vancouver Sun*, February 14, 1914.

8 *The Vancouver Province*, September 12, 1933.

9 Most young people in the Valley were temporarily involved in some aspect of the fruit industry: picking, packing, canning, or making boxes. In the early '50s, Kelowna resident, Senator Ross Fitzpatrick, partnered with his cousin, Hugh, to make enough boxes early in the day to earn $25 between them and then take off to spend the rest of the day at the beach.

10 The tin used to make tintops was razor-sharp and the operators often complained about cut fingers, and having to wrap rags around each finger for protection. Liberal amounts of Pond's Cold Cream would be slathered on their hands at night, which helped a bit, though most women just stuck it out and their hands toughened up by the end of the season.

11 Unpublished Simpson family files.

12 At one point, either the industry or S. M. decided different coloured box tops would be a good idea and Horace was given the job of dipping each top in either a barrel of red or green dye. The coloured top was placed on a drain board to dry and Horace was left to deal with the task of getting his brightly coloured hands back to normal. He said it was one of his worst jobs. Unpublished Simpson family files.

13 See Captain Len's Ferry Tales by his son, Bob Hayman, for many of his stories.

14 Those who did included Jack Reilly, Klondike (Mike) Paly, Andy Gaspardone, Fred Kitsch, Shigge Kawahara, Art Marty, Bill Nikon, and Kay Kawahara.

15 In conversation with Arthur Marty.

16 Okanagan Telephone Directory, 1937.

17 Pierre Burton, *The Great Depression*, p. 131.

18 *The Kelowna Courier*, April 13, 1939.

19 Ibid, April 13, 1939.

20 *The Kelowna Courier*, April 20, 1939.

21 Ibid., April 13, 1939.

22 Unpublished Simpson family files.

CHAPTER FIVE

1 The first Forest Act came into existence as a result of the Fulton Royal Commission of 1909-1910, which also recommended that a Chief of the Forest Service position be created. MacMillan was the first person to fill that role and during his four-year tenure, focussed on completing an inventory of B.C.'s forest resources and establishing a policy to manage the province's timber sales. (In conversation with John Cuthbert, Chief Forester of B.C. 1985-1994. February 26, 2003.)

2 K. Bernsohn, *Slabs, Scabs and Skidders*, p. 11.

3 Old employees Bill Knowles and Bert Janzen remember travelling with Stan to the defunct BC Spruce Lumber Co. plant in Lumberton, the Adams River Timber Company in Chase, and the mining ghost town of Tulameen to pick up used boilers and planers for the mill.

4 Drushka, *Tie Hackers to Timber Harvesters*, p. 115.

5 When rail cars were not immediately available, the company stacked shook up to the rafters in the Hollywood Orchards packinghouse, which had been owned by the Rowcliffe brothers and had gone into receivership. Simpson's took over the building in lieu of payment for previously supplied shook. Unpublished Simpson family files.

6 Part of a letter from Horace Simpson, April 14, 1940. Unpublished Simpson family files.

7 *The Kelowna Courier*, September 24, 1942.

8 Sometimes it took the men and women who worked in the box factory years before they had full-time jobs, and many spent their working years moving between the box factory, the orchards, and the packinghouses.

9 Jack Wigen in conversation, August 2001.

10 Newspapers used the terms 'saw mill' and 'sawmill' interchangeably. Because what would now be known as the company logo – KSM – became the common way the Kelowna Saw Mill was referred to. The more generic term, sawmill, refers to any lumber operation.

11 Though David Lloyd-Jones was referred to as Kelowna's "grand old man" and tribute was paid in the *Courier* to his "good citizenship and unpublished kindnesses," there are also memories of a somewhat rough frontiersman who exhibited few of the gentlemanly qualities other early immigrants brought to the area.

12 *The Kelowna Courier*, December 10, 1942.

13 When Stan started in the business in 1923, a complete apple box sold for 14¢. 20 years later the price had only increased by 2¢. With the onset of war and escalating logging and processing costs, box prices quickly jumped to 20¢ each, with the approval of the Wartime Prices and Trade Board.

14 Minutes from the Box Shook Committee of the Wood Containers Administration, March 26, 1945. National Archives of Canada.

15 *The Kelowna Courier*, October 19, 1944.

16 From two separate sources, both of whom requested anonymity.

17 *The Kelowna Courier*, September 23, 1943.

18 The Simpson bargaining committee included: M. A. Plant, President of the CCL Woodworkers Union Local No. 4; T. Welder; V. Leier; J. Krimmer; and P. Howard, the CCL organizer from Penticton. On the Kelowna

Saw Mill Employees Association were G. Walker, S. Deck, C. Buber, M. A. Plant, and P. Howard.

19 Comprised of M. A. Plant, J. J. Krimmer, Anthony Welder, and Valentine Leier.

20 Unpublished Simpson family files – copy of agreement.

21 Those signing on behalf of the employees were W. H. Sands, E. E. Wilkison, A. A. Schleppe, F. Schwertza, and W. H. Whitson, over the union seal.

22 Unpublished Simpson family files – collective agreement.

23 In 1949, Marion and Peter, just married in Alberta and broke, were returning to Kelowna where Peter had a job in the mill. Marion's father had given her enough money to return to Kelowna but refused to pay for her husband. Marion called Stan, who lent them the money so they could travel back together. On their return, Marion met Stan to repay the money and thank him: "He was a very kind man."

24 From notes written by Sadie Gregory, July 1999.

25 In 1944, the average monthly wage for a male worker was $37.19, an increase of $1.95 over the previous year. According to Canadian statistics at the time, a working family needed at least $36 a week to maintain a frugal standard of living.

26 The first slate of officers for Local – 423 was: President, Mel Fulton; First Vice President, George Walker; Second Vice President, R. J. Ainslie; Financial Secretary, Val Leier; Recording Secretary, Marion Holtem; conductor, Valentine Hungle; Warden, Charles J. Thompson; Trustees, Joe Marty, A. Mcinroy, and M. Popoff.

27 This was the union's rallying cry for the 1946 strike – a 25¢-an-hour increase, a 40-hour work week, and union security – meaning only union member could work at the mill, though the check-off of union dues would be voluntary. If these demands were not met, they would go on strike.

28 *The Kelowna Courier*, May 16, 1944.

29 Ibid., May 16, 1944.

30 Ibid., May 16, 1944.

31 The rate payable to the railway for failure to unload within the time allowed.

32 *The Kelowna Courier.* June 20, 1946.

33 Ibid., June 20, 1946.

34 Ibid., June 20, 1946.

35 Ibid., June 20, 1946.

36 *The IWA in British Columbia*, p. 35.

37 Most of the activity took place in B.C.

38 I. M. Abella, *Nationalism, Communism, and Canadian Labour*, 1973.

39 A. Neufeld and A. Parnaby, *The IWA in Canada, the Life and Times of an Industrial Union*, p. 300.

40 The other companies were Armstrong Sawmills, Long Bros. Sawmills, Kamloops Lumber Company, Ponderosa Pine Lumber Co. Ltd., H. Sigalet. Co. Ltd., Shuswap Lumber Co. Ltd., Vernon Box and Pine Lumber Co. Ltd.

41 *The Kelowna Daily Courier*, March 2, 1960.

42 Presentation by S. M. Simpson to The Hon. Mr. Justice Gordon Sloan, Commissioner of Inquiry into B.C.

Forest Resources. October 21-23, 1944. Unpublished Simpson family files.

43 Ibid.

44 Findings of The Royal Commission of 1945. p. 162.

45 Unpublished Simpson family files.

46 *The Kelowna Courier*, December 14, 1944.

47 Ibid., May 10, 1945.

48 Ibid., May 3, 1945.

49 V-E Day is the acronym for Victory in Europe – the day the Allies announced the surrender of German forces in Europe. V-J Day – Victory in Japan – was August 14, 1945, and brought an official end to WWII.

50 Unpublished Simpson family files.

51 The same referendum also approved the expenditure of a further $20,000 for the purchase of the Dickson Ranch in Ellison, now Kelowna International Airport.

52 Harland Bartholomew was one of the few acknowledged town planning experts at this time and was hired by many Canadian cities and towns to give them advice on how to plan their growing communities.

53 Restrictive Covenant #108302, City of Kelowna. Unpublished Simpson family files.

54 Unpublished Simpson family files.

55 This parcel of land has recently been identified as Kelowna's Centennial Project and plans are underway for the development of a unique park on the site.

56 *Hardware and Builder*, April 1950, Volume 3, Number 4, Vancouver.

57 The building worked much better for its original owner than for subsequent occupants, as both *The Kelowna Courier* and RCMP put up a number of partitions to exclude the same public the KSM had invited in.

58 Promotional booklet published by the Kelowna Board of Trade, 1949. p. 45.

59 Kelowna Board of Trade booklet, p. 59.

CHAPTER SIX

1 "The Most Fully Integrated Forest Industry in Interior British Columbia", *The Lumberman*, December 1951.

2 Unpublished Simpson family files.

3 July 2001 correspondence from W. G. Burch, who was Chief Forester of B.C. Forest Products Ltd. during the time Alan was Woodlands Manager at S. M. Simpson Ltd.

4 *The Kelowna Courier*, November 1, 1951.

5 Copy of letter dated November 1, 1951. Unpublished Simpson family files.

6 Unpublished Simpson family files.

7 Copy of letter dated November 9, 1951. Unpublished Simpson family files.

8 The Okanagan's crop production varied annually but the number of boxes required continued to be substantial. In 1950, it was 8,008,073 boxes of apples and 346,780 pears vs. 6,183,730 boxes of apples and 571,450 of pears in 1951. *The Kelowna Courier*, August 27, 1951.

9 The IWA's demand for a union shop – meaning that all employees had to belong to the union to work at a sawmill or in the industry – usually went along with the demand that employers automatically deduct union dues from their employees' paycheques,

whether the employee wanted to join the union or not. The union argued that since all employees benefited from its negotiations, all should pay to support its efforts.

10 *The Kelowna Courier*, November 3, 1952.

11 *The IWA in British Columbia.* Issued by Western Canadian Regional Council No. 1, International Woodworkers of America. AFL-CIO-CLC February, 1971. p. 45.

12 *The Kelowna Courier*, June 29, 1953.

13 Ibid., October 8, 1953.

14 Ibid., October 15, 1953.

15 Editorial, *The Kelowna Courier*, October 22, 1953.

16 After three weeks on picket duty, single men received $7 a week strike pay, married men, $12, with an additional $2 per child. No IWA member would go hungry, but the union could not make house or car payments and Coastal workers each began to contribute one dollar a month to the Interior Strike Fund.

17 *The Kelowna Courier*, October 26, 1953.

18 Ibid., November 9, 1953.

19 Copy of the injunction – Unpublished Simpson family files.

20 *Slabs, Scabs and Skidders – A History of the IWA in the Central Interior.*

21 *The Kelowna Courier*, December 24, 1953.

22 The IWA executive involved in the disputes became familiar in the following years: Joe Morris, Clayton Walls, Jack Strong, and George Mitchell, among others.

23 Strikes were very hard on the employees. Some went hungry and during one strike, the union went to Armstrong and found a farmer with a barn full of potatoes and bought up the whole lot. It also got some bulk cheese at the same time and cut it into slabs and handed it out to some families with their strike pay. In conversation with Ray Ottenbreit.

24 A huge fire broke out at the mill a few days later, but was fortunately contained before it consumed the buildings and machinery.

25 *The Kelowna Courier*, March 29, 1956.

26 Ibid., March 29, 1956.

27 The rest of the team included: Bill Sakala, a local engineering genius who was responsible for laying the steam system; Larry Gorby, chief electrician; Jack Birch, production control analyst; Cy McLean, shift foreman; Norm Murray, shift foreman; Larry Preston and John Sharpe, department foremen; Godfrey Rice, maintenance foreman; and Jack Strong, timekeeper and first aid man.

28 In conversation with Ray Ottenbreit.

29 *The Kelowna Courier*, April 29, 1957.

30 British Columbia Lumberman, June 1957. p. 64.

31 *The Kelowna Courier*, April 29, 1957.

32 Conversation with Bill Crooks, June 17, 2002.

33 IWA Bulletin – Undated (likely May 1957) – Unpublished Simpson family files.

34 Information Bulletin – Re: S&K Plywood Dispute – November 1, 1957 – Unpublished Simpson family files.

35 In conversation with Bob Bain. June 19, 2002.

36 In conversation with Ray Ottenbreit.

37 Unpublished Simpson family files.

38 Premier Bennett had personally committed to build the Okanagan Lake Bridge against considerable opposition from other parts of the province. In 1955, construction began and in July 1958, Princess Margaret joined Premier Bennett in cutting the ribbon to officially open the amazing new transportation link that would finally solve Kelowna's perpetual problem of getting across Okanagan Lake.

39 Guests included representatives from MacMillan & Bloedel, Canadian Western Lumber Co., Canadian Forest Products Ltd., Plywood Manufacturers Association of BC, Vernon Box and Pine, Boundary Sawmills (Midway), Armstrong Sawmill, Pioneer Sash and Door (Vernon), Sooke Lake Lumber, Canadian Colleries, Columbia Engineering, Knight Lumber (Crow's Nest), Inland Building Supplies (Kamloops), Canadian Manufacturers Assoc., Cascade Saw Co. (New Westminster), and BC Forest Service, among others.

40 Stan Simpson was the fifth recipient of Kelowna's Freedom of the City (there have been nine since), which is the highest award bestowed by City Council upon individuals or groups in recognition of their outstanding contributions to the community.

41 From the City Council motion dated April 15, 1957. Unpublished Simpson family files.

42 From a copy of the Mayor's speech. Unpublished Simpson family files.

43 From a copy of Stan's letter in response to the award, May 3, 1957. Unpublished Simpson family files.

44 *The Kelowna Daily Courier*, February 5, 1959.

45 *B.C. Lumber Worker*, Editorial, Second issue, January, 1954.p.4.

46 Peeler logs used in making plywood as they were large enough that thin sheets of veneer could be 'peeled' off and glued together to form plywood. S. M. used this same process for making veneer fruit containers.

47 *The Kelowna Daily Courier*, November 2,1961.

48 *British Columbia Lumberman's Western Lumberman and Woodworker.* November 1962. p.46.

49 Hugh Dendy, *A Fruitful Century.* p. 104/5.

50 *Bulk Handling of Fruit in British Columbia*, A. D. McMechan, Canada Dept of Agriculture, Summerland. 1959.

51 A design and marketing team was established to address the local industry's needs. It consisted of: Design and engineering, Bill Buss and Dan Hill; Brochures and Patents, Dan Hill and Alex Davidson; Wood parts production and part assembly operations, Jim Charpentier; Plywood Production, Bill Crooks; Metal parts purchasing, Fred Day; Sales, Len Smith. Field representatives Bas Jennens, Cedric Boyer, and Terry Harding became trouble-shooters and goodwill ambassadors for the company during the following years. Eventually domestic and export sales, including the U.S., were looked after by Bill Buss and Bas Jennens.

52 Canadian Patent No. 684, 598 – Materials and Produce Handling Container

53 From the unpublished "Harvesting Bin Story – 1957 – 1978" by Len Smith. Unpublished Simpson family files.

54 While awaiting the decision, Gorman Brothers established a bin and pallet company in Oroville, Washington, which continues to operate today as Oroville Remand & Reload.

55 *The Daily Courier*, Editorial, March 23, 1959.

56 Ibid., March 23, 1959.

57 Ibid., March 23, 1959.

58 Ibid. March 23, 1959.

CHAPTER SEVEN

1 Unpublished Simpson family files.

2 *The Kelowna Daily Courier*, April 28, 1960.

3 Ibid., May 27, 1960.

4 S. M. Simpson Ltd. had been M & B's Interior agent for building products, and had partnered with the forest giant on the international sales and marketing of Simpson's plywood and bins.

5 *The Kelowna Daily Courier*, October 2, 1962.

6 During the early '60s, the Raboch family, which for the previous two decades had been logging in the area east of Enderby and buying up small sawmills in the area, joined forces with William H. Steele Lumber Co., a Vancouver lumber wholesaler, to form Riverside Forest Products. The new company began expanding by purchasing a number of small operators in the Southern Interior, which set the stage for its more substantial expansion in the years that followed.

7 Unpublished Simpson family files.

8 Between 1962 and 1971, the number of sawmills in B.C. dropped from 1,627 to 627, even as lumber production increased by 49 per cent. Druska, *Tie Hackers*, p. 194.

9 Unpublished Simpson family files.

10 *The Executive Magazine*, September 1961, p. 37.

11 Crown Zellerbach's departure from Canada preceded the demise of McMillan Bloedel, once the province's most recognizable forestry company; M & B was taken over by U.S. multi-national Weyerhaeuser in 1999. Thousands of once-independent smaller forest companies have also disappeared as the industry evolved over the years.

12 Crown Zellerbach's corporate records were donated to the Bancroft Library at University of California, Berkley in 1988 by the James River Corporation, and subsequently added to by the Zellerbach family. They can be found on the Online Archive of California.

13 The three years date from the 1962 agreement between S. M. Simpson Ltd. and CZ to supply the pulp maker with chips from Simpson's Manhattan Beach operation.

14 *The Kelowna Daily Courier*, April 12, 1965.

15 In mid-September 2003, the giant Coastal forest companies, Weyerhaeuser, Interfor, and Timberwest, announced that without significant rationalization and restructuring, the once-vibrant Coastal forest industry could not be profitable into the future. They did not mention that the Interior industry had now become the mainstay of the province's forest industry.

CHAPTER EIGHT

1 In conversation with Jack Munro, past International President of the IWA.

2 Part of the reason the '67 strike took so long to settle was a turf war dating back to the 1964 agreement when the Cranbrook local, with Jack Munro at the head and Bill Schumacher in the same position in Kelowna, disagreed with the IWA's Coast policy committee over the terms of settlement. The legacy of that disagreement carried over to the 1967 negotiations, when the IWA policy committee again insisted that wage parity should be high on the list of negotiable issues. Later in *The Barker*, the official publication of Vancouver Local 1-217 IWA, the policy committee admitted that "hindsight is always easier than foresight but nevertheless it is now also obvious that the slogan of parity was wrong. This slogan placed the Union in a corner where there was no way out … Inept bungling leadership has no place in the labor [*sic*] movement."

3 In conversation with Jack Munro.

4 This was replaced with a new lumber mill and planer.

5 In conversation with Gordon Steele, President and CEO of Riverside Forest Products, and John Marritt, Vice President of Woodlands, September 2002.

6 S. M. Simpson Ltd owned the land now known as Sutherland Park in 1944, and Stan agreed to exchange it with the city for the property immediately adjacent to the mill site that had been George Sutherland's home. The city gained a new park and picnic ground, and the Sutherland name was appended to the new north-end park. The mill acquired a portion of land and lakeshore contiguous to its main location.

7 In conversation with Bill Schumaker, President IWA Local 1-423, Kelowna, 1960-1990.

8 The grandstanding days are gone and if an outsider walked into negotiations today, they'd think it "was a bloody love-in." Bill Schumaker, September 2002.

9 Letter from Stan Simpson to Mayor J. J. Ladd after he had received the Freedom on the City, May 3, 1957. Unpublished Simpson family files.

Bibliography

Abella, Irving M. *Nationalism, Communism, and Canadian Labour: The CIO, the Communist Party, and the Canadian Congress of Labour.* University of Toronto Press, Toronto, 1973.

Battye, Clement. *Reminiscences of a Nonagenerian throughout the 20th Century.* Okanagan Falls: Published by Partners in Print.

Bealby, J. T. *Fruit Ranching in British Columbia.* MacMillan and Co., Toronto, 1911.

Berton, Pierre. *The Great Depression 1929-1939.* McClelland & Stewart Inc., Toronto, 1990.

Bernsohn, Ken. *Slabs, Scabs and Skidders: A History of the IWA in the Central Interior.* Prince George: Published by IWA Local 1-424, 1970?

Broadfoot, Barry. *The Pioneer Years: 1895 – 1914: Memories of Settlers Who Opened the West.* Doubleday Canada, Ltd., Toronto, 1976.

Dendy, David and Kyle, Kathleen. *A Fruitful Century. The British Columbia Fruit Growers Association 1889 – 1989.* British Columbia Fruit Growers Association, Kelowna, 1990.

Drushka, Ken. *Tie Hackers to Timber Harvesters: The History of Logging In British Columbia's Interior.* Harbour Publishing, Madeira Park, 1998.

Halleran, Mike. *Loggers and Lumbermen: The Evolution of the Forest Industry in the Southern Interior of British Columbia.* ILMA, 1994.

Hayman, Bob. *Captain Len's Ferry Tales of the Okanagan. The Early Okanagan seen through the eyes of a Ferryman, Captain L. A. Hayman.* Bob Hayman, Kelowna, 1988.

Kelowna Board of Trade, The. *Kelowna, British Columbia.* 1949.

Knowles, C. W. (Bill). *According to Bill: The Times and Tales of C. W. (Bill) Knowles.* Manhattan Beach Publishing, Kelowna, 2001.

Naicam, Saskatchewan, Canada, The Town of. *Gleanings Along the Way; A History of Naicam, Lac Vert and Surrounding Districts.* Inter-Collegiate Press, Winnipeg, 1980.

Sanford, Barry. *McCulloch's Wonder: The Story of the Kettle Valley Railway.* Whitecap Books, Vancouver, 1978.

Tracey, Mary. *Gorman Bros. From Boxes to Boards.* Gorman Brothers Lumber, Westbank, 2001.

Waiser, Bill. *All Hell Can't Stop Us.* Fifth House Ltd., Calgary, 2003.

Webber, Jean and the Okanagan Historical Society. *A Rich and Fruitful Land: A History of the Valleys of the Okanagan, Similkameen and Shuswap.* Harbour Publishing, Maderira Park, 1999.

Western Canadian Regional Council No.1 – International Woodworkers of America AFL-CIO-CLC. *The IWA in British Columbia.* Vancouver, 1971.

Zuehlke, Mark. *Scoundrels, Dreamers and Second Sons: British Remittance Men in the Canadian West.* (Second Edition) The Dundurn Group, Toronto, 2001.

Periodicals

The Kelowna Courier, as cited

The Kelowna Courier and Okanagan Orchardist, as cited

The Kelowna Daily Courier, as cited

The Kelowna Record, as cited

The Penticton Herald, as cited

The Vancouver Province, as cited

The Vancouver Sun, as cited

The Vernon Daily News, as cited

Annual Reports of the Okanagan Historical Society, as cited

Other sources

The Okanagan Telephone Directory

The Vernon and Okanagan Telephone Directory

The Wrigley's *Provincial Directory*

Minutes of the Box Shook Committee, National Archives of Canada

B. C. Ministry of Forests, Victoria. (Robin Brown and Robin Corner)

Oral History Sources

Beth Allen – by telephone, September 20, 1999.

Marion Brown – by telephone, September, 1999.

Bob Bain – in conversation on several occasions.

Jake Bartel – at mill reunion, September 26, 1999.

Frank Bartel – at mill reunion, September 26, 1999.

Mrs. Baker – by telephone, September. 1999.

Bob Brown-Clayton – in conversation.

W. G. Burch – by letter, July 16, 2001.

Bill Cameron – by telephone, September 23, 1999.

Gwen Campbell – at mill reunion, September 26, 1999.

Leonard Campbell – in conversation, April 9, 2002 and October 10, 2000.

Bob Christie – in conversation and photos.

Ernie Cowan – in conversation, September 23, 1999.

Bill Crooks – by telephone.

Gary Crooks – in conversation.

Reno Culos – by telephone, March 16, 2000.

John Cuthbert – by telephone, February 26, 2003.

Bob Demara – by telephone, July 18, 2001.

Charlie Dore – in conversation, September 20, 1999.

Kitty Drought – in conversation, January 23, 2002.

Dick Ford – in conversation.

Hillas Francis – by telephone, September 23, 1999.

Bill Greenwood – in conversation March 22, 2002, October, 1999, and other occasions.

Dale Gregory – written anecdotes.

Sadie Gregory – written anecdotes, July 1999.

Bob Harrison – in conversation.

Dick Hartwick – at mill reunion, September 26, 1999.

Doug Herbert – in conversation, August 26, 1999.

Clare Holford – in conversation, September 20, 1999.

Arthur Hughes-Games – in conversation, March 23, 2002.

Bill Huggins – by fax, November 27, 2001.

Lexi (Goodman) Jamieson – by letter.

David Jeffries – written anecdotes, October 5, 1999.

Gordon Jennens – in conversation, September 23, 1999.

Joan Jennens – in conversation, April 16, 2001.

Bob Jones – at mill reunion, September 26, 1999.

Leona Jones – by letter, November 28, 2001 and January 7, 2002.

Eileen Judd – by telephone, September 25, 1999.

Bill Knowles – in conversation on various occasions.

Dru Langton – in conversation, April 16, 2001.

Jack Leier – in conversation, January 28, 2000.

Gerry Lord – at mill reunion, September 26, 1999.

Eunice Lundeen – by telephone, September 24, 1999.

John Marritt – in conversation.

Arthur Marty – in conversation and written anecdotes, on many occasions.

Bill McGhee – in conversation.

Jim McMynn – in conversation, December 6, 2000.

Jennie McMillan – in conversation, September 26, 1999.

Mary Miller – early map of KSM, October 5, 1999.

Min Mori – at mill reunion, September 26, 1999.

Jack Munro – by telephone, June 22, 1999.

Tillman Nahm – in conversation, March 1, 2000.

Larry Neave – in conversation, October 10, 2001.

Margaret Newick – in conversation, September 20, 1999.

Mary Olinger – in conversation, February 20, 2001.

Ray Ottenbreit – in conversation and written anecdotes, on several occasions.

Helen Ottenbreit – in conversation.

J. Parminter – articles re Interior forest practices

Spen and Mary Price – in conversation, October 12, 2001.

Evelyn Radomski – at mill reunion and in conversation, May 5, 2000.

Arthur and Lori Rogers – in conversation and tour of packinghouse, October 2001.

Marion Sallenback – by telephone, September 1999.

Don and Barbara Sandburg – in conversation, September 23, 1999 and January 28, 2000.

Reg Saunders – in conversation, August 27, 2000 and September 8, 2000.

Bill Schumaker – in conversation.

Peter and Fran Simpson – in conversation, October 3, 1999.

Chris Sladen – SMS Crest, September 2001.

Len Smith – written history, May1999.

Betty Sperle – copy of memo re. Bob Ryder.

Gordon Steele – in conversation.

Harry Tupman – in conversation, October 28, 1999.

Jim Whillis – in conversation, July 31, 2001.

Theresa White – at the ILMA on various occasions.

Jack Wigen – in conversation, August 14, 2001.

Old-timers lunch gatherings on March 20, 2000, and April 27, 2000, where the voices and stories of Bert Jansen, Barney McIvor, Jack Lomax, Ray Ottenbreit, and Evert Does blended together .

Biographies

The Author

Sharron was born and grew up in Kelowna when it was a much smaller city than it is today. She left to attend university and travel around the world, after which she lived in Vancouver, Montreal, and Toronto before finally returning home in 1984. With an eclectic work background as a social worker, stock broker, politician, and teacher (among others), she has become a vocal advocate for preserving family memories and community stories. In addition to developing and teaching a series of writing workshops entitled *Memories into Memoirs* through the Kelowna Museum, Sharron has compiled the Museum Writers Group's award-winning volumes, and edited and published the best-selling book *According to Bill – the life and times of C.W. (Bill) Knowles*. She is a member of the Simpson and Jennens families, both of which settled in the Okanagan during the early years of the last century.

The Editor

Stuart Kernaghan was born in Toronto, but has been moving around British Columbia for the last two decades looking for the right sized city to call home. He has a Master of Arts degree from the University of Victoria and has spent the past several years working as a writer/journalist and editor in both print and online environments. Stuart never tackles any piece of editing without a red pen in hand, and he enjoys discussing the finer points of grammar and copy editing with anyone who will listen. A firm believer in the serial comma, Stuart currently balances the challenges of freelance wordsmithing with an office job. He lives in Vancouver with his four bikes.